True

Hermann Simon

True Profit!

No Company Ever Went Broke Turning a Profit

Copernicus Books is a brand of Springer

Hermann Simon
Bonn, Nordrhein-Westfalen, Germany

ISBN 978-3-030-76701-3   ISBN 978-3-030-76702-0   (eBook)
https://doi.org/10.1007/978-3-030-76702-0

Translation from the German language edition: *Am Gewinn ist noch keine Firma kaputt gegangen* by Hermann Simon, © Campus Verlag GmbH 2020. Published by Campus Verlag GmbH. All Rights Reserved.

This Copernicus imprint is published by the registered company Springer Nature Switzerland AG
The registered company address is: Gewerbestrasse 11, 6330 Cham, Switzerland

Preface

Profit is the cost of survival. If a company does not earn profits, it will go under sooner or later. This happens to thousands of companies every year.

A company must file for insolvency when it cannot pay its current liabilities. Illiquidity is the proximate cause, but it is not the reason for insolvency. The real reason is continued losses, which means that the resources a company puts in exceed the value it produces. That is unsustainable for private companies in the long run.

Starting a business is not too difficult. The bigger challenge is to run it profitably over time. Nine out of ten start-ups go bankrupt within the first 3 years. Why does this happen? The visible reason is a lack of liquidity. Ultimately, however, they go under because they have no profit prospects. Founders should therefore remember that turning a profit is a necessity, not a nice-to-have.

Profit is the opposite of waste. It is and will remain the sole criterion for the sustainable success and viability of a company. It is a company's bedrock pillar of support.

With those views in mind, one would expect to find a lot written about profit. But as a glance at amazon.com indicates, there is no book explicitly on the subject of profit. This book is the first one devoted exclusively to the topic. It illuminates the many dazzling facets of profit: its terminology, pursuit, ethics, causes, and drivers.

The contents of this book derive equally from my experiences as an academic researcher and as a practitioner. Perhaps one can fully explore the complexities of profit only if one knows profit firsthand from its theoretical and its real-world sides. The book's numerous case studies and quotes from around the world reveal that profit has a deeply emotional side, and not only an economic one. Sometimes, an entrepreneur's fate ends tragically because he or she has relegated or neglected the profit motive.

I take a clear stand and leave no doubt about my conviction that entrepreneurs should be resolutely profit-oriented. Making a profit is not only the best long-term goal for a company but also a business leader's ethical responsibility.

With this book, I would like to put profit at the heart of what entrepreneurs, managers, and ambitious founders strive to accomplish. No company ever went broke from turning a profit.

In the summer of 2021   Prof. Dr. Dr. h.c. mult. Hermann
Bonn, Germany   SimonFounder and Honorary Chairman,
Simon-Kucher & Partners

Contents

1

Profit: What is It?

"I'm for profit maximization!"

If you want to infuriate large portions of society and turn people against you, uttering that sentence is a very effective way to do it.

Few phrases are more explosively controversial than "profit maximization." Some people even go berserk when they hear the word "profit." During a large demonstration against the German industrial giant Bayer AG at its annual shareholders meeting on April 26, 2019, I became involved in a discussion with the protesters. When I mentioned that a company needs to earn profits in order to survive, I was aggressively taunted and berated.

This kind of aggressive reaction seems to be universal. The maximization of profit—or perhaps worse, the maximization of "shareholder value"—is considered by many observers to be the root of all economic evils. Of course, most rank-and-file employees oppose profit maximization. But beyond that, it doesn't matter whether the listeners are teachers, doctors, lawyers, or civil servants, not to mention the critics among political scientists, sociologists, or philosophers. There isn't even general consensus in favor of the "profit" concept among businesspeople.

But in its essence, profit maximization is simply the antithesis of waste. One could also equate profit maximization with "waste minimization." Critics claim that the maximization of profit and shareholder value is responsible for the exploitation of resources and workers, for disparities in income and assets, for the offshoring of jobs to low-wage countries, for the relocation of corporate headquarters to tax havens, and many other abuses.

© The Author(s), under exclusive license to Springer Nature
Switzerland AG 2021
H. Simon, *True Profit!*,
https://doi.org/10.1007/978-3-030-76702-0_1

These criticisms stand in stark contrast to the theoretical groundwork of microeconomics. If a company doesn't strive to achieve the highest possible profit, it faces the risk that its competition will wipe it out. To co-opt the mantra from the scientific community, the ultimate law of business is "profit or perish."

Profit is the reward for undertaking business risks. Profit is what is left over after a company meets all of its contractual obligations to its employees, suppliers, banks, other creditors, and the various national, state, and local governments that levy taxes. Profit is thus a residual that belongs exclusively to the company's owners. As soon as the company has met all of its obligations to outside parties, no one else can make any additional claims.

This simple and incontrovertible definition of profit is by no means generally accepted. During his tenure as French president, Nicolas Sarkozy "declared that it is unfair that shareholders and owners get to keep all of a firm's profit, and that it would be more fair for company profits to be divided into three equal parts: one for the shareholders, one for employees, and one for re-investment into the company."[1] In Sarkozy's view, it is unacceptable that the owners of a company claim all of the profits for themselves. But isn't that tantamount to saying that it is unacceptable for employees to keep their net wages for themselves and allow no other parties to lay claim to their money? Nonetheless, populist statements such as Sarkozy's enjoy broad public appeal.

So What is Profit Anyway?

The simplest and easiest-to-understand definition is the one above: profit is the residual amount left over after a company has met all its financial obligations. But the reality is unfortunately more complicated.

There is a variety of definitions for profit, and it is not an exaggeration to say that some of these definitions are confusing or even misleading. When we talk about profit, we should know *exactly* what we are talking about. Otherwise it is easy to be deceived. For that reason, I cannot let the reader off the hook by glossing over the prevailing definitions of profit that are in common use. At first glance, the upcoming parts of this chapter may come across as a bunch of boring accounting and financial jargon. But the clarifications and distinctions we make in this chapter should be indispensable to you when we

---

[1] https://www.wsj.com/articles/SB10001424052748703922804576301090149677206.

get to the hopefully more exciting chapters on what profit truly represents, not what it is mathematically.

Profit is defined as follows:

$$\text{profit} \ = \ \text{revenue} - \text{costs} \tag{1.1}$$

Revenue comprises sales or operating revenue, defined as the product of price and unit volume:

$$\text{revenue} \ = \ \text{price} \times \text{unit volume} \tag{1.2}$$

Revenue also includes financial components such as interest income, income from securities, and extraordinary income from asset sales, tax refunds, or other similar financial holdings.

Profit depends on three drivers, namely, price, sales volume, and costs. Costs break down into fixed costs and variable costs. If a country imposes a sales or value-added tax (VAT), revenue is usually expressed without those taxes included. But some practices deviate from this standard.

In addition to the operating revenue and operating costs, financial aspects such as the ones mentioned above (interest income, proceeds from asset sales, etc.) can flow into the profit calculation.

Revenue occupies the first line in standard financial reporting, which is why it is commonly referred to as the "top line." Profit after taxes—the true profit in line with our definition above—typically is the last line of the report, or the "bottom line."

Is Profit Actually a Cost?

An insightful perspective is to interpret profit as a cost. "Profit is the cost of survival," Peter Drucker once said.[2] According to his view, profit comprises three types of costs:

— costs of capital
— costs of business/entrepreneurial risk
— costs of securing future jobs and pensions.

---

[2]See Peter Drucker [1].

In this sense, profit should not be understood as a residual that hopefully has a plus-sign at the end of the business year. Instead, profit should be factored in upfront, like cost, in order to secure the company's survival.

The wide range of nouns and adjectives to identify profit adds confusion rather than transparency. First, we see results, earnings, gains, surplus, profit, income, yield, and margin. Then we compound the problem with the inclusion of modifiers such as operating, from continuing operations, preliminary, nominal, real, inflation-adjusted, extraordinary, plus distinctions across different organizational levels (corporate, group, business unit) and time periods (quarterly, annual). There is also "book" profit, based on the operating revenue and costs that are covered explicitly in the company's books. Finally, we have profit concepts such as normal profit and economic profit, with the latter taking the opportunity cost of capital into account.

Do you see now why we need clarity and focus when it comes to profit?

In press reports and meetings, it is often not precisely clear what kind of profit is being discussed. In the finance community, certain profit measures have established themselves, but they have nothing in common with the definition of true profit, namely, the residual amount of money after a company meets its obligations. One is inclined to think that this jargon arises from intentional obfuscation tactics so that the general public—and in some cases even insiders—struggles to understand the different concepts and terms and to distinguish among them. This jargon is at least partially responsible for the widespread confusion and misperceptions about the profit situation of individual companies or industries.

The goal of this book is not to engage in a comprehensive examination of profit calculations in all their complexity. That is what specialized accounting literature is for. My goal with these sections is to provide the reader with brief explanations of the most common profit terms and concepts. But I leave you with one recommendation: in any discussion when the word "profit" comes up, you should ask, for the purpose of clarity, what that term includes and excludes.

Clearing Up the Alphabet Soup of Profit

In addition to the terms mentioned above, reports often come filled with an alphabet soup of acronyms, such as EAT (earnings after taxes), EBT (earnings before taxes), EBIT (earnings before interest and taxes), and EBITDA (earnings before interest, taxes, depreciation, and amortization). Let's look into these in some detail.

- Earnings after Taxes (EAT): This is often referred to as net profit or net income. It is ultimately the most relevant profit term, because it is the amount the shareholders retain. When we refer to net profit or net income throughout the book, we mean EAT.
- Earnings before Taxes (EBT): As the name implies, the income taxes have not yet been subtracted from this profit number. Thus, it does not represent the true profit in the sense of what the firm's owners can retain for themselves.
- Earnings before Interest and Taxes (EBIT): This key profit figure is often referred to as operating profit, but it is not used consistently. If the company's debt, and thus its interest payments, is high, then the EBIT amount will look much more impressive than EAT, or net profit. That is one reason EBIT is a very popular metric in corporate financial reports.
- Earnings before Interest, Taxes, Depreciation, and Amortization (EBITDA): In contrast to EBIT, this amount is higher because it includes the depreciation and amortization of plant and machinery and intangible assets. This term is likewise often referred to as operating profit. Sometimes the number will be adjusted to reflect extraordinary expenditures and income. In that case, one uses the term "adjusted EBITDA". EBITDA has next to nothing to do with EAT, as we defined it above. Nonetheless, the valuation of an individual firm is often expressed as a multiple of EBIT or EBITDA. For EBITDA, depreciation and amortization not only encompass physical assets, but also write-downs of the company's value after an acquisition, a term known as goodwill. These sums are often quite large.

Figure 1.1. shows the relationship between the different levels of "profit."

These explanations underscore once again how important it is to pay close attention to what profit term or concept someone is using. Otherwise, one can be easily fooled or misled.

The amount of imagination expended to enhance or inflate profit numbers seems limitless. One business journalist sent me this comment: "I regularly attend annual shareholder meetings. The managers toss around all kinds of key numbers and indicators, apparently in an effort to mask their mistakes. One such number is EBITDAR (R stands for restructuring.) Sometimes it sounds as if these numbers were made up just for an earnings conference. In the New Economy, CFOs have played up the 'burn rate'[3] of their companies

---

[3]The term "burn rate" or "cash burn rate" is most often used in connection with start-ups. The cash burn rate indicates the rate at which the financial resources of a company decline.

EAT (Earnings after Taxes)

+ Taxes

- Tax refunds

= EBT (Earnings before Taxes)

+ Interest expenses

- Interest income

= EBIT (Earnings before Interest and Taxes)

+ Depreciation and amortization of assets

- Asset impairments

- Asset write-ups

= EBITDA (Earnings before Interest, Taxes, Depreciation, and Amortization)

+ Non-operating income

- Non-operating expenses

= Adjusted EBITDA

Fig. 1.1 Interconnections between the different levels of profit

as a success factor. This confused me, and started to make me think that profit is more of a 'nice to have' instead of a 'must have.'".[4]

The aftermath of the New Economy bubble of the early 2000's did not diminish the creativity at all. I recently heard about a new variant called EBITDAL. The L stands for leases, meaning that the firm has apparently added the cost of its leases to its "profit" number. It seems there is no limit to the number of letters one can add to these definitions.

Then again, why should one worry, when "losses are 'sexy' again," according to one magazine. More than 80% of all companies that have recently launched an initial public offering (IPO) in the US have never turned a profit.[5] The ride-sharing company Uber launched its IPO on May 10, 2019. But in 2018, Uber posted a loss of $3.8 billion, according to figures at the time. At the same time, Uber declared a "core platform contribution profit" of $940 million.

In the same year, WeWork, a provider of shared office space, recorded a loss of $1.9 billion on revenue of $1.8 billion. So the firm came up with a new metric called "community adjusted EBITDA," which excluded items such as marketing expenditures. Then there is Groupon, the global e-commerce platform for discounted goods and services. It announced an "adjusted consolidated segment operating income" of $61 million, although

---

[4] Personal mail from Finn Mayer-Kuckuk on December 12, 2011.

[5] See   https://www.wiwo.de/finanzen/boerse/stelter-strategische-verluste-sind-wieder-sexy/24253188.html.

the company's loss totaled $420 million. The creative new metric did not include the acquisition costs for new customers. Groupon considered those costs to be an investment in its future.[6]

Under the ironic title "Profit before Costs," a journalist elaborated on this modern tendency to put an upbeat face on what is, in reality, a miserable profit situation. "In some years, the true profit is miniscule or fully unsatisfactory. That's when the companies get very imaginative. They will add taxes and interest to their net profit, or the depreciation. And when that is still not a number worthy of presenting, they will add in 'special items' or one-time expenses. A company revises the profit number upwards for so long, using whatever items it wants, until it reaches a number that looks good relative to the competition. But that number no longer says anything about the company's true profitability."[7]

The journalist added: "Many companies consider EBITDA to be relevant. But to me, this number says absolutely nothing. If a company can't even earn its depreciation, it is destroying capital and very likely heading toward its demise."[8]

Expressing Profit as Returns

One preferred way to express profits is in the form of returns, which enable better comparisons across companies, business sectors, and industries. A return is a ratio with the profit level—no matter how it is defined—as the numerator and the reference or comparison basis as the denominator. Any of the profit metrics mentioned above could be used to determine returns. The ratios are usually expressed as percentages.

The most commonly used returns are the following:

$$\text{return on sales (ROS)} = \text{profit/revenue} \qquad (1.3)$$

This ratio indicates what percentage of revenue is left over as profit. If one uses net income or EAT in (1.3), the resulting percentage is the net return on sales. In the same spirit, we will refer to this number as "net profit margin."

One can also measure profit (income) relative to capital invested. This ratio uses the total amount of capital invested (=assets) and the profit (regardless

---

[6]Regarding these examples, see Rolf Winkler [2].
[7]Georg Giersberg [3].
[8]Personal e-mail from January 6, 2013.

of which definition) in order to calculate the return on total capital invested:

$$\text{return on assets} = \text{profit/assets} \tag{1.4}$$

Commonly used in practice is the variant of Eq. (1.4) that includes interest. The rationale is that the yield on total capital is comprised of profit and interest. Using this method, we get the equation:

$$\text{return on assets} = (\text{profit} + \text{interest})/\text{assets} \tag{1.5}$$

Because interest is deductible as an expense, the following variant is also used:

$$\text{return on assets} = \left(\text{profit} + \text{interest}\left(1 - s\right)\right)/\text{assets} \tag{1.6}$$

The s represents the corporate tax rate.

Other variants for these kinds of equations include return on investment (ROI), return on capital employed (ROCE), and return on net assets (RONA). For ROCE and RONA, the calculation uses total capital, or total assets adjusted for accounts payable and accounts receivable.

The return on equity (ROE) expresses profit as a percentage of equity:

$$\text{return on equity} = \text{profit/equity} \tag{1.7}$$

Equity is defined as total assets less liabilities (usually debt). As with the other equations, this one can have different variants of profit in the numerator.

The following relationship exists between the various types of returns:

$$\text{return on sales} = \text{return on assets/capital turnover} \tag{1.8}$$

Capital turnover is defined as revenue divided by total assets, and indicates how often the capital is turned over in one year. The capital turnover varies considerably across industries. Figure 1.2 shows how strong these differences in capital turnover are for large companies in different industries and countries.

If capital turnover is less than 1, it means that the return on sales is greater than the return on assets. If we solve Eq. (1.8) for return on assets, we get:

$$\text{return on assets} = \text{return on sales} \times \text{capital turnover} \tag{1.9}$$

Company	Country	Revenue in $bn	Assets in $bn	Capital Turnover
Walmart	USA	524	236	2.22
Volkswagen	Germany	283	548	0.52
Amazon	USA	281	225	1.25
Exxon Mobil	USA	265	363	0.73
Apple	USA	260	339	0.77
Samsung Electronics	South Korea	198	305	0.65
AT&T	USA	181	552	0.33
Hon Hai	Taiwan	173	111	1.56
Alphabet	USA	162	276	0.59
JPMorgan Chase	USA	142	2687	0.05
Bank of China	China	135	3269	0.04
Allianz	Germany	130	1135	0.11
Lukoil	Russia	115	96	1.20
Hitachi	Japan	81	92	0.88
Vodafone Group	UK	50	185	0.27
Sanofi	France	42	127	0.33

Fig. 1.2 Revenue, assets, and capital turnover for companies in various industries and countries (2019 fiscal year, Source: Fortune, August 2020)

This equation shows that the return on assets rises proportionally with return on sales and capital turnover.

For the interrelationship between return on equity and return on assets, the debt-to-assets ratio plays an essential role. This ratio is defined as debt divided by total assets.

$$\text{return on equity} = \text{return on assets}/(1 - \text{debt/total assets}) \qquad (1.10)$$

We'll use a numerical example to illustrate this. Total assets are $100 and $50 of that is borrowed, leaving a debt-to-assets ratio of 0.5. Profit before interest is $10 (we will ignore taxes for now) and the interest rate on the debt is 5%. That means that the $50 of debt cost $2.50 in interest.

The profit after interest is therefore $7.50. Using Eq. (1.4), we get a return on assets of 7.5%. According to Eq. (1.7), the return on equity is 15%. If we use Eq. (1.5) for the return on assets, with the interest included in the numerator, we get a return on assets of ($7.50 + $2.50)/$100 = 0.10 or 10%. If we use Eq. (1.6) and assume a corporate tax rate of 30%, we get a return on assets of ($7.50 + $2.50 × 0.7)/100 = 0.0925, or 9.25%.

Now, what happens when we increase the amount of debt from $50 to $60, which reduces equity to $40? Revenue and profit before interest remain unchanged. In this case, the amount of interest due is $3, so that profit after interest is $7 and the return on assets declines to 7%. Equation (1.10) leads to a return on equity of $7/0.4 = 17.5\%$. This demonstrates the so-called leverage effect. If the interest rate is lower than the return on assets, a higher level of debt will increase the return on equity. A higher level of debt, however, also increases the firm's risk. And when the interest rate is higher than the internal rate of return, the leverage effect becomes negative, i.e. higher debt decreases return on equity.

Indicators such as return on sales, return on total assets, and return on equity have advantages compared to the reporting of absolute profits. They allow comparisons across business units, companies, industries, and even across countries, although each measures different aspects of profit achievement. We will get back to these in later chapters.

To illustrate all of these financial indicators together, we use the example of a midsized manufacturer of consumer goods. Figure 1.3 shows the key figures for their previous fiscal year. This company has total assets of $134 million and revenue of $91 million. Capital turnover is therefore 0.67 times per year. The company's net return on sales is 10.3%. The net return on assets is 7.0%. The ratio of debt to assets is 58.2%, which means the return on equity is 16.8% according to Eq. (1.10). Overall, this company has a solid profit and financial picture.

Key figures	$m	in percent
Assets	134	100
Equity	56	41.8
Debt	78	58.2
Capital turnover		67.9
Revenue	91	100
Depreciation	5.9	6.5
Interest	1,5	1.6
Tax	3.8	4.2
Earnings before interest, taxes, depreciation, amortization (EBITDA)	20.6	22.6
Earnings before interest and tax (EBIT)	14.7	16.2
Earnings before tax (EBT)	13.2	14.5
Earnings after tax (EAT)	9.4	10.3
Return on assets based on EBIT		11.0
Return on assets based on EAT		7.0
Return on equity		16.8

Fig. 1.3 Profit indicators for a midsized consumer goods company

Nominal versus Real Profit

Thus far we have only considered the nominal, accounting-based profit. That means that the profit figures—no matter which ones we choose—are expressed in current currency units. If one adjusts the nominal profit for inflation, one gets the so-called real profit. In periods of relatively low inflation, like what we have experienced since 1994, the difference between nominal and real profit is small. During that 25-year period to 2019, the annual inflation rate in the United States exceeded 3% only five times, and was under 2% in 12 years. That is much different from the 1970s. The annual inflation rate was above 6% in eight years between 1971 and 1982. Europe has experienced similar inflation rates during the same periods.

Let's assume that a company has revenue of $100 million and an after-tax profit of $10 million. The company's machinery, which cost $50 million to purchase, is depreciated over five years and then replaced all at once. The annual depreciation was thus $10 million. The business remains steady over the five-year period, i.e. the nominal revenue and profit remained unchanged from year to year at $100 million and $10 million respectively. What is the effect of an annual inflation rate of 5%, which means that the machinery becomes 5% more expensive every year? Replacing the machinery after five years would not cost $50 million, but rather $63.8 million. This difference of $13.8 million is a "phantom profit."

One can also express this in another way. The profit declines every year by 5% in real terms. In the fifth year, the company earns a real profit of only $7.8 million on a nominal profit of $10 million. The company would have had to increase its tax-reducing level of depreciation by a total of $13.8 million to offset the effects of inflation and maintain the same level of purchasing power in real terms. But the tax basis for depreciation is solely the original purchase costs, and the total amount of depreciation cannot exceed them.

Taxes are levied against nominal profit. The phantom profits are therefore subject to taxation, even though they do not contribute to an increase in real value. Regarding additional effects of inflation, such as the question of passing on higher input costs in the form of higher prices, we refer the reader to specialized literature.[9] In times of high inflation, companies should strive to protect their real profit and not get blinded by the allure of phantom profits.

---

[9]See Hermann Simon and Martin Fassnacht [4].

Profit and Opportunity Costs

Let's assume that an existing business would generate a return on assets (ROA) of 8%. Should the company continue with that business? Should someone invest in a proposed project with an expected ROA of 8%? Is it wiser to continue such a project or pull the plug?

There are no absolute black-and-white answers to such questions. Instead, the answers depend on the available alternatives. If one expects a return of only 6% from other investments—assuming similar risk profiles—than yes, the company should continue the existing business or invest in the proposed project. But if other opportunities offer returns of 10%, it makes more sense to invest in those opportunities instead of continuing the business in question or pursuing the new project.

Some concepts about profit are not oriented toward the accounting-based costs, i.e. the actual amount of money spent, but rather toward the opportunity costs of capital. These opportunity costs are defined as the achievable returns from other investments, assuming comparable levels of risk. The so-called "normal profit" is the profit that owners or investors must earn in order to cover their opportunity costs. If the venture is less profitable than expected, equity investors will divest their money and re-invest it where they can earn higher returns. In competitive capital markets, a company must earn at least the "normal profit" in order to attract an adequate amount of equity.

The so-called "economic profit" (also called "excess profit") measures whether a business has earned more than its opportunity cost of capital. In other words, economic profit represents the difference between the ROA and the total cost of capital, multiplied by the company's total assets. The economic profit (EP) is thus defined as:

$$EP = \text{total assets} \times (ROA - WACC) \qquad (1.11)$$

where WACC is the weighted-average cost of capital. What plays a vital role in determining normal profit and economic profit is the risk-adjusted minimum return required by capital investors. This makes the variable WACC relevant for both equity and debt investors. WACC is defined as:

$$WACC = e(\text{equity/assets}) + f(1 - s)(\text{debt/assets}) \qquad (1.12)$$

where equity, debt, and assets are measured at market value rather than at book value.

e = the return demanded by equity investors.

f = the interest demanded by debt investors.

s = the corporate tax rate.

The value of debt is treated as after tax, because the interest (cost of capital) is tax deductible.

A critical variable in Eq. (1.12) is e, which expresses the return demanded or expected by equity investors. Its value is calculated using the Capital Asset Pricing Model (CAPM) as a risk-free capital investment plus a risk premium.[10] This is where the risk-related components of profit are expressed.

Historical WACC numbers are easy to find online. At the start of 2020, the WACC for Apple was 8.39%, while IBM's was 7.95% and ExxonMobil's was 7.7%. The Chinese firm Alibaba had a significantly higher WACC of 13.35%. Japanese firms, in contrast, tend to have lower WACC's. Sony's is 5.34% and Toyota's merely 2.12%.

WACC can vary by business unit in order to reflect differences in risks. Daimler (Mercedes) uses a WACC of 8% for its classic automotive business, but 15% for the new businesses grouped under "Daimler Mobility."[11] WACC can also vary by country for the same company. Compugroup Medical S.E. uses 6.1% for Germany, 7.0% for Poland, and 8.7% for Turkey.[12]

We illustrate the effects with a numerical example. Let's assume that a company has total assets of $100 million, generates a return on assets of 10%, and has a WACC of 8%. The economic profit is then $100(0.1 - 0.08) = \$2$ million. In other words, the company earned $2 million more than its capital costs.

The concept of economic profit is frequently used in practice in the form of economic value added (EVA), an idea promulgated by the consulting firm Stern Stewart.[13] Many companies use the EVA concept to manage their businesses. Economic profit even plays a central role in privately held businesses. Koch Industries, the world's largest family-owned business with annual sales of $110 billion, uses the opportunity cost of capital as the key metric for managing the business, according to CEO Charles G. Koch.[14] The basic idea to use the opportunity cost of capital as the basis of comparison is not new.

---

[10] See Louis Perridon, Manfred Steiner und Andreas W. Rathgeber [5].

[11] See https://www.daimler.com/dokumente/investoren/berichte/geschaeftsberichte/daimler/daimler-ir-jahresfinanzbericht-2017.pdf, p. 251.

[12] CompuGroup Medical S.E., annual report 2017; see https://www.bundesanzeiger.de/ebanzwww/wexsservlet

[13] See Joel M. Stern and John S. Shiely [6] as well as Bennet Stewart [7].

[14] See Charles G. Koch [8].

It has its roots in a recommendation from Alfred Marshall in 1890.[15] The same thinking is reflected in the discounted cash flow (DCF) method.

Profit and Risk

One of the basic laws of economics says that profit and risk have a positive correlation. In other words, opportunities for higher profit carry a greater burden of risk. We can distill this law into a simple rule for decision making. For a given level of profit, one should choose the alternative with the lower risk. Conversely, one should pick the alternative with the highest potential profit if risks are equal. Harry M. Markowitz received the Nobel Prize in 1990 for his groundbreaking work on this topic, originally published in a paper in 1952. Markowitz shows that one can achieve a more favorable profit-risk profile through diversification than through one single investment.[16] Numerous models would later expand on Markowitz's basic principle. One of the best-known of those models is the Capital Asset Pricing Model (CAPM) based on the work of William F. Sharpe.[17] This model addresses the question of what portion of the overall risk of an investment cannot be eliminated through diversification. It explains how capital markets evaluate higher-risk investment opportunities.

Profit Determination in Practice

In practice, determining the profit for accounting and tax purposes is a difficult undertaking. The reason is that there are so many factors that influence profit yet are laden with uncertainty and hard to quantify. For example, what is the appropriate amount of goodwill to write off after acquiring another firm? How should future risks be assessed, when they require the firm to set aside provisions which adversely affect profit in the current period? What time periods should be established for determining the profit for ongoing projects, when events that occur in one period affect profit in a subsequent period?

Those are just a few of the numerous valuation questions that come up in practice when one tries to determine the profit. Many of these are subject to accounting principles and tax codes. The rules may differ from country to country. In this book, we will not go into detail on such problems or on

---

[15]See Alfred Marshall [9].

[16]See Harry M. Markowitz [10].

[17]See William F. Sharpe [11].

the more intricate definitions of profit. Instead, we will concentrate on the "true" profit. Unless otherwise stated, that is the after-tax profit, also called net profit or net income.

Profit and Value Creation

A company purchases raw materials, consumables, and energy from suppliers, as well as a wide array of services such as consulting, advertising support, facilities management, or software as a service (SaaS). When one subtracts the costs of these inputs from the company's revenue, the difference is the so-called added value, i.e. the amount of value the firm has created. This metric expresses how much value a firm's production and service processes add to the inputs it procures. The value added essentially comprises four components: gross wages, interest, taxes, and profit.

The value added forms the basis in many countries for the familiar value-added tax, or VAT. The sum of the added values of all the companies in a given country, plus the amount of investment and government activity, is the country's gross domestic product or GDP. Occasionally the revenue of giant companies will be compared to the GDP of small countries. Such comparisons are apples-to-oranges and thus not very useful, because they compare revenue with a measure of value creation. In any case, profits are a component of value added. That is true at the corporate level and the national level.

Profit and Liquidity

Profit and liquidity are two different things. Liquidity indicates the ability of a company to meet its current payment obligations. Can a company go bankrupt even if it is profitable? The answer is yes. If insufficient liquidity is available when debt comes due, the company must declare itself insolvent, regardless of how high its profits are. On the other hand, if a company is liquid, this does not automatically mean that it is profitable. Amazon posted either losses or only minimal profits in the first 20 years since its founding in 1994. Salesforce.com had a similar track record. Established in 1999, it ran up a cumulative loss of $339 million in its first 18 years. Despite these losses and high levels of investment, neither Amazon nor Salesforce.com ever experienced problems with liquidity. In such situations, however, a company cannot meet its obligations solely using its own available resources. It is in constant need of money in the form of loans, debt, or equity capital increases.

In other situations, parent companies must step in and close the liquidity gaps of their subsidiaries. General Motors kept its former German subsidiary Opel afloat by continually injecting capital, even though Opel racked up a cumulative loss of $19 billion between 1999 and 2016. But even GM eventually had enough, and sold Opel to the French group PSA (now Stellantis) in 2017.[18] As long as banks, shareholders, or parent companies are willing to make money available to a company, a weak or non-existent level of profitability does not pose a threat to liquidity.

The reverse situation—that a company generates a profit but faces liquidity problems—can also occur, although it is very unusual. The moment a company issues an invoice for work completed or goods sold, it can record the invoiced amount as revenue and have it contribute to profit. But as long as the customer does not pay, the company's liquidity will suffer despite its profit on paper. But over a longer-term perspective, the combination of profit and a lack of liquidity is rare.

Some liquidity actions such as payments, disbursements, collections, or capital inflows have no effect on profit. When a company pays back a loan, money leaves the company's coffers, but profit remains unchanged. The change is manifested in a contraction of the balance sheet, as the assets are reduced by the amount repaid, and the liabilities by an equal amount. Taking out a loan or drawing on a line of credit likewise has no effect on profit. Both sides of the balance sheet expand as the liabilities rise, offset by the actual money that flows into the company as an asset. Profit remains unchanged until the first interest payment is due. When customers pay for shipments or for services rendered, those payments also have no influence on profit.[19] They represent only a shift in assets, as accounts receivable becomes smaller and cash larger by the same amount.

Conversely, there are measures or actions that drive profit, but do not affect a firm's liquidity. Such measures include depreciation. The payment was made at the moment of purchase, but from an accounting standpoint, the costs are spread over a longer period.

Liquidity is often compared to the air we breathe. Cut off the "air" of a business, and it will die quickly. Even a single day of insolvency can spell the end of a business. In contrast, profit is more akin to a nutrition supplement. Under some circumstances, a person—like a company—can survive for years without it, but at some point, the deficiency becomes dangerous.

---

[18] After merging with FiatChrysler in 2021, the group now has the name Stellantis.

[19] If a company uses cash-based accounting, the timing of payments against accounts receivable has a strong effect on profit, not only on liquidity.

Cash Flow

The most common metric for assessing liquidity is cash flow. The simplest definition of cash flow is the difference between cash inflows and cash outflows in a given period. Cash flow can be positive or negative. In the indirect method for calculating cash flow, one takes the net profit and adds back the expenses that did not involve actual payments. The most important of such expenses are depreciation and amortization. Cash flow is therefore often also defined as net profit plus depreciation and amortization. Conversely, there can be actions that increase profit—such as the sale of goods on credit—that do not trigger an immediate payment and therefore do not affect the cash flow. The ratio of cash flow to revenue is referred to as the cash flow margin.

An important process in determining how advantageous investment opportunities are is the discounted cash flow (DCF) method. The DCF corresponds to the sum of all future cash flows, discounted by a chosen discount rate. That discount rate represents the return on relevant alternative investments. The basic thought behind DCF is similar to the economic profit concept. If the net present value is positive, then the investment or project will earn more than its alternative. If one uses the WACC as the discount rate in the DCF model, the result is the economic profit.

Free Cash Flow

Similar to profit, there are many variants of cash flow in use in practice. It is therefore advisable to ask for the precise definition in any given discussion. The so-called free cash flow (FCF) is especially important in financial reporting to the capital markets (banks, investment funds, analysts) as well as to investors in general. The FCF refers to a company's freely available cash flow and is the sum of the cash flow from operations and the cash flow from investment activities. It indicates how much money the company has available to pay dividends, make distributions, or pay down debt. FCF is an indicator of a company's capacity for financing. It plays its strongest role in times when financing capacity is tight, such as during periods of strong growth. Jeff Bezos, the founder of Amazon, got straight to the point when he said: "Percentage margins are not one of the things we are seeking to optimize. It's the absolute dollar free cash flow per share you want to maximize, and if you can do this by lowering margins, we would do that. Prioritizing free cash flow will allow you to experiment and innovate quickly."[20] In this spirit, FCF reflects how much financial leeway a company has and is a particularly important factor in a company's early stages.

The FCF stories of two groups of internet companies are eye-opening.[21] The first group comprises the "older" companies Google, Apple, Facebook, and Amazon. Google's FCF was never significantly negative, nor was Apple's. Facebook was FCF-negative only in two years, 2007 and 2008. The sum of Amazon's negative FCF between 1999 and 2001 was $813 million, which is a small amount relative to its revenue. So in the early years, these four firms altogether had a negative FCF of around $1 billion.

Now let's look at the "younger" group of start-ups in the internet era: Tesla, Uber, Lyft, and Snap. Companies such as these are so-called cash burners. In contrast to the four older companies, these four younger ones have collectively "burned up" $23.9 billion in cash through 2019, covering 22 separate years with FCF deficits. Beyond that, roughly 84% of all companies that went public in 2019 reported no profits.[22] It is a legitimate question to ask whether investors will ever recoup the money already invested and earn a profit that covers the cost of capital.

Free cash flow is considered to have a strong effect on shareholder value. One advantage of free cash flow is that, for all practical purposes, it cannot be manipulated by accounting "tricks."[23] But metrics such as cash flow or free cash flow do not give any direct indication about the level of a company's profits.

Profit is Profit

The numerous profit terms and concepts that we have discussed in this chapter have hopefully not led to further confusion. When one deals with profit, it is absolutely essential to know what term and which kind of profit is under discussion.

Some metrics such as EBITDA or EBIT do not measure profit in the sense of how we defined it at the outset: the residual amount that the company has after fulfilling all its obligations to third parties. At the same time, despite all of the refinements that the other definitions of profit supposedly bring, it

---

[20]Cited from Carsten Linz, TIS Customer Day, Frankfurt, November 2018, p. 23.
[21]See "The Biggest Burners", *Fortune*, July 29, 2019, pp. 16–17.
[22]See "Herd Instincts", *The Economist*, April 20, 2019, pp. 23–26.
[23]See. http://boerse.ard.de/boersenwissen/boersenlexikon/freier-cash-flow-100.html.

remains true that "profit is profit." That is because the individual profit variations tend to go in the same direction, or statistically speaking, they tend to be highly correlated. A company that earns a high after-tax profit typically achieves an economic profit. For economic profit to be positive, the company must earn at least its weighted-average cost of capital (WACC). For accounting profit the break-even point is zero, while in economic profit it is defined by WACC. But in either case, a higher profit is preferable to a lower profit.

Summary

The goal of this chapter was to provide the reader a concise overview of common profit terms and concepts, as well as their derivations and interrelationships. This book, however, doesn't aim to dig more deeply into complex accounting and finance questions. Instead, we focus on the economic, managerial, and ethical aspects of profit.

Profit is what a business or entrepreneur can retain after fulfilling all obligations to third parties. By the simplest definition, profit is the difference between revenue and costs, in some cases adjusted for other aspects unrelated to business operations. Profit is an important component of value added.

Profits are interpreted by some authors as the cost of survival. More broadly-defined terms for profit have become popular, but they include factors that mask the determination of true profit. They should be viewed with caution.

Profits can be expressed in absolute terms or in the form of returns. In the latter case, commonly used metrics are return on sales, return on equity, and return on assets. There are also terms such as normal profit and economic profit which take the opportunity cost of capital into account. If a company does not recover its cost of capital, it may report an accounting profit but does not generate an economic profit.

A company can be liquid, but not profitable. This case is quite frequent in early stages. Conversely a profitable company can be illiquid and end up insolvent. This case is rare. Cash flow and liquidity-based metrics play an important role in practice, but they offer no direct insights into a firm's profitability. Over time, however, profit and liquidity tend to go in the same direction.

References

1. Drucker, P. (1975). The Delusion of 'Profits', *The Wall Street Journal*, 10.
2. Winkler, R. (2019). Uber and Lyft Get Creative with Numbers, but Investors Aren't Blind to the Losses, *Wall Street Journal Online*.
3. Giersberg, G. (2017). Gewinn vor Kosten, *Frankfurter Allgemeine Zeitung*.
4. Simon. H., & Fassnacht, M. (2019). *Price Management,* Springer: New York.
5. Perridon, L., Steiner, M., & Rathgeber, A. W. (2016). *Finanzwirtschaft der Unternehmung*, (17th edn), Munich: Vahlen.
6. Stern, J. M., & Shiely, J. S. (2001). *The EVA Challenge: Implementing Value-added Change in an Organization*, New York: Wiley.
7. Stewart, B. (1991). *The Quest for Value: the EVA Management Guide*, New York: Harper Business.
8. Koch, C. G. (2007). *The Science of Success: How Market-Based Management Built the World's Largest Private Company*, Hoboken: Wiley.
9. Marshall, A. (1890). *Principles of Economics*, (1st edn), London: Macmillan.
10. Markowitz, H. M. (1971). *Portfolio Selection*, New Haven: Yale University Press.
11. Sharpe, W. F. (1970). *Portfolio Theory and Capital Markets*, New York: McGraw Hill.

2

In Search of Profit

Marcel Proust became famous thanks to his monumental work *In Search of Lost Time*. In this chapter we set out in search of profits.

We will begin that journey by asking about profit perceptions in the general population. Then we will compare profits across countries, industries, and companies of various sizes. We will see that returns vary extremely by country, industry, and company. At the company level, we will learn that there are a few extremely profitable companies that account for a large share of profits. But on the other hand, a great many companies constantly generate low returns and do not earn their cost of capital (WACC). Our considerations in this chapter are essentially based on after-tax profits. This corresponds to our definition of true profit, the money that the owners can keep for themselves after all obligations are met. We note, though, that comparisons of pre-tax and after-tax profits can lead to different evaluations and trends, because tax rates differ across countries.[1]

Overestimated Profits

What does the average citizen think about profit? Numerous studies have explored that topic. We'll start with what people think in the United States, where a survey posed the following question to a representative sample: "Just

---

[1] https://www.wsj.com/articles/huge-disparity-in-corporate-profits-hints-at-something-amiss-115763 28400.

© The Author(s), under exclusive license to Springer Nature Switzerland AG 2021
H. Simon, *True Profit!*,
https://doi.org/10.1007/978-3-030-76702-0_2

a rough guess, what percent profit on each dollar of sales do you think the average company makes after taxes?"[2] The average response was 36%! This is very consistent with research that advertising guru David Ogilvy cites in his book *Ogilvy on Advertising:* "the average shopper thought Sears Roebuck made a profit of 37% on sales."[3] Sears' true profit at that time was less than 5%.

Responses to similar questions in nine different polls between 1971 and 1987 ranged from 28 to 37% and averaged 31.6%. What is the truth? The actual average after-tax profit margins of US companies over the long term is around 5%. In other words, the respondents overestimated the level of corporate profits by a factor of six. We found very similar perceptions in a study conducted in Italy in 2019. Respondents there estimated net profit margins to be 38%.[4]

People in Germany have also responded to surveys with similar questions.[5] The answers varied between 15.75 and 24.15% with 20% on average.[6] In Austria, a comparable number was 17%.[7] In other countries we could not find similar surveys.[8]

In light of these astounding findings, I decided to conduct my own survey and personally asked 100 people whom I approached randomly in pedestrian zones or similar places. Such a sampling is known as a convenience sample, from which one cannot expect to draw representative conclusions. My interest was not only to collect the individual numerical answers from each person, but also to observe their reactions when I posed this question: "How much remains as profit after costs and taxes when a company collects €100 in revenue?".

People with some business sense may find this question relatively easy. But a significant number of the respondents found the question to be difficult. Some were flustered and admitted that they had never once given any thought to the topic. Some resolutely insisted they could not or would not name a number, explaining that they did not have even the slightest clue about profit

---

[2] Survey from May 2013, https://www.aei.org/carpe-diem/the-public-thinks-the-average-company-makes-a-36-profit-margin-which-is-about-5x-too-high/.

[3] David Ogilvy [1].

[4] Study conducted by Simon-Kucher & Partners, Milan 2019.

[5] We note that the role of value-added taxes was not addressed in this study or the subsequent ones. That can lead to some skewing of results, but not at a magnitude that would fundamentally change the misconceotions and incorrect estimates.

[6] 19.97%, to be exact.

[7] https://www.lifepr.de/inaktiv/raiffeisenlandesbank-oberoesterreich-aktiengesellschaft/Wir-muessen-das-Schmuddelimage-des-Gewinns-ueberwinden/boxid/233688.

[8] We looked for similar studies in the following countries: UK, France, Spain, Japan, Netherlands, Belgium, Poland, Sweden, Denmark.

margins. Others refused to answer the question on ideological grounds, with some citing their absolute aversion to profits.

This survey was a new and unusual experience for me. It dawned on me that every student of business or economics should be required to ask normal people about the topic of profit. I never did that myself in my time in academia, neither as a student nor as a professor.

What did the results look like? On average (arithmetic mean) the respondents estimated a net profit margin of 22.8%. Despite the small sample size, this result is well in line with the results of previous representative surveys. But the average doesn't tell the whole story. Figure 2.1 shows the distribution of the respondents' answers.

It was hard to believe, but the answers ranged from 0 to 80%. The standard deviation was also very high, at 19%. This spread demonstrates—similar to the United States—that there is widespread uncertainty and unfamiliarity driving these estimates of net profit margins. Figure 2.1 also shows the true

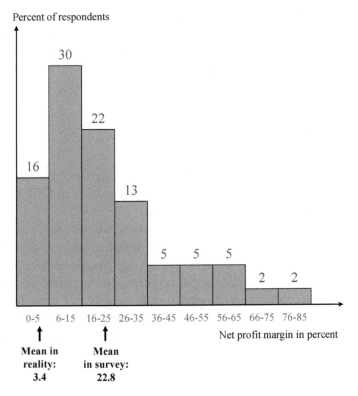

Fig. 2.1 Distribution of estimates of net profit margins (Germany)

average net profit margin of German firms over a span of 14 years. It is a mere 3.4%. People overestimated profit margins by a factor of six.

The similarities between the estimates in the US and Germany strike me as both noteworthy and extremely interesting. In both countries, the actual net profit margins were overestimated by a factor of six, i.e. by 500%. The general and widespread lack of knowledge about actual profits is cause for concern.

How does one explain such extreme misperceptions? I have no convincing answer. But we can say that such distortions exist in many aspects of society. In a representative study conducted in 37 countries, participants were asked how high the unemployment rate was in the country. The average estimate across all countries was 34%, while in reality the mean unemployment rate was only 7%. Amazingly, this misjudgment was also off by a factor of five.[9] In his highly regarded book *Factfulness*, the late Hans Rosling cited countless examples of misperceptions permeating a broad spectrum of daily life and diagnosed a "devastating global ignorance."[10]

The perceptions of the general population regarding profits deviate massively from reality. One could even argue that the population has lost its sense of reality when it consistently makes estimates that are off by a factor of five or six. In the next section, we will take a closer look at the true profit situation.

Profits by Country

We now look at corporate profits by country. Figure 2.2 shows the net profit margins (after-tax return on sales) for companies in OECD member countries. The relevant period is eight years.[11]

Because the economic strength of the countries shows a wide variance, we use the gross domestic product (GDP) as a weighting factor to determine the average margin. That results in an overall average margin of 5.71%. The net profit margins vary significantly across countries. In the period we examined, the profit margins of Russian companies were roughly five times higher than those generated by Japanese firms. US firms were slightly below average at 4.9%. German and Japanese firms showed the lowest net profit margins.

---

[9] See "Perils of Perception 2018," IPSOS, https://www.ipsos.com/en-my/perils-perception-2018.
[10] See Hans Rosling [2].
[11] This data set is available for the years 2003 to 2010, after 2010 the publication was discontinued.

Margins of Industrial Firms

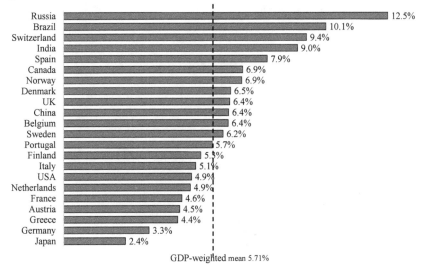

GDP-weighted mean 5.71%

Fig. 2.2 Net profit margins of companies in OECD countries

Smaller Country, Higher Margin

If we plot the average national net profit margins against the rank of the gross domestic products (GDP) of the respective countries, we can observe a slightly negative correlation between the economic size of a country and the profit margins of its companies. Figure 2.3 shows this relationship.

This relationship is in fact statistically significant.[12] Net profit margins tend to be lower in larger countries and higher in smaller countries. This finding contradicts the concept of economies of scale. One explanation could be that larger countries have more intense competition, which puts downward pressure on margins. If this hypothesis is true, it means that the intensity of competition has a stronger influence on profit margins than economies of scale.

One also has the impression that profit margins are strongly correlated with the risks in the respective countries. That would reflect the general relationship between profits and risk. One can achieve higher margins in countries such as Russia, Brazil, and India, which can be classified as high-risk economies. Switzerland is a notable exception.

Figure 2.3 also shows that the net profit margins in member countries of the European Union (EU) tend to be lower. Including EU membership as a

---

[12]$R^2 = 0.694$, overall significance 99%.

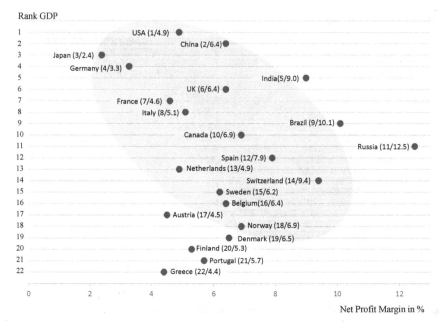

Fig. 2.3 Net Profit Margin versus Gross Domestic Product (GDP) rank

variable in the regression analysis does in fact yield a somewhat better explanation.[13] Membership in the EU leads to a reduction of net profit margin of 2.4 percentage points. Companies in the EU earn lower profits relative to companies outside the EU. Tax rates, which are generally higher in the EU, help explain this phenomenon.

Profit Dynamics

Also interesting is the way the net profit margins changed over the eight-year period. Figure 2.4 illustrates this dynamic.

The average margin over the eight years was 6.05%, but there were considerable differences from year to year. In the best year, 2007, the net profit margin was more than twice as high as in the worst year, 2003. Profits in that year still presumably suffered from the lingering effects of the internet bubble's burst and the terrorist attacks on September 11, 2001. One will note that in the two years of the Great Recession—2008 and 2009—the profit declines were relatively moderate.

---

[13]$R^2 = 0.718$, overall significance 90%.

After-tax return on sales in %

2003-2005 19 countries, 2006 21 countries, 2007-2010 22 countries

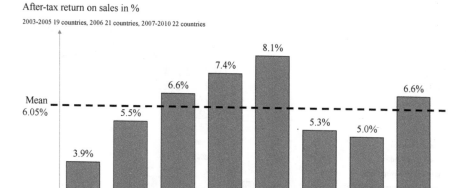

Fig. 2.4 Profit dynamics in OECD countries over an eight-year period

Sector Margins

The insight that profit margins differ vastly across countries and years also applies to industrial sectors. These margins are subject to many factors, including the intensity of competition, the extent of value creation, capital turnover, and the velocity and intensity of research and development. Even within a sector, margins can be very volatile from year to year. Print media is one example. The sector's previously high margins, which were at 10.4% in 2007, collapsed due to the rise of the internet and went negative to −1.6% in 2019. In cyclical industries such as oil and gas, price fluctuations can have a strong effect on annual profit margins. In contrast, other sectors such as pharmaceuticals show sustained high margins.

There are numerous studies on margins by sector, but unfortunately their comparability is limited. We cite here one New York University study which comprised 7,053 companies in the United States across 93 sectors.[14] Figure 2.5 shows the net profit margins for 14 selected industry sectors.

The median net profit margin across all 93 sectors stood at 5.9%, which lies within the range of the values we have cited so far. Software showed the highest value among the selected sectors at 20.53%, while green and renewable energy brought up the rear at −11.39%.

---

[14]http://pages.stern.nyu.edu/~adamodar/New_Home_Page/datafile/margin.html.

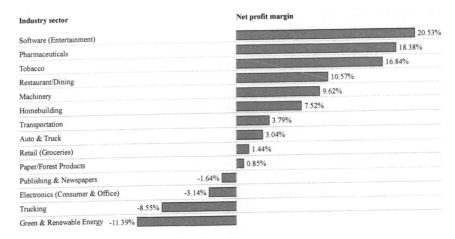

Fig. 2.5 Net profit margins for 14 selected industry sectors

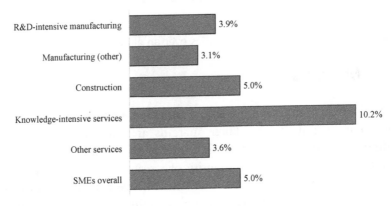

Fig. 2.6 Net return on sales for German SMEs, by industry sector

The German bank KfW issued a report on profit margins for small and mid-sized (SME) businesses across many sectors.[15] Figure 2.6 shows the net return on sales for five large sectors as well as for the SME businesses as a whole.

This study reveals wide variance across sectors. For the "manufacturing (other)" sector, the return was only 3.1%, while SMEs overall posted a net return on sales of 5.0%. Within the service sector, large differences are apparent across sub-sectors. While knowledge-intensive services had an average return of 10.2%, other services mustered only 3.6%. Return on sales

---

[15]https://www.kfw.de/PDF/Download-Center/Konzernthemen/Research/PDF-Dokumente-KfW-Mittelstandspanel/Mittelstandspanel-2017-%E2%80%93-Tabellenband.pdf. The original numbers were pre-tax. They were adjusted using a tax rate of 30%.

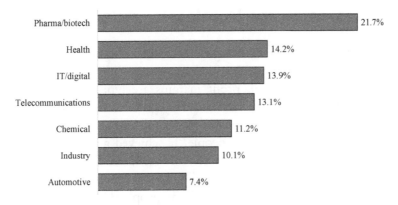

Fig. 2.7 Return on sales (EBIT-based) by industry for research-intensive companies

in this study showed a negative correlation with company size, meaning that smaller companies earned higher returns on average than larger ones.

In a global study of 500 research-focused, publicly traded companies, the accounting and consulting group EY studied the return on sales for selected industries. But in the spirit of our caveat from Chap. 1, we need to define precisely what type of profit the study looked at. In this case, they compared EBIT margins (Earnings before Interest and Taxes) instead of net margins.[16] Figure 2.7 shows the results. The differences in returns are once again considerable. The pharma/biotech industry has almost three times the return as the automotive industry. The different levels of R&D intensity are one explanation for these stark differences. Pharma/biotech companies spend on average 17.1% of sales on R&D, whereas the automotive OEMs devote only 4% of their sales to R&D.

We can draw a few conclusions from these studies. First, return on sales— or other measures of margin or profit—vary significantly by industry sector, with research-intensive industries achieving higher margins. Some findings support the hypothesis that margin is negatively correlated with the size of the company (measured by revenue). But comparing margins across industries is only of limited use. Comparisons of companies within a particular industry provide more meaningful benchmarks. While an individual company can, through good management, improve the overall average of its sector, it does not conduct business in a vacuum and is subject to the conditions in its sector. In that sense, margins by sector or industry provide an important reference point.

---

[16]See "Top 500 F&E: Wer investiert am meisten in Innovationen," EY, July 2019.

Returns in Retail and Wholesale Trade

Companies in the retail trade can generate massive amounts of revenue, but their margins tend to be low. Nonetheless, margins in the sector vary widely.

In food-and-grocery retail, profit margins are typically below 3%, and often even under 1%. Walmart, the world's largest retailer and also the world's largest company in terms of revenue, generated revenue of $524 billion in 2019 and employed 2.2 million people. It achieved a net profit margin of 2.84%. The German food-and-grocery retail group REWE posted revenue of €49.4 billion and net profit of €338 million. That corresponds to a net profit margin of 0.68%. REWE employed 345,434 people. The retail group Metro's revenue totaled $41.4 billion and it lost $142.1 million. Metro employed 97,606 people.

Retailers outside of food-and-grocery have recorded significantly higher margins, The Swedish furniture retailer IKEA, which employs 208,000 people, is an excellent example. It earned a net profit of €2.47 billion on revenue of €36.3 billion, for a net profit margin of 6.8%.[17] The net profit margins of so-called "fast fashion" retailers are even more robust. Inditex, which operates the Zara chain, has a net profit margin of 13.7%.[18] Right on their heels are Primark with 12.4%, H&M with 11.3%, and Uniqlo with 10.4%. All of these chains are low-price retailers with extremely efficient operations and high inventory turnover.

We also observe sharp differences in wholesale trade. The largest company in Switzerland in terms of revenue, Glencore, is a global, diversified producer and trader of natural resources. It earned an after-tax profit of $2.6 billion on revenue of $220 billion, for a net profit margin of 1.18%. With around 70,000 employees, the pharmaceutical wholesaler McKesson had revenue of $231 billion, but its net profit was only $900 million for a net margin of 0.4%. The German pharmaceutical wholesaler Phoenix Pharma SE, with 34,000 employees, had revenue of €30.5 billion, but its net profit of €6 million left it with a net profit margin of 0.02%. But within wholesale, there are also exceptions. The world's largest industrial goods wholesaler, Würth, has a workforce of 77,080 worldwide and earned €687 million on sales of €13.6 billion, which results in a relatively high net profit margin of 5.0%.

These examples demonstrate that within the retail and wholesale trade, the net profit margins as well as the structures of the value chains show significant differences.

---

[17]Numbers are for 2017.

[18]Vgl.   https://de.statista.com/statistik/daten/studie/510433/umfrage/netto-umsatzrenditen-globaler-fast-fashion-filialisten/.

The Profits of the Giants

After the analysis of profits by country and by sector, we will now take a closer look at the profit situation of the world's largest corporations. The basis is the data for the Fortune Global 500, which comprises the world's 500 largest companies in terms of revenue.[19] In 2019, they came from 32 countries, with China (124), the United States (121), and Japan (53) alone accounting for 60% of the companies. The Global 500 employ 69.9 million people around the world and serve as a barometer for the world economy.

The Fortune Global 500 earned an aggregate net profit of $2.061 trillion on revenues of $33.294 trillion. That works out to a net profit margin of 6.19%. On average, each company on the list achieved a revenue of $66.59 billion and a profit of $4.12 billion. The arithmetic mean of profits, however, is influenced by the extremely high profits of a handful of companies that skew the overall picture. The profits of Saudi Aramco, which totaled $88 billion, contribute $176 million to the average on their own. More insightful is the median figure, which eliminates the distorting effects of outliers such as Saudi Aramco. The median net profit of the Fortune Global 500 is $2.03 billion, and the corresponding median net profit margin is 3.68%. The median value is much more representative of the average profit performance of these giant companies than the arithmetic mean.

Arithmetic mean and median consolidate a large amount of data into one numerical parameter. But in this process, a large amount of information gets lost. A more informative way to understand the profit performance is to look at the distribution of net profit margins for the Global 500. The distribution in Fig. 2.8 shows data for the 2019 business year.

The most striking aspect of this distribution is the wide range of margins. They range from -30.8% for Schlumberger to + 33.1% for Taiwan Semiconductor Manufacturing. The distribution also reveals a much more differentiated view than we could gain from looking at the arithmetic mean and the median. Out of the 500 companies, 45 of them, or 9%, posted a net loss in 2019. The average loss of those companies was $2.255 billion, and the aggregate total loss was $101 billion.

The share of companies with a positive net profit margin of less than 2.5% is also high. Almost one third, exactly 29.0%, fall into this category. And about every fifth company (exactly 20.2%) earned between 2.51 and 5% on sales. When we include these two categories and those that lost money, the

---

Number of Fortune Global 500 companies

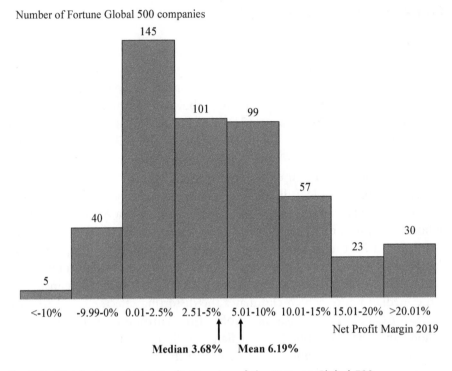

Fig. 2.8   Distribution of Net Profit Margins of the Fortune Global 500

total comes to 291 companies or 58.2% of the list. Most of these corporations, i.e. more than half of the Fortune Global 500 companies, are unlikely
to have earned their capital costs (measured as WACC) in 2019,[20] and thus
did not produce any economic profit. That is an alarming finding. All of these
companies should urgently shift their focus to profit maximization.

Profit Dynamics of the Global 500

Over the 10 years from 2010 through 2019, the profit margins of the
Fortune Global 500 showed a remarkable stability. Figure 2.9 traces the profit
development.

The arithmetic means of the net profit margins were above 5% in all years,
with the best performance of the decade in 2018. The average margin over the
entire period was 5.65%. In comparison to Fig. 2.4, which shows the annual
margins for OECD countries, the profit margins of the world's corporate

---

[20]Weighted Average Cost of Capital, see Chap. 1.

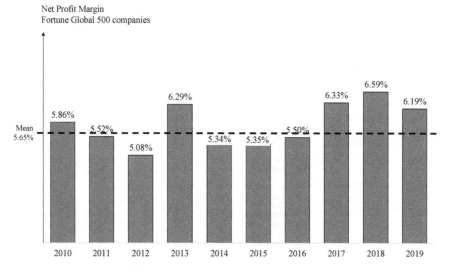

Fig. 2.9 Profit Dynamics of Fortune Global 500 over 10 years

giants showed less volatility than the margins by country. One explanation for this finding is that the Fortune Global 500 generally have operations throughout the world. Globalization acts as a risk diversifier, which leads to lower volatility. Please also note that Figs. 2.4 and 2.9 cover different time periods. The difference might appear to be slight at first glance, but the world economy grew more evenly in the 2010s than it did in the first decade of the millennium.

Profit Stars

The attention of the general public tends to fixate strongly on companies that earn very high profits. Figure 2.10 shows the 25 members of the Global 500 with the highest profits. We call them the Profit Stars.

Because the absolute numbers for the year shatter the outer limits of most people's imaginations, we have also included the profits per day in Fig. 2.10. Even at that scale the numbers are breathtaking. These Profit Stars represent only 5% of the Global 500, but racked up a grand total of $764 billion in profits. That corresponds to more than one third (37.1%, to be exact) of all the profits earned by the Fortune Global 500 corporations. This percentage is up from 33.1% the year before, indicating an even higher concentration of profits.

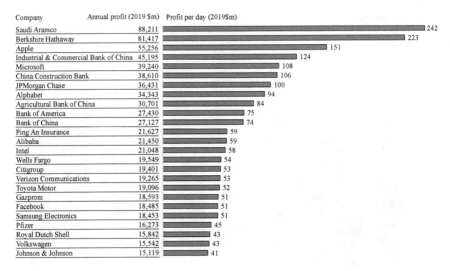

Fig. 2.10 The 25 Profit Stars of the 2019 Fortune Global 500

Several things stand out on the list of Profit Stars. The 25 companies come from only eight countries. But 13 of the 25 are from the United States and six from China. All other countries (Saudi Arabia, Japan, Russia, Korea, the Netherlands and Germany) have only one Profit Star. Eight of the 25 are banks, four each from China and the US. The next largest group is the tech companies, comprising Apple, Samsung Electronics, Microsoft, Alphabet, Alibaba, Intel, Verizon, and Facebook. That means that two thirds of the Profit Stars come from just two sectors: banking and technology/telecom, again confirming the high concentration of profits.

Margin Stars

While the list of stars in absolute profits is not identical with the list of companies that achieve the highest net profit margins, there is substantial overlap. Figure 2.11 lists the 30 corporations among the Global 500 which achieved net profit margins of more than 20%. We call them Margin Stars.

Once again there is a heavy concentration with ten corporations in banking, nine in technology, and five in pharmaceuticals. These three sectors alone comprise 80% of the list. Pharmaceuticals is another strong sector with five companies. In terms of regional distribution, the US (16 corporations) and China (seven) dominate the list. Only four Margin Stars are from Europe, none of them from the European Union. This analysis of profit in absolute and percentage terms leads to the conclusion that is

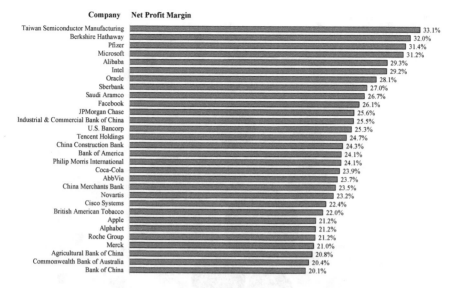

Fig. 2.11 The 30 Margin Stars of the 2019 Fortune Global 500

appropriately summarized in this statement from Bridgewater: "US Superstar Phenomenon: When we scan around the world, the US stands out as having a disproportionate share of 'superstar' companies: large firms with very strong market positions, high margins, and substantial profits."[21]

In this regard, it is illuminating to take an additional look at the 500 largest US companies, which are compiled in a separate list by *Fortune*. Figure 2.12 illustrates the net profits for the US companies on that list.[22]

The surface of each circle represents the net profit. The picture demonstrates the extreme concentration of profits among a small number of Profit Stars. These highly profitable companies also come from just a few sectors, such as technology and banking. This phenomenon of extreme profit concentration in the hands of just a few companies from a few sectors has become more pronounced in recent years. It has led to a corresponding divergence in market capitalizations and raises troubling questions about competitive practices. In October 2020, the US Department of Justice filed an anti-trust lawsuit "to stop Google from unlawfully maintaining monopolies through anticompetitive and exclusionary practices in the search and search advertising markets and to remedy the competitive harms."[23]

---

[21] https://www.bridgewater.com/research-library/daily-observations/peak-profit-margins-a-global-perspective/peak-profit-margins-a-global-perspective.pdf.

[22] *Fortune*, July 1, 2019, p. F25, please observe that only the 455 companies with profits are shown.

[23] https://www.justice.gov/opa/pr/justice-department-sues-monopolist-google-violating-antitrust-laws.

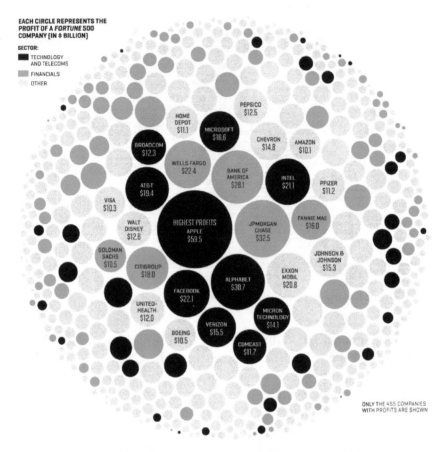

EACH CIRCLE REPRESENTS THE
PROFIT OF A *FORTUNE 500*
COMPANY (IN $ BILLION)

SECTOR:
■ TECHNOLOGY
  AND TELECOMS
▨ FINANCIALS
▧ OTHER

PEPSICO $12.5

HOME DEPOT $11.1

MICROSOFT $16.6

CHEVRON $14.8

AMAZON $10.1

BROADCOM $12.3

WELLS FARGO $22.4

BANK OF AMERICA $28.1

INTEL $21.1

PFIZER $11.2

AT&T $19.4

VISA $10.3

WALT DISNEY $12.6

HIGHEST PROFITS APPLE $59.5

JPMORGAN CHASE $32.5

FANNIE MAE $16.0

GOLDMAN SACHS $10.5

CITIGROUP $18.0

EXXON MOBIL $20.8

ALPHABET $30.7

JOHNSON & JOHNSON $15.3

FACEBOOK $22.1

UNITED-HEALTH $12.0

BOEING $10.5

VERIZON $15.5

MICRON TECHNOLOGY $14.1

COMCAST $11.7

ONLY THE 455 COMPANIES
WITH PROFITS ARE SHOWN

Fig. 2.12 Visualization of 2018 Profits of American Fortune 500 Companies

Global Superstars

Thus far we have looked primarily at the Global 500, the world's largest corporations. One study that extended beyond the Global 500 examined the profits of 5,750 companies with at least $1 billion in annual revenue.[24] This study delivers a more representative view of the global profit situation. One criterion the study used to rank the companies was economic profit, i.e. the profit earned beyond the amount of money needed to cover the company's capital costs (WACC). Companies that ranked in the top 10% (top decile) in economic profit among the 5,750 companies were labeled Superstars. The findings of the study are surprising and very interesting:

---

[24]See "Superstars—The Dynamics of Firms, Sectors, and Cities Leading the Global Economy," Discussion Paper, McKinsey Global Institute, October 2018. See also the summary version at: https://www.mckinsey.com/featured-insights/innovation-and-growth/what-every-ceo-needs-to-know-about-superstar-companies.

- The distribution of economic profits is extremely uneven. The top decile, i.e. the Superstars, accounted for 80% of all the economic profits earned by the companies on the entire list. This is reminiscent of the earning power of Apple, which rakes in more than 80% of the profits in the smartphone market despite having a market share of "only" 15% on a unit basis.
- The top 1% among the Superstars, i.e. 57 companies, alone bring in 36% of all the economic profits of the 5,750 companies.
- The middle 60% of all companies earned essentially little or no economic profit, meaning that in the best cases they barely covered their WACC.
- The lowest decile, comprising the weakest earners that make up the bottom 10%, suffer economic losses and, in aggregate, destroy as much value as the Superstars generate. Many of these companies can only survive because they receive support from their national governments. They are often referred to as "zombie" companies.
- The gap between the Superstars and the median company widens over time. The same applies for the lowest decile. The economic profit margins, in other words, are drifting apart. Superstars and "Super Losers" are much farther apart from each other nowadays than they were 20 years ago.
- The Superstar segment is very dynamic. Almost half of the companies drop out of the top decile within 10 years. Some 40% of those fallen stars, or 20% of all the Superstars, plummet all the way down to the lowest decile. The old stock exchange slogan "never grab a falling knife" seems confirmed by this dynamic.
- Superstars are by no means limited to a small number of industries. The diversity of sectors has actually increased, with these sectors growing in importance: finance, professional services, real estate, pharmaceuticals and medical technology, and internet/media/software.
- The spread of regions has also grown, with the Superstars concentrated more and more in megacities. The study identified 50 "Superstar Cities" whose per capita income is 45% higher than the income in the surrounding regions.

The Superstar Study not only confirmed the findings from the analysis of the Fortune Global 500, but also established those insights on a much broader basis. A few Superstars account for the lion's share of the profits earned in their respective markets. The majority of large companies either barely earns their cost of capital or suffers economic losses. We can observe an increasing dynamic and volatility in profit positions, driven by trends such as digitalization, greater research-and-development intensity, and the emergence of new companies in the developing world.

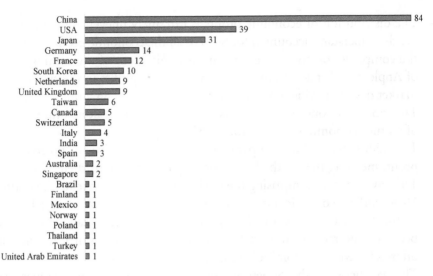

Fig. 2.13 Companies in the troupe of mediocrity, by country

The Troupe of Mediocrity

It is understandable that the companies with the highest profits attract the most attention from the public and the capital markets. This selective focus of attention explains in part the public's great overestimation of profit margins, which we described at the outset of this chapter. The profit reality for most companies is far more modest. As we know from Fig. 2.8, roughly half of the Global 500 or 246 companies earn a net profit margin between 0 and 5%. This view is consistent with the findings of the Superstar Study, according to which 60% of the analyzed companies earn no economic profit. Such firms are much more representative of the overall global profit picture than Profit Stars or Superstars, whose net profit margins are usually in excess of 20%.

What is the profit reality for this "troupe of mediocrity" in the Global 500? Their average revenue is $70 billion, somewhat higher than the overall average of $66.6 billion. Their median revenue of $46.3 billion is almost identical to the overall median of $47.1 billion. So from a revenue stand-point they play in the same league as the Profit Stars. But their profit margins are extremely modest, at 2.3% (average) and 2.1% (median).[25] Most of the companies in this category do not earn their WACC. Their profit situation is highly unsatisfactory.

Interesting are the countries of origin of the troupe of mediocrity. These are shown in Fig. 2.13.

---

[25]The arithmetic mean and the median are close to each other in this case, because limiting the interval ti between 0 and 5 excludes the possibility of outliers.

Among the Fortune Global 500, 84 companies are based in China and earn net profit margins of less than 5%. This corresponds to 68% of the 124 Chinese firms in the Global 500. The share of Japanese companies with such low net profit margins is 58%, while the percentages for Germany (52%) and the UK (41%) are somewhat lower. France (39%), Canada (38%) and Switzerland (36%) have similar shares of mediocre performers. Among countries with substantial numbers of Global 500 corporations, the US ranks best with only 32% among the troupe of mediocrity. The mediocre performers would be well advised to pay more attention to profit improvement.

The Money Losers

Below the troupe of mediocrity, we find the 45 companies among the Fortune Global 500 that lost money. Figure 2.14 lists the 25 largest money losers for 2019, ranked by loss margin.

Europe has nine money losers, seven of which are from the European Union. While Europe is strongly represented among the Money Losers, it has

Company	Revenue ($m)	Profit ($m)	Country	Net Profit Margin
Schlumberger	32,917	-10,137	USA	-30.80%
Pemex	72,820	-18,039	Mexico	-24.77%
Deutsche Bank	41,780	-6,033	Germany	-14.44%
U.S. Postal Service	71,154	-8,813	USA	-12.39%
SoftBank Group	87,440	-8,844	Japan	-10.11%
Repsol	47,544	-4,271	Spain	-8.98%
Nippon Steel Corporation	54,465	-3,969	Japan	-7.29%
Nissan Motor	90,863	-6,174	Japan	-6.79%
JFE Holdings	34,305	-1,819	Japan	-5.30%
General Electric	95,214	-4,979	USA	-5.23%
Tata Motors	37,242	-1,703	India	-4.57%
Centrica	28,934	-1,305	UK	-4.51%
Vale	37,570	-1,683	Brazil	-4.48%
Korea Electric Power	50,257	-2,013	South Korea	-4.00%
ArcelorMittal	70,615	-2,454	Luxembourg	-3.48%
Toshiba	31,179	-1,054	Japan	-3.38%
Dow	42,951	-1,359	USA	-3.16%
Bunge	41,140	-1,280	USA	-3.11%
Auchan Holding	54,672	-1,638	France	-3.00%
Marubeni	62,799	-1,816	Japan	-2.89%
Continental	49,783	-1,371	Germany	-2.75%
SNCF Group	39,308	-897	France	-2.28%
ENEOS Holdings	75,897	-1,729	Japan	-2.28%
Vodafone Group	49,960	-1,022	UK	-2.05%
Airbus	78,883	-1,524	Netherlands	-1.93%

Fig. 2.14 The 25 companies in the Global 500 with the highest loss margins

few Profit Stars. Seven Japanese companies are among the big money losers in terms of return on sales. The US is next with five companies. Note that there is no Chinese company among the 25 biggest money losers.

The Fortune Global 500 corporations are an important mirror of the world economy. Their profit margins have been relatively stable over the years, though 2018 was a record-high year. Nonetheless, the median of the net profit margins for 2019 was only 3.71%, which means that many of these large corporations do not earn back their cost of capital and thus turn no economic profit. The Superstar Study came to similar conclusions. Among the world's largest companies, there are a few Superstars that attract considerable public attention and earn more than one third of all global economic profits. The profit rankings are very dynamic, meaning that the views and analyses for a given year are only a snapshot. The United States is strongly represented among the Profit Stars, while China and Japan have many firms with mediocre results. Europa, in turn, accounts for many of the Money Losers, but has hardly any superstars.

A Look At Asia

The fact that Asia has been the growth region makes it worthwhile to take a closer look at the profit situation there. A study of the world's 5,000 largest companies revealed that between 2005 and 2017, more than half of all new investments flowed to Asian companies.[26] The profit on these investments in Asia, however, has been below average. While the investment in North American companies generated an aggregate economic profit of $245 billion, the investments in Asia generated an economic loss of $206 billion.

Asian companies are underrepresented among the most profitable firms, but their share of money-losing firms is disproportionately high. The authors of the study attribute this relatively weak performance to several reasons. First, Asia still lags behind other regions in terms of development, in particular in high value-added segments, high tech, and the presence of strong brands. These are exactly the segments where US-based firms achieve high profits. The predominance of such segments, in which Asian companies are less profitable, accounts for two thirds of the profit difference. Another factor behind the relatively low profit performance in Asia is the prevalence of companies

---

[26] https://www.mckinsey.com/featured-insights/asia-pacific/getting-the-measure-of-corporate-asia?cid=podcast-eml-alt-mip-mck&hlkid=a7ed7ae31b7e4407ab929ac029f838b7&hctky=10318136&hdpid=9408c2be-66dc-41d3-8451-3d2b3f72abd3.

that are either state-owned or not exchange listed. Publicly traded companies tend to be more profitable, and that holds true around the world. This situation led to the following diagnosis from McKinsey: "Asia could unlock billions of economic profit by turning around troubled companies"[27] These assessments are more or less applicable to European companies as well.

Hidden Champions

So far we have focused on large companies. In the United States, these companies play an outstanding role. The US Fortune 500 account for 42% of the revenue and 53% of the profit of the Fortune Global 500.[28] In other countries, large companies have significantly less economic weight, and small and mid-sized enterprises (SMEs) play a correspondingly greater role. Germany is a typical example. The so-called Mittelstand companies are a major force behind the country's position as one of the world's top exporting nations. For this reason, we will take a closer look at the profit situation of SMEs in Germany.

In international comparisons, German companies generally find themselves at the low end of the lists, with an average net profit margin of 3.3% (see Fig. 2.2). Germany's central bank came to similar results in its survey of corporate profits between 2003 and 2016. The average net profit margin in that dataset was 3.24%. The average profit margins for 27 German companies that rank among the Global 500 for 2019 are identical at 3.25% and well below the average margins for the Global 500 of 6.19%. In short, German companies are notoriously weak performers in terms of profits.

However, within Germany's *Mittelstand* there are many highly profitable companies. The first group we will look at in detail are the Hidden Champions. A Hidden Champion is a company that is either among the top three in its global market or number one on its home continent, has less than $5 billion in annual sales and is not well known to the general public.[29] Germany has 1,573 Hidden Champions, accounting for 46% of the 3,406 Hidden Champions that I have detected around the world.[30] Germany thus has far more Hidden Champions than any other country. They form the

---

[27] https://www.mckinsey.com/featured-insights/asia-pacific/corporate-asia-a-capital-paradox.

[28] *Fortune*, July 1, 2019 for American 500 and *Fortune*, August 26, 2019 for Global 500.

[29] See Hermann Simon [3]

[30] Hermann Simon, *Hidden Champions—The New Game in the Chinese Century*, New York: Springer 2021.

Company	Sector	Revenue in €m	Net profit in €m	Net return on sales in %
Publity AG	Real estate services	34.6	14.9	43.1
CTS Eventim	Ticketing	225	95.4	42.4
Teamviewer	Remote screen control	157	61.9	39.4
Chemetall	Chemical coatings	188	59.8	31.8
Payback	Rebate systems	281	87.9	31.3
Lohmann Therapiesysteme	Transdermal therapy systems	226	69.3	30.7
Kryolan	Professional make-up	25	7.5	30.0
Eppendorf	Laboratory equipment	425	120.9	28.4
FTI Ticketshop	Ticketing	15.4	4.3	27.9
Puls	Rail power supplies	108	28.9	26.8
Rational	Professional cooking systems	491	129	26.3
Pulsion	Medical technology	25.6	6.7	26.2
Lange Uhren	Luxury watches	114	28.8	25.3
RIB Software	Construction software	54	12.8	23.7
Lamy	Writing utensils	112	26.0	23.2
Scout24	Advisory Sales	480	110.9	23.1
Buhl-Data-Service	Software	85	19.5	22.9
Evotec	Pharmaceutical development	375	84.1	22.4
Weng Fine Art	Art dealer	4.4	0.97	22.0
Dr. Falk Pharma	Pharmaceuticals	324	71.4	22.0
Prisma Verlag	Print media supplements	25.6	5.56	21.7
Motel One	Hotels	487	104	21.4
Mast-Jägermeister	Spirits	412	87.7	21.3
Horst Brandstätter Holding (Playmobil)	Toys	642	133	20.7
Scheubeck Holding (Reinhausen)	Electronics	745	151	20.3
Lotto 24	Online lottery	38.3	7.7	20.1

Fig. 2.15 Selection of Profit Stars in Germany with a net return on sales of more than 20%

elite of the country's Mittelstand and the backbone of the "German export machine."

Since the start of the 1990's, I have conducted numerous studies on these Hidden Champions. Through 2019 they have earned an average net profit margin of 8%, an outstanding performance. This makes them 2 ½ times more profitable than the average company in Germany and roughly 25% better on average than the companies that comprise the Fortune Global 500. It is clear that the German Hidden Champions have delivered outstanding profitability over the years, relative to other companies.

Despite the generally rather bleak profit situation in Germany, the country still has some Profit Stars that can hold their own in international comparisons. Figure 2.15 lists 25 companies that all achieve a net profit margin of more than 20%.[31] Within those 25, there is a very wide range of profit margins. Only 6% of the Global 500 earn margins at least that high. All of the companies in Fig. 2.15 have less than $1 billion in annual sales, making them

---

[31] Sources include reports in the *Bundesanzeiger*, various corporate reports, and the newspapers *FAZ* and *Handelsblatt*.

true SMEs. Quite a few of them are Hidden Champions, e.g. Teamviewer, Chemetall, Lohmann, Eppendorf, Puls, and RIB Software.

Revealing here is the fact that these small and mid-sized Profit Stars are by no means limited to a few industries such as pharmaceuticals or luxury goods, where people expect high profit margins. Instead, they come from a wide cross section of industries. The highest net return on sales, at 43.1%, was achieved by the publicly-traded real estate services firm Publity AG. The list also includes Rational, the global market leader for professional cooking systems, the electronics firms Puls and Scheubeck Holding, the rebate system provider Payback, software and internet companies such as Teamviewer and Scout24, the ticket agent CTS Eventim, a chemical company (Chemetall) and a hotel chain (Motel One). Mast-Jägermeister is a Profit Star from the food-and-grocery sector. Even the crisis-riddled print media sector has a representative on the list with the publisher Prisma-Verlag. Despite its small size, the highly profitable Weng Fine Art AG is publicly traded.[32]

I want to emphasize three points with these cases. First, smaller companies can succeed in earning high profits, just as large companies can. The second is that even in a relatively weak profit climate such as Germany's, there are companies that indeed earn very high margins. Third, the selected companies in Fig. 2.15 show that high profits are possible across a wide spread of industries. Competing in a particular industry cannot serve as a blanket excuse for weak profit performance. It always comes down to the company itself and its competencies. I hope that message encourages Mittelstand companies in other countries to adopt the Hidden Champions approach and pursue the same kinds of very ambitious profit goals.

Return on Capital

So far in this chapter we have compared net profit margins or net return on sales. One can legitimately ask whether that is the relevant metric for comparing profit performance. Wouldn't it make more sense to compare companies by their return on equity or their return on asset? Shouldn't the firm's owners, i.e. the shareholders, be more interested in return on equity than in return on sales? As mentioned before, return on equity or return on assets are definitely meaningful to compare companies across industries. From the perspective of investors, such comparisons make a lot of sense.

---

[32]The data for Chemetall are for the 2016 fiscal year. The company was acquired by BASF in 2017 and consolidated into BASF's group results. The data for Eppendorf are from 2016. The data for Motel One and Weng Fine Art are from 2018.

Return on sales (net profit margin), return on assets, and return on equity are interrelated. If we solve Eq. (1.8) for Return on Assets, we get:

$$\text{return on assets} = \text{return on sales} \times \text{capital turnover} \qquad (2.1)$$

If the capital turnover is 1, the return on assets equals the return on sales. If capital turnover is higher, the return on assets is correspondingly higher. Walmart has a capital turnover of 2.22 times per year, so that its return on sales of 2.84% translates into a return on assets of 6.30%. In contrast, a very asset-intensive company such as AT&T turns its capital over only 0.33 times per year. It has a return on sales of 7.67% and therefore a return on assets of 2.53%. Apple has a capital turnover of 0.77, which means it has a return on assets of 16.3% based on a return on sales of 21.2%. The revenue structure and the capital structure of each of these firms are very different.

For an investor, however, the return on assets is less important than the return on equity, because that metric reflects the return that investors earn on their own money. From Eq. (1.10) we can derive the following relationship.

$$\text{return on equity} = \text{return on sales} \times \text{capital turnover}$$
$$\times \left(1 + \text{debt-to-equity ratio}\right) \qquad (2.2)$$

The debt-to-equity ratio plays a central role in the relationship between return on sales and return on equity. If capital turnover and the debt-to-equity ratio both equal 1, then the return on equity is twice the return on sales. If the debt-to-equity ratio is 2 and the capital turnover is 1, then the return on equity is three times the return on sales. If the company has no debt, a rare case, and capital turnover is 1 the return on sales and equity are the same. For a given return on sales, the higher the debt-to-equity ratio, the higher the return on equity will be.

Applying the relationships to the three example companies, we get the following debt-to-equity ratios and return on equity:

	Debt-to-Equity Ratio	Return on Equity
Walmart:	1.75	17.33%
AT&T:	1.73	6.91%
Apple:	1.12	34.65%

These cases show that the returns on equity vary greatly between companies.

Germany is an interesting case with regard to the influence of debt and equity. German companies have a return on sales (net profit margin) of 3.3%, which is low by international standards. But German companies also tend to have high debt-to-equity ratios of around 4. If we assume capital turnover of 1 and apply Eq. (2.2) we get a return on equity of 16.5%. This is close to the result of an empirical study which reported an average return on equity for German companies of 15.4%.[33] This is in the same ballpark as the return on equity in the United States (16.9%) and Europe (12.9%).[34]

Thus, the German business world seems to be in order with respect to return on equity, in contrast to how it stacks up in terms of return on sales. But this is due to the high debt-to-equity ratio. This ratio drives the return on equity up, but has a negative side effect: the higher the debt-to-equity ratio, the higher the risk. The satisfactory performance in terms of return on equity, compared with return on sales, has been "bought" by taking on more risk.[35]

The Hidden Champions deviate from this pattern, however. Their return on equity of 25% is significantly above the average of 15.4%, but there is an important difference. That higher return on equity is not the result of a higher debt-to-equity ratio. The Hidden Champions, in fact, have a debt-to-equity ratio of 0.72, meaning that they are predominantly equity-financed. The high profitability of the Hidden Champions derives instead from continuous innovation, top performance, and high prices, not from a high debt-to-equity ratio. A pervasive cost-consciousness, another trait of Mittelstand companies, also contributes significantly to the higher profitability. Strong profits form the basis for accumulating equity capital, which reduces the need for debt and thus mitigates risk.

Summary

Our search for profits turned up many surprises. The general public has a complete misperception of how profitable companies truly are. The average person on the street overestimates net profit margins by more than 500%. These misperceptions prevail both in Europe and in America.

The most striking discoveries about profits are the large differences across countries, industry sectors, and individual companies. For countries, net profit margins tend to be higher when the country lies outside Europe and when its tax rates are lower. Two other aspects hold true: the smaller a country is, and the riskier it is, the higher net profit margins tend to be.

---

[33] See "Erfolgskennziffern deutscher Unternehmen," Deutsche Bundesbank.

[34] See http://pages.stern.nyu.edu/~adamodar/New_Home_Page/datafile/roe.html.

[35] There are numerous financial formulas for quantifying these risk costs, but they are inevitably based on averages and historical values and thus relatively useless when applied to an individual case.

Industry sectors also show sharp differences in net profit margins. Those with a higher intensity of research tend to have higher margins, while the wholesale and retail trades generally have lower margins.

Among the world's largest companies, a small number of Profit Stars accounts for the majority of all profits. This skewed distribution of profits among the Fortune Global 500 is evident in the difference between the average net profit margin (6.19%) and the median of 3.68%. More broadly speaking, the top one percent of large companies earns roughly one third of economic profits. The profit performance among large companies is also highly dynamic. It is not unusual for Profit Stars to fall to the bottom category within just a few years.

The majority of companies belongs to the Troupe of Mediocrity, whose average net profit margins is only 2%. These companies do not earn back their weighted-average cost of capital (WACC) and, thus, do not turn any economic profit.

The imbalance in the distribution of profits is widening. That is true for countries, industries, and companies. The United States has the most Profit Stars, while one third of all large Chinese and Japanese companies land in the Troupe of Mediocrity. Europe has the most Money Losers. But even within a region with relatively low profits, one can still find Profit Stars. The analysis of German small and mid-sized businesses such as the Hidden Champions illustrates this.

For investors and lenders, capital-based profit metrics such as return on assets (ROA) or return on equity (ROE) can be more relevant than the return on sales. The return on sales forms the basis for calculating these capital-based metrics, but one also needs to know capital turnover rates and equity ratios. The various metrics can result in different profit rankings for companies, but one must also take the level of risk into account. A higher debt-to-equity ratio increases return on equity, but at the same time induces higher risk.

We conclude that we observe large and increasing profit discrepancies between countries, industry sectors, and individual companies. In Chap. 5 we will explore in detail causes of these discrepancies and ways to address them strategically.

References

1. Ogilvy, D. (1983). *Ogilvy on Advertising*, New York: Random House, 74.
2. Rosling, H. (2018). *Factfulness—Wie wir lernen, die Welt so zu sehen, wie sie ist*, Berlin: Ullstein.
3. Simon, H. (2009). *Hidden Champions of the 21st Century*, New York: Springer.

3

The Goal

In this chapter we will deal with the economic aspects of earning profits and of profit orientation. We will explore the ethical questions surrounding profit in Chap. 4.

All economic action requires an objective or target.[1] Or as the Roman philosopher Seneca said: "If one does not know to which port one is sailing, no wind is favorable." There are two answers regarding the question of why profit is the most sensible—perhaps even the *only* sensible—objective for guiding and managing a company.

The simple answer, and the easiest to understand, is that profit is the only metric that takes all the consequences of economic activity—the revenue side and the cost side—equally into account. All other potential goals for a firm—such as sales volume, market share, or preserving jobs—consider only some aspects of economic activity and are therefore limited in their use as corporate goals or objectives.[2] At best, one should view them as secondary or temporary objectives, and even then, one should impose an additional profit-oriented constraint or condition, such as a minimum level of profit.

The second answer derives from economic theory, which makes certain assumptions regarding the behavior of consumers and companies. These

---

[1]See Goldratt [1].

[2]The idea from William R. Baumol, that managers should pursue revenue maximization, is also widely known. Baumol says: "Businessmen see some connection between scale and profit. In my dealings with them I have been struck with the importance they attach to the value of their sales." Baumol [2]. For a deeper discussion, see also Sandmeyer [3] and Anderson [4]. This working paper can be found on numerous homepages.

assumptions include rationality, the existence and accessibility of complete information, and the desire of consumers to maximize their utility. These modeling assumptions lead to the goal of profit maximization for companies, a goal that is a fundamental element of the market economy.

But the significance of the profit goal goes beyond these aspects. It affects the overarching, and often only implicit, goal of survival and preservation. Peter Drucker succinctly described this key role of profits: "Profit is a condition of survival. It is the cost of the future, the cost of staying in business."[3]

As we mentioned already in Chap. 1, one can interpret profit as "the cost of survival." Whoever wants to secure the future of a company must build in a calculation for these "survival costs" and endeavor to cover them the way a business tries to cover all its other costs.[4] So with respect to planning and management, profit can by no means be considered simply as a residual amount of money—hopefully with a plus sign before it—or as a mere "nice to have" at the end of a particular business period. It should be treated upfront as another cost the company must cover. This turns profit into a proxy for the ability of a company to survive.

Theory versus Reality

A huge gulf lies between the economic models and theories that lead to the goal of profit maximization and what actually happens in practice. Of course, the real-life goals of a company are more complex and diverse than what the textbook theories state. Most companies pursue several goals simultaneously. Researchers and academics have looked intensively at the topic of multiple, often competing business goals.[5] But these efforts have not had a significant impact on business practice, at least not at the strategic level that we are focusing on here. The Balanced Scorecard (BSC) developed by Robert S. Kaplan and David P. Norton attempted to provide an integrated way to manage multiple goals.[6] But the BSC is not viewed as a model for success

---

[3] Drucker [5].

[4] Drucker has also interpreted profit as the cost of future risks, by asking: "What is the minimum profitability needed to cover the future risks of the business?," Drucker [6].

[5] We refer the reader to the standard text Keeney and Raiffa [7]. There are also several journals devoted to this theme, such as *Journal of Multi-Criteria Decision Making, International Journal of Multicriteria Decision Making, Multiple Criteria Decision Making*.

[6] See Kaplan and Norton [8].

and has failed to work in many companies. Some authors explain these failures by saying that such comprehensive, integrated management of goals is too complicated.[7]

Distinguishing between short- and long-term goals has proven on the one hand to be highly relevant, but on the other hand, extraordinarily difficult. The first of many questions is: what precisely is meant by short term and long term? Is the short term a month, a quarter, or one full year? Does long term mean five years, or ten years? Could it even mean a lifetime, in the spirit John Maynard Keynes, who said that "in the long run we are all dead"?

The retail trade has sometimes given me the impression that short term means "one day." In an earlier phase of my career I conducted management seminars for retail managers. Each seminar began at 8 a.m. and I invariably noticed that the participants were very restless. At 9 a.m., many of them left the room, and some disappeared during the coffee break that followed shortly thereafter. When I asked what was going on, I was told that "the results from the previous day come out at 9 a.m. and I need to see them."

Publicly traded companies are obligated to issue quarterly reports. This gives rise to a short-term orientation toward quarterly results. General Electric reported revenue and profit growth in every single quarter during the tenure of CEO Jack Welch, which ran from April 1981 to September 2001. But it is hard to believe that such a trend would be possible without a certain amount of "accounting cosmetics."

At the other extreme are companies that experience robust revenue growth over a long period, but do not earn any profits. The best-known example is Amazon. The firm turned its first profit, albeit a tiny one, in the fourth quarter of 2001, seven years after it was founded. It took Amazon 13 years until the sum of its cumulative profits and losses netted out to a positive number. In 2019, however, Amazon earned an impressive $11.6 billion in net profits. Through the 2019 business year, Amazon's cumulative profit stood at "only" around $34 billion, well below Google's (now Alphabet), which was founded two years later but has accumulated $190 billion in net profits.[8] Nonetheless, Amazon's strategy has been very successful. Amazon's market capitalization stood at $1.56 trillion in early 2021.

Then there is the case of the software company Salesforce.com, which was founded in 1999 and posted revenue of $13.3 billion in fiscal 2019. Its cumulative loss after its first 20 years was $276 million, but its market capitalization reached $200 billion in January 2021, more than 11 times its annual revenue at the time. The shared office space provider WeWork, founded in 2010,

---

[7] See Schäffer and Weber [9].

[8] See "Transformation der Tech-Riesen," *Frankfurter Allgemeine Zeitung*, May 4, 2019, p. 24.

showed a loss of $1.9 billion in 2018 on revenue of $1.8 billion. WeWork had never achieved a profit through 2018. That situation is possible when investors continually pump in money. Japan's Softbank alone has invested $10 billion in WeWork, which was valued at $47 billion at the start of 2019. Then in November 2019, Softbank announced that it would be writing off $4.6 billion on its WeWork investment.[9]

These examples show that a company's objectives can depend very strongly on its life cycle. Short-term losses—and "short term" here can mean several years—can indeed be in line with long-term profit maximization. But a prerequisite for success with this approach is the willingness of banks or investors to ensure the company maintains adequate liquidity. Ultimately, the long-term profit goals must take precedence. A long-term profit orientation is essentially identical with the concept of shareholder value, which we will discuss in detail later.

Goals in Practice

Strategy development starts with the company's goals, from which specific objectives for managing all aspects of the business can be derived. Clear goals and the resulting guidance are indispensable requirements for professional management. That is easy to say, but the development of clear strategic goals often proves difficult in practice. Goals are not always expressed clearly and unequivocally, a situation that sometimes leads to unspoken goals receiving more weight than the explicitly formulated objectives.

Typical corporate goals include:

- **Profitability** (profit, return on sales, return on equity, return on assets, shareholder value): Most companies pursue profit goals that are stated in more or less clear form.
- **Volume and growth goals** (volume, market share, customers, revenue, or revenue growth): Volume, revenue, and growth goals often serve as proxies for long-term profit maximization or the increase of shareholder value. For years, Volkswagen set itself a volume goal, namely, to sell more cars than Toyota. In the New Economy around the year 2000, companies almost exclusively prioritized these kinds of goals. In recent times, volume growth or customer growth have again become important goals for start-ups.

---

[9]See "Softbank Takes a $4.6 Billion Hit from WeWork," *New York Times*, November 6, 2019; see also https://www.wsj.com/articles/the-money-men-who-enabled-adam-neumann-and-the-wework-debacle-11576299616.

- **Financial goals** (liquidity, creditworthiness, indebtedness): These goals play important roles for new companies that may not have sufficient capital, or for companies that are facing a crisis.
- **Power goals** (market leadership, market dominance, social or political influence): Many Hidden Champions not only pursue the goal of market leadership, but view it as an element of their identity. It is often said that Google wants to dominate any market it enters. In his best-selling book Zero to One, investor Peter Thiel encourages companies to find niches that they can dominate, with the ultimate goal "to first dominate a specific niche and then scale to adjacent markets."[10] Right from the outset, Flixbus established and pursued the goal of dominating the deregulated market for long-distance bus travel in Germany. Fighting and beating the competition is a popular goal among managers, and in my own experience, that goal is most pronounced in the United States. One of many examples is Southwest Airlines, which since its founding has sought market leadership on all the routes it serves.
- **Social goals** (creating or preserving jobs, avoiding layoffs or furloughs, employee satisfaction, supporting social causes, sustainability, climate objectives): Based on their social goals, companies sometimes sell their products or services at prices that do not cover costs, but allow them to avoid cutting jobs. Many companies, but especially small and mid-sized businesses, followed that route during the Great Recession of 2008-09. This behavior runs contrary to short-term profit maximization, but can definitely be in synch with long-term profit orientation and shareholder value. For example, keeping qualified staff on board during a crisis may allow the company to recover faster when the crisis ends.

Companies can also cross-subsidize products and services, in order to make them accessible to customer segments that could otherwise not afford them. Common examples include discounts for students and seniors. Some pharmaceutical companies offer their products at much lower prices in poorer countries than in wealthier regions. The firm Patagonia, a manufacturer of outdoor clothing and gear, has made ecological sustainability a central tenet of its corporate mission. Patagonia donates employee time, services, and at least one percent of its revenues to environmental groups throughout the world. The INGKA Foundation, based in the Netherlands, is the owner of the global furniture company IKEA. It is only allowed to invest its funds in IKEA or make donations to charitable causes.

---

[10]Thiel [10].

Goals affect the choice of instruments that a company employs. In pursuit of growth goals, a company can focus on innovation or on aggressively low prices. Profit and other financial goals can be realized through cost cutting or price increases. Companies can try to achieve their power goals by starting price wars, by taking control of a sales channel, or by taking over competitors.

Goal Conflicts

In practice, most companies pursue multiple goals simultaneously. It is not uncommon for some of these goals—and the functions responsible for them—to be at odds with each other. Profit goals, for example, can be incompatible with goals for volume, revenue, or market share. Such conflicting priorities represent day-to-day reality in most companies. I once asked one of the top managers at a well-known home appliance manufacturer how business was going, and his answer was revealing: "Our volumes have shifted toward higher-value models. That is good for profit, but it's not so good for our staff, because we are selling fewer units. Our capacity utilization goals and our profit goals are out of synch at the moment."

Figure 3.1 illustrates the typical dilemma. The vertical axis shows profit growth, while volume growth is depicted on the horizontal axis. The intersection of the two axes represents the status quo.

Quadrant I is the "manager's dream" because both profit and volume are growing. Managers generally underestimate the difficulties in reaching this quadrant. The best chances occur in strongly growing markets or with new

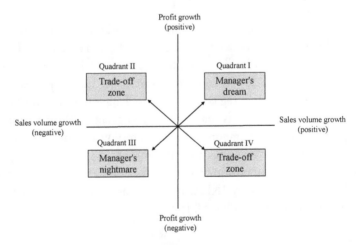

Fig. 3.1 The goal conflict between profit growth and volume growth

products whose unit costs decline as volumes rise. In mature or no-growth markets, the manager's dream is only possible when a company cuts prices that were previously too high. In that case, the lower prices boost volume to an extent that more than compensates for the lower unit contribution margin. The result is a higher profit.

In practice, the situations in Quadrants II and IV are most common. A company achieves either profit growth or volume growth, but not both at the same time. Quadrant II shows rising profits and declining volumes. This effect arises when a company's current prices were below their optimal levels. Raising the prices reduces volume, but the higher unit contribution margin offsets the volume decline and ultimately yields a higher profit. Quadrant IV shows the opposite effect, namely that profits decline while volumes rise. This happens if prices are below their optimal levels.

Managers should avoid Quadrant III at all costs. Companies land in the "manager's nightmare" when they raise prices even though the prices are already too high. This causes both volume and profit to decline. That can happen when companies more or less blindly follow a cost-plus approach to price setting.

Volume and Market Share Goals

Volume and especially market share goals play a prominent role, both in academic and business literature as well as in practice. Such goals are indispensable for planning. A company cannot properly plan and allocate its production capacity without volume targets. Volume targets are also necessary for planning logistics and distribution. Setting clear, ambitious targets for volume and market share is also an effective way to motivate salespeople. But these aspects only partly explain the popularity of volume and market share goals. There are a number of additional justifications for these goals, and some of them seem to border on being inviolable natural laws.

The best-known justification for market share goals goes back to the PIMS Study. PIMS stands for Profit Impact of Market Strategy, and Fig. 3.2 shows its most important insights.[11] According to the study's findings, there is a significant positive correlation between market share and returns. The market leader earns a pre-tax return on investment (ROI) that is more than three times as high as the smallest competitor's return. The strategic conclusion

---

[11] Buzzell and Gale [11].

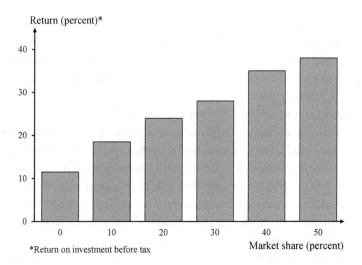

Fig. 3.2 Market share and returns

seems obvious: strive for the highest possible market share and become the market leader with the highest profit!

A second justification for pursuing high volumes and market shares comes from the concept of the experience curve. This concept states that the cost position of a company is a function of its relative market share, which is defined as one's own market share divided by the market share of the strongest competitor. The experience curve states that the larger the relative market share of a company is, the lower its unit cost will be. The market leader thus has the market's lowest cost and will earn the highest profits, assuming it and its competitors charge the same prices.

The experience curve and the PIMS Study are the mothers of all market share philosophies. Jack Welch, the CEO of General Electric from 1981 to 2001, became its most prominent advocate. When he began his tenure, he declared that General Electric will withdraw from all businesses in which it could not become the number one or number two.

The central question here is whether the link between market share and profitability represents a valid causal relationship, or merely a correlation. More recent studies have cast doubt on whether a causal relationship truly exists to the extent shown in Fig. 3.2. In any event, the newer results demonstrate a weaker link between market share and returns than the one postulated by the authors of the PIMS Study. Farris and Moore concluded that: "Once the impact of unobserved factors is econometrically removed, the remaining effect of market share on profitability is quite small."[12] These "unobservable" influencing factors include management competence, corporate structure, and the existence of sustainable competitive advantages. As the authors of one study explained it: "Although high market share, by itself, does not increase profitability, it does enable high share firms to take certain profitable actions that may not be feasible for low share firms."[13] What the authors are saying is that a higher market share does not automatically increase returns, but it does afford the larger company opportunities that small companies would not have. One example is access to important distribution channels. Another study came to the conclusion that the absolute size of a company explains no more than 50% of its profitability. Other factors likely play a more important role in driving ROI: "While a typical firm's absolute size matters for its profit experience, perhaps some other factors matter even more."[14]

Edeling and Himme have published a comprehensive meta-analysis of the link between market share and profit.[15] They calculated a market-share-to-profit elasticity for 635 business units. These elasticities reflect the percentage change in profit when market share increases by 1‰. The average elasticity turned out be 0.159, which is very low but still significantly different from zero. What does this tell us? Let's assume that a company has a market share of 50% and a profit margin of 10%. If the market share increases by 1 to 50.5%, the profit margin would rise to 10.0159. If the market share increases by 10 to 55%, the profit margin rises to 10.159%. In a subsequent analysis, Edeling eliminated methodologically induced distortions and came to a slightly negative but still statistically significant market-share-to-profit elasticity of −0,052.[16] These results call into the question the "market share is everything" philosophy.

Digitalization

A current and important question is how digitalization affects the interaction between market share and profit. In this case, different and sometimes contradictory factors come into play. Network effects confer an advantage on large suppliers. At the same time, economies of scale and experience curve effects may become less important, because marginal costs are minimal. Customers

---

[12]Farris and Moore (editor) [12].
[13]Ailawadi et al. [13].
[14]Lee [14].
[15]Edeling and Himme [15].
[16]Edeling [16].

are better informed, and companies' competitive orientation becomes keener. A particular niche—the so-called "long tail"—is easier to reach via the internet. Personalization increases. Distribution costs decline. The so-called "Superstar Theory" implies that profits will be concentrated in the hands of a small number of suppliers.

A recent study is looking at the influence of market share on the financial performance of 91 companies in the Standard & Poor's' Index with "strong digitalization" and 116 companies with "weak digitalization."[17] The dataset covers 2,497 observations for the years 1998 to 2017. The authors came to some surprising findings. Market share in digitalized sectors not only has even less influence on financial performance than it does in traditional industries. The market-share-to-profit elasticity is actually slightly negative, albeit not significantly. In digitalized sectors with a moderate or high concentration, the elasticity is significantly negative. The authors conclude: "In digital and highly concentrated industries, a strong focus on market share can have a negative impact on the company's performance. Managers should focus directly on profits rather than on market-oriented objectives such as market share."[18]

Competitive Orientation

How do competition-oriented goals—such as dominance or "beating the competition"—affect profits? Lanzilotti discovered that the pursuit of competition-oriented goals has a negative effect on margins.[19] Armstrong and Green came to a similar conclusion: "Competition-oriented goals are damaging. But the evidence has had only a modest influence on academic research, and has been essentially ignored by managers."[20] A study by Rego, Morgan, and Fornell also found empirical indications for a negative correlation between competition-oriented goals and a company's profitability.[21] These are only a few of the many studies that examine the effects of market share goals, the experience curve, or portfolio management based on the "Boston" matrix. The book *The Myth of Market Share* by Miniter offers additional arguments against the predominance of market share goals.[22]

---

[17] See Sklenarz et al. [17].
[18] Ibid., p. 9.
[19] Lanzillotti [18].
[20] Scott Armstrong and Green [19]; see also Scott Armstrong and Collopy [20].
[21] Rego et al. [21].
[22] Miniter [22].

In short, pursuing goals based on volume, market share, or harming the competition—especially in highly competitive or saturated markets—is problematic. They probably hinder companies from realizing their full profit potential.

What matters is the "how?" behind the market share, as in "how was it achieved?" In my view, the absolute level of market share itself is not the most important point. What matters more is how the company achieves that market share. If the company builds its strong market position through aggressively low prices without correspondingly low costs, then it is "buying" market share at the expense of profit. Cespedes expressly calls out the danger that can arise from the combination of market share growth and negative economic profit when he says that "additional investments accelerate the destruction of value."[23] If, on the other hand, the company earns its high market share through innovation and quality at appropriate prices, profits and margins should likewise be healthy. Furthermore, the high profits enable the company to make fresh investments in innovation and product quality. Newer studies on the links between market share and profitability affirm that strategy. Companies can boost their profitability by developing new service offerings or technologies, or by using mergers and acquisitions in the pursuit of market share goals.[24]

Striking a balance between short- and long-term effects of the respective goals remains difficult. Aggressive actions to increase market share can lead to short-term declines in profit, but can also re-adjust the market in a way that makes higher long-term profits possible. The need to balance the twin objectives of profit increases and volume increases is self-evident. In the early stages of a market or a life cycle, a greater emphasis on volume, revenue, or market share goals is normally advised, if not necessary. In the maturity stage of the product life cycle, the profit goal should come to the forefront. Then in the final stages of a product life cycle, the profit goal can become extremely short-term oriented. This is referred to as a harvesting strategy.

Profit Goals

Profit can be measured in absolute terms or in percentage terms as a margin or return. As we described in Chap. 1, there are many different margin metrics, such as return on equity, return on assets, or return on sales. Which profit

---

[23]Cespedes [23].
[24]Chu et al. [24].

indicator is best suited for a company depends on the prevailing conditions as well as the nature of the decision.

If we find ourselves in a situation in which profit must be optimized within a defined context or framework, then a profit goal in absolute terms makes the most sense. Such a situation arises when other decisions about investments capital structure, etc. have already been made. The company must then only plan parameters such as price, production, and sales volume, and costs in such a way that profit is maximized.

If a company sets a goal based on margins or returns, one must not only monitor the numerator, but also the denominator. Maximizing return on sales can lead to different outcomes than maximizing absolute profit. In the former case, a company will try to realize the projects that bring the highest profit per dollar of revenue. Higher revenues reduce the return on sales, which means that if a company wants to adhere strictly to the goal of maximizing its return in sales, it will inevitably forgo some projects, even though they are profitable in absolute terms.

Maximizing return on equity was already suggested 100 years ago as a meaningful goal.[25] That makes sense when the focus is on investments, and it applies for private investors in the stock market just as much as it applies to industrial firms. Assuming no difference in the perceived risk profiles, investors will place their money in the securities that promise the highest return per dollar invested. Industrial firms behave the same way. They invest their scarce resources in the projects that will generate the highest return on equity. For banks, the return on equity is the most important profit metric. Equity generally represents around 10% of a bank's total assets. That means that if a bank has a return on assets of 2%, it translates into a return on equity of 20%. But one should also keep an eye on the denominator in this calculation. For a given return on assets the return on equity will depend on the equity ratio. If the bank in question lowers its equity ratio to 8% of total assets, its return on equity *ceteris paribus* rises to 25%. Conversely, if the equity ratio rises to 12%, the return on equity would drop to 16.7%. But as we explained in Chap. 1, shifts in the debt-to-equity ratio affect the level of risk. So if one sets a target for return on equity, one is not only making a decision about profit optimization, but also about the firm's financing and risk structure.

---

[25] See Rieger [25].

Long-Term Profit Maximization

Long-term profit optimization ultimately comes down to one question: how willing is a company to sacrifice short-term profits in order to achieve higher long-term profits? From a pure rate-of-return viewpoint, that question is answered by using the discounted cash flow (DCF) method. But trying to forecast future volumes, prices, and costs poses considerable real-world difficulties. Another challenge is that inter-relationships are hard to quantify across time. One example is customer acquisition. If a firm uses monetary incentives to attract customers today, how much profit will those customers generate in three or five years? Long-term profit maximization always depends on forecasts, and the longer these forecasts extend into the future, the more uncertainty they harbor. Price strategies such as skimming or penetration exemplify this dilemma. The skimming strategy emphasizes short-term profit orientation. In contrast, the penetration strategy calls for lower prices during the introductory phase, in order build up a market share position that hopefully generates high future profits. But at the beginning of the product life cycle, it is uncertain whether those hopes will ever be realized.

Another important issue is how much you are willing to invest in keeping customers. Horst Schulze, the hotelier who created Ritz Carlton, empowered every employee to spend up to $2,000 to make sure a guest is happy. Schulze says: "When I announced this policy, my peers nearly fainted." So Schulze told them: "Look, the average business traveler will spend well over $100,000 on lodging during their lifetime. I am more than willing to risk $2,000 to keep them coming back to our brand of hotels."[26]

My experience over decades has taught me that there is hardly ever a crystal-clear set of actions or a definitive roadmap to make a long-term profit orientation successful. Instead, the subjective estimates and assessments of management play a dominant role.

Shareholder Value

Long-term profit orientation essentially coincides with the concept of shareholder value proposed in 1986 by Alfred Rappaport.[27] The value that the company's shareholders receive comes in the form of dividends and the increase in the share price. According to the shareholder-value concept, the central goal of management—and its measure of success—is the long-term

---

[26]Schulze [26].
[27]See Rappaport [27].

enrichment of the shareholders, a goal which is essentially identical to long-term profit maximization. The concept, in that sense, has been broadly accepted in business. In the foreword to the second edition of his book, published in 1998, Rappaport states that "corporate boards and CEOs almost universally embrace the idea of maximizing shareholder value."[28]

The most important drivers of shareholder value are profit and—depending on the company's maturity—the growth in revenue, free cash flow, volume, or number of customers. In a company's early phases, the focus is typically and foremost on growth. A statement from Yan Fei, the head of strategy for the Chinese coffee house chain Luckin, captures this sentiment: "What we want right now is size and speed. It doesn't make any sense to talk about profit."[29] Luckin has announced that it aims to open 2,500 new stores in a year and that it wants to knock Starbucks out of first place in China. In a similar vein, the CEO of YouTube, Susan Wojcicki, answered the question "Are profits a priority?" with a short and swift response: "Growth is the priority."[30]

But behind this apparently single-minded thirst for customer, volume, or revenue growth lies nothing other than the hope that this growth will become the wellspring for higher long-term profits. This phenomenon is by no means new. In the New Economy phase around the turn of the century, the emphasis on growth at the expense of profit reached extreme levels. For many start-ups, the only goal was acquiring more customers. The actual sales volume didn't matter, and profits were ridiculed as something that could spoil a company's growth prospects.

It didn't take long for the bill for these excesses to come due. The Nasdaq Composite Index peaked at 5,048 points on March 10, 2000, but by October 2002 it had plunged to 1,380 points, a decline of 73%. The share prices for some companies saw even steeper declines, with tech equipment maker Cisco down by 86‰. The trend in Germany was even worse. The "new market" index NEMAX rose from 1,000 points on December 31, 1997 to 9,666 points on March 10, 2000. Within several months it lost more than 95‰ of its value, and by October 9, 2002 it stood at a mere 318 points. The NEMAX was shut down on June 5, 2003, leaving the destruction of hundreds of billions of dollars in shareholder value in its wake.

Similar distortions seem to be emerging again, especially in the US and Chinese markets, as some people plead for extreme growth at the expense

[28] Rappaport [28].
[29] "Chinas Kaffeehauskette expandiert—Luckin will Starbucks auf den zweiten Platz verdrängen", *Frankfurter Allgemeine Zeitung*, January 4, 2019, p. 19.
[30] "YouTube CEO takes on TV, Web Rivals," *The Wall Street Journal*, June 8, 2016, p. B5.

of short-term profit. They justify their claims by citing low capital costs, meaning that future profits will be not be discounted as heavily as they would in an environment of higher interest rates. Amid these low rates, they believe in rationales such as: "The promise of more dollars tomorrow through growth exceeds the value of a few extra dollars today."[31]

Many companies that have recently gone public received very high valuations, even though they posted huge losses and remain far away from the profit zone. One example is the initial public offering for the ride-sharing service Uber in May 2019. Despite a quarterly loss of $1.1 billion, Uber's market capitalization reached $75 billion. The Chinese market for bike rentals is another extreme example of wildly optimistic growth expectations. Backed by massive amounts of capital, around 40 companies had entered this new market and stocked China's large cities with hundreds of millions of bikes. Renting a bike costs between 8 and 14 cents per hour. But these fees were often waived, and in some cases, prices went negative, meaning the firms paid customers to rent the bikes.[32] The only objective was to grow the number of customers. None of the companies turned a profit, and most of them have gone bankrupt in the meantime. The result is that Chinese cities became cluttered with enormous "bicycle graveyards." It is unclear whether it's possible to earn a sustained profit in this business, and that is not confined to China.

Today, shareholder value is a contentious topic. The debates often position shareholder value and the so-called "stakeholder value" as contradictory concepts.[33] Stakeholders are all parties who have some role in the fate of the company including employees, suppliers, banks, governments (local, state, national), and in some cases, society at large. But the superiority of the shareholder value concept—a long-term profit orientation rather than short-term profit maximization—has been confirmed scientifically. The researchers Mizik and Jacobson of Columbia University found that short-term profit maximization can reduce a company's market value significantly, by around 20%: "Firms that appeared to make short-term adjustments to inflate earnings ended up losing profits in the long run, causing their market value to drop by more than 20% four years out."[34] In the next chapter, "The Ethics of

---

[31] Mankins [29].

[32] See Simon [30].

[33] For a deeper treatment, see Blanpain et al. [31].

[34] Mizik and Jacobson [32]; see also "Myopic Marketing Management: Evidence of the Phenomenon and Its Long-Term Performance Consequences in the SEO Context," *Marketing Science*, May–June 2007, pp 361–379 as well as Mizik [33].

Profit", we will take a deeper look at the controversial concept of shareholder value.

Goals and Incentives

The entrepreneur or business owner-manager determines the goals that he or she will pursue. The economic incentive is profit, or rather shareholder value, rendering other incentives unnecessary. But the implementation of incentives can differ on the ownership side. Shares can carry different voting rights or distribution rights, as represented by classifications such as A, B, and C shares.

A completely different problem arises when the company is managed by hired employees who may have a much smaller equity stake, or none at all. In such cases, the company must ensure the best possible alignment between the goals of the owners and the goals of the managers. This problem is not a modern 20th century invention. In 1868, Arwed Emminghaus raised the issue and suggested that managers should have a stake in both the profits and losses of the companies they lead.[35] Nowadays practically all large companies have an incentive system for their managers.[36] Many of these systems offer stock options. But many stock option models fail to align the goals of owners and managers, because they induce asymmetrical incentives. Establishing and maintaining consistency across goals has proven difficult to achieve and unintended consequences are common.

This problem of goal alignment, however, is not limited to managers. It exists in any part of the company where employees earn variable compensation. It applies to investment bankers, who can take home insanely large bonuses, depending on how successful their deals are. It also applies to salespeople, whose commissions are often a direct function of the revenue they generate. In all these cases, there is a risk that the incentive will not promote profit, but another objective.

Summary

Profit is the most important and ultimately the only sensible corporate goal, because it is the only metric that encompasses all the consequences of a company's economic activity. It takes into account both the revenue and the

---

[35]See Emminghaus [34]; as well as Brockhoff [35].
[36]See Lahlou [36].

cost side. Under certain conditions, absolute profit should serve as the objective. When capital is scarce, capital return-based metrics should be applied. These metrics comprise a numerator (the company's profit measure of choice) and a denominator (equity, assets). The denominator plays a role in optimizing the return, because adjustments to it affect the company's capital and risk structure.

In practice, companies generally pursue multiple goals. In addition to profit, the goals often include sales volume, revenue, or market share. These additional goals play an important role for volume planning, incentivization of the salesforce, or in the run-up to an IPO. They often serve as proxy variables for long-term profit maximization. But the true link between these proxies and actual long-term profit is uncertain. Concepts such as PIMS and the experience curve have come under more intense scrutiny and are today viewed with skepticism. It's not so much the size of the market share that matters, but how it was achieved [1]. One recent study even challenges long-held beliefs in the advantages of economies of scale.[37] Ultimately, long-term profit orientation—which corresponds to the shareholder value concept—appears to be the most sensible objective.

References

1. Goldratt, E. P. (1992). *The Goal*, Great Barrington: North River Press.
2. Baumol, W. J. (1967). *Business Behavior, Value and Growth*, revised edition, New York: Harcourt, Brace & World, 45.
3. Sandmeyer, R. L. (1964). Baumol's Sales-maximization Model: Comment, *American Economic Review*, 54, 1073–1080.
4. Anderson, W.L. (unpublished). Profit maximizing versus revenue maximizing firms? Only Time will Tell, working paper, College of Business, Frostburg State University, Frostburg.
5. Drucker, P. (2001). *The Essential Drucker*, New York: Harper Business, 38.
6. Drucker, P. (1975, February 5). The delusion of 'profits'. *The Wall Street Journal*, 10.
7. Keeney, R. L, & Raiffa, H. (1993). *Decisions with Multiple Objectives: Preferences and Value Tradeoffs*, Cambridge: Cambridge University Press.
8. Kaplan, R. S., & Norton, D. P. (1996). *The Balanced Scorecard: Translating Strategy into Action*, Boston: Harvard Business School Press.
9. Schäffer, U. & Weber, J. (2019). Kennzahlen sollten die Realität zeigen, *Frankfurter Allgemeine Zeitung*, 16.

---

[37]See "Efficiencies of Scale May Be a Myth," *Harvard Business Review*, March–April 2019, p. 22; see also Ertan et al. [37].

10. Thiel, P. (2014). *Zero to One: Notes on Startups or How to Build the Future*, London: Virgin Books, 591
11. Buzzell, R. D., & Gale, B. T. (1987). *The PIMS Principles: Linking Strategy to Performance*, New York: The Free Press.
12. Farris, P. W., & Moore, M. J. (eds) (2004). *The Profit Impact of Marketing Strategy Project: Retrospect and Prospects*, Cambridge: Cambridge University Press.
13. Ailawadi, K. L., Farris, P. W., & Parry, M. E. (1999). Market Share and ROI: Observing the Effect of Unobserved Variables. *International Journal of Research in Marketing*, 16(1), 31.
14. Lee, J. (2009). Does Size Matter in Firm Performance? Evidence from US Public Firms. *International Journal of the Economics of Business*, 16(2), 200.
15. Edeling, A., & Himme, A. (2018). When Does Market Share Matter? New Empirical Generalizations from a Meta-analysis of the Market Share-Performance Relationship. *Journal of Marketing*, 82(3), 1–24.
16. Edeling, A. (2015). Does Market Share Matter? New Empirical Generalizations from a Meta-analysis, working paper, Economics and Social Science Faculty, University of Cologne.
17. Sklenarz, F. A., Himme, A., & Edeling, A. (2019). Digital transformation and marketing performance measurement–How the 'old' market share-performance relationship does not hold anymore. In: Paper presented at the annual conference of the European Marketing Academy, Hamburg.
18. Lanzillotti, R. F. (1958). Pricing Objectives in Large Companies, *The American Economic Review*, 48(5), 921–940.
19. Armstrong, J. S., & Green, K. C. (2007). Competitor-oriented Objectives: the Myth of Market Share. *International Journal of Business*, 12, 117–136.
20. Armstrong, J. S., & Collopy, F. (1996). Competitor Orientation: Effects of Objectives and Information on Managerial Decisions and Profitability. *Journal of Marketing*, 2, 188–199.
21. Rego, L. L., Morgan, N. A., & Fornell, C. (2013). Reexamining the Market Share-Customer Satisfaction Relationship. *Journal of Marketing*, 77, 1–20.
22. Miniter, R. (2002). *The Myth of Market Share: Why Market Share Is the Fool's Gold of Business*, New York: Crown Business.
23. Cespedes, F. V. (2014). *Aligning Strategy and Sales: The Choices, Systems, and Behaviors that Drive Effective Selling*, Boston: Harvard Business Review Press, 45.
24. Chu, W., Chen, C., & Wang, C. (2008). The Market Share–Profitability Relationships in the Securities Industry. *The Service Industries Journal*, 28(6), pp. 813–826
25. Rieger, W. (1928). *Einführung in die Privatwirtschaftslehre*, 1st edn (unchanged 2nd edn (1959)), Palm & Enke, Nuremberg: Palm & Enke.
26. Schulze, H. (2019). *Excellence Wins*, Grand Rapids: Zondervan, 32.
27. Rappaport, A. (1986). *Creating Shareholder Value: A Guide for Managers and Investors*, New York: The Free Press.

28. Rappaport, A. (1998). *Creating Shareholder Value: A Guide for Managers and Investors*, New York: The Free Press, foreword.
29. Mankins, M. (2017). Stop focussing on Profitability and Go for Growth. Harvard Bus Rev. Accessed on 1 May 2017, https://hbr.org/2017/05/stop-foc using-on-profitability-and-go-for-growth
30. Simon, H. (2016). Negative Preise – ein neues Phänomen, *Marketing Review St. Gallen*, 2, 76–81.
31. Blanpain, R., Bromwich, W., Rymkevich, O., & Senatori, L. (eds) (2011). *Rethinking Corporate Governance: From Shareholder Value to Stakeholder Value*, New York: Wolters Kluwer.
32. Mizik, N., & Jacobson, R. (2007). The Cost of Myopic Management. *Harvard Business Review*, July-August, p. 22
33. Mizik, N. (2010). The Theory and Practice of Myopic Management. *Journal of Marketing Research*, 47/August, 594–611.
34. Emminghaus, A. (1868). *Allgemeine Gewerkslehre*, Berlin: F. A. Herbig, S. 69.
35. Brockhoff, K. (2013). Was bedeutet eigentlich 'Shareholder Value'?, speech, WHU Koblenz, June 5.
36. Lahlou, I. (2019). *Corporate Board of Directors: Structure and Efficiency*, Cham: Springer Nature.
37. Ertan, A., Lewellen, S., & Thomas J. K. (2018). The Long-run Average Cost Puzzle. Accessed 1 May 2018 on https://ssrn.com/abstract=3178202

4

The Ethics of Profit

One could also title this chapter "Profit and the Market Economy." I will get less into general questions of ethics, morals, or philosophy, and concentrate instead on economic aspects related to profit. Earning profit is an integral component of the market economy and plays out within a specific legal framework. In many countries, however, the government "corrects" the market's distribution of profits by imposing taxes and social measures.

The prospect of making money represents the most important, though not the only, incentive to develop innovations, found start-ups, improve efficiency, generate growth, and create jobs. As I've mentioned several times already, profits are a prerequisite for the long-term survival of a company. In the long run, there is no liquidity without profit. Sustained losses will inevitably lead to bankruptcy, job destruction, debt defaults, and lost tax revenue.

The Superiority of Capitalism

In the book *The Power of Capitalism*, Rainer Zitelmann lays out a comprehensive and convincing case for the superiority of capitalism.[1] Rather than falling back on theoretical arguments, he relies on empirical and historical analyses that compare the results produced by socialist and capitalist systems.

---

[1] Zitelmann [1].

© The Author(s), under exclusive license to Springer Nature
Switzerland AG 2021
H. Simon, *True Profit!*,
https://doi.org/10.1007/978-3-030-76702-0_4

He contrasts Chile with Venezuela, South Korea with North Korea, and West Germany with East Germany. No one who takes an unbiased look at this history can seriously dispute the superiority of capitalism. It has proven itself time and again to be an extremely efficient system of wealth creation. With an eye toward the future—especially with respect to growth and to mastering the challenge of climate change—I believe in the power of capitalism. An economic historian writes: "Appeals that call for a future of self-restraint rather than growth are either well-intended personal advice or ill-considered sociopolitical visions, if not illusions. How should an economy deny itself something that may never happen or may not even be possible? As long as the problems created by population growth and technological change persist, a capitalist economy—assuming political stability—will also endure, because it has demonstrated the highest problem-solving elasticity. The actual risk factor is not capitalism, but rather principled policies that strive for final solutions where only transitional or temporary solutions are possible."[2]

I'm not trying to dive into a deep, fundamental discussion about economic systems here. I have no illusions that I could sway the opinion of someone who is a dedicated opponent of capitalism. Such opposition is driven by emotion in most cases, and these emotions can be stronger than rational arguments backed by historical facts. At the same time, I admit that emotions play a role in my own attitude toward the market economy and capitalism. I am an "emotionally convinced" market economist.

If we ask why capitalism or the market economy is such an "efficiency machine," we will inevitably end up at the profit motive. Driven by the profit motive (or profit maximization), an organization should generate a certain level of performance with the minimum expenditure of resources, i.e. with as little waste or "idling" as possible. Put another way, the organization will aim for the highest possible level of performance, given a fixed level of resources. In practice, these two perspectives go hand in hand. Nothing expresses the condition for maximum profit better than "marginal revenue = marginal cost." Profit maximization is the minimization of waste. In that sense, it conserves resources instead of wasting them, and leads to optimal wealth creation. Ultimately, a society can only distribute the wealth it creates.

It is indisputable that the distribution of wealth under capitalism is not always perceived as fair, and some will never perceive it as fair. That is why governments intervene massively in almost all countries. In this context, one speaks of a "social market economy" in Germany. At the level of market income, the income distribution in Germany has a Gini coefficient of 0.51,

---

[2]Plumpe [2].

which is almost identical to the Gini coefficient in the United States.[3] But in Germany, "the disparity of incomes is reduced by almost 42% due to government redistribution, including social security contributions, income taxes, and transfers."[4] That brings the net-income Gini coefficient for Germany down to 0.29, which represents a rather even distribution of income, relative to other countries. In the US, the respective Gini coefficient is 0.39.

These two effects—wealth creation and wealth distribution—should be kept separate conceptually. Pursuits driven by the profit motive contribute to maximum wealth creation, but not necessarily to the socially desired level of wealth distribution. It is up to politics to intervene and redistribute wealth or income. But if the corrective measures of government go too far, they suppress the profit motive and lead to lower wealth creation. Socialist systems have provided empirical evidence that this causality exists and is strong. Wealth redistribution is an eternally controversial theme in politics. But the topic of social equity with respect to income distribution is not a topic of this book.

In a book published in 1947, Professor Alfred Müller-Armack argued vehemently in favor of individual freedom, but also demanded at the same time that society address its social issues. His justification went beyond purely economic reasons: "With respect to personal freedom, the market economy would still be preferable, even if its economic output were less than under a command economy. While it has not come down to this, it seems necessary to note that the ultimate criterion for an economic order also lies in the spirit and not solely in the economics."[5] In other words, the roots of profit orientation run deeper than pure economics. Profit orientation is a decisive factor behind the high productivity of capitalist systems. Without profit, we would not have the standard of wealth we enjoy today.

Profit and Freedom

One pleasant moral and ethical effect of a capitalist-market economy is that profit begets freedom. Business owners who generate a profit reduce their dependence on banks, customers, and suppliers. They can decide on their own what they do with their profits. They can distribute them, re-invest them in the existing business, build new businesses, or donate them to a cause or charity of their choice. Profit grants freedom. The opposite also

---

[3]The Gini Coefficient is a way to measure inequality. It ranges from 0 (=no inequality in income distribution) to 1 (=maximum inequality in the distribution of incomes).
[4]Niehues [3].
[5]Müller-Armack [4].

applies. The business owners who generate losses will sacrifice freedom and autonomy. Banks will restrict the entrepreneur's leeway, and the company becomes increasingly dependent on every single order or job. Employees fear for their jobs, and the working atmosphere deteriorates. In the case of insolvency, the freedom of the owners and their business comes to an end, as a court-appointed trustee takes control. This outcome has left many entrepreneurs broke and broken.

Profits also create freedom for managers within an organization. Carlos Tavaros, CEO of the French-Italian car manufacturer Stellantis, expressed that point when his firm acquired Opel from General Motors: "The higher the profit, the greater the freedom."[6] Reinhold Würth, the founder of the eponymous world market leader for assembly products, feels similarly: "The greater the success, the greater the freedom."

Owners and businesses gain additional degrees of freedom when they use their profits from better times to build reserves for worse times. Those reserves are essential for survival in cyclical businesses. It is problematic to solely evaluate those businesses on the basis of annual profit. One can assess the true profit situation only by observing an entire cycle, which can last several years

Profit, Ethics, and Decency

In a market economy, businesses and their owners have a responsibility to earn a profit. Milton Friedman, who was awarded the Nobel Prize in economics in 1976, made that point explicitly when he wrote: "The social responsibility of a business is to make profits."[7] Nitin Nohria, dean of the Harvard Business School from 2010 to 2020, once told me: "The first ethical responsibility of a business leader is to make a profit."[8] He elaborated by saying that if a business leader does not earn a profit, the company consumes resources without adding value. Losses are tantamount to the destruction of value.

Peter Drucker described this responsibility in a similar way: "There is no conflict between profit and social responsibility. It is not the business that earns a profit adequate to its genuine costs of capital, to the risks of tomorrow and to the needs of tomorrow's workers and pensioners, that rips off society.

---

[6]"Peugeot verspricht Opel Hilfe zur Selbsthilfe," *Frankfurter Allgemeine Zeitung*, March 8, 2017, p. 19.

[7]Friedman [5].

[8]Personal conversation, Boston, April 3, 2019.

It is the business that fails to do so."[9] Even the Jesuit Oswald von Nell-Breuning, a professor and thought leader in Catholic social teachings and an open critic of capitalism, was convinced that only economic prosperity and profits would ensure the security of the working class.[10] Korean Professor Pil Hwa Yoo writes: "The social cost of paying not enough attention to profits is growing. Korea's shipbuilding and shipping industries were shining stars. Now they are in terrible shape. A major reason is their over-emphasis on market share at the expense of profits."[11] Heinz Dürr, the primary shareholder of the eponymous world market leader in automotive paint systems, expresses the same idea: "A business is social when it makes profits."[12] One can turn that statement around and say that a business that generates losses is anti-social. Profits contribute to society, while losses steal from it.

Can one prescribe ethical rules for business? Professor Theodor Baums, an expert in corporate governance and the ethics of capital markets, has found that "laws must be followed, but all other demands above and beyond the law are theoretical. Kant's Categorical Imperative—'Act according to the maxim that you would wish all other rational people to follow, as if it were a universal law'—is hard to apply to the behavior of businesses. The reason is that businesses are supposed to do something special or unique that should not apply to others or be imitated."[13]

Corporate Social Responsibility

Why do businesses nonetheless practice Corporate Social Responsibility (CSR), which can encompass everything from generosity toward employees, to diversity and inclusion, climate protection, promoting development projects, or support for political causes? There are many answers to this question. First, in a free market economy, entrepreneurs can choose on their own whether to promote and pursue such causes. To the extent that the law allows, they can integrate those goals into their normal business activities. They can also choose to devote a portion of their profits—which are theirs and theirs alone—to support the causes of their choosing. I prefer the second variant, which doesn't commingle business activities with philanthropy. IKEA is one example of that approach. The INGKA Foundation, which owns the vast

---

[9]Drucker [6].

[10]See Emunds and Hockerts [7].

[11]Personal mail from Prof. Pil Hwa Yoo on May 9, 2019.

[12]Heinz Dürr, speech held at the USW, October 6, 1986.

[13]Speech on the 25th anniversary of Simon-Kucher & Partners, Frankfurt/Main, September 7, 2010.

majority of IKEA, can only do two things with its profits: re-invest them in IKEA or donate them to the causes identified in the foundation's bylaws.[14]

Another reason why companies practice CSR activities is self-interest. They feel the activities are advantageous and in line with the profit maximization over the long term, though not necessarily in the short term. If these activities make a company more attractive to potential employees, increase employee retention and loyalty, reduce sick days, and enhance brand reputation or the company's social acceptance, then it is certainly plausible that the long-term profit improvements will more than offset the CSR investments in the short run.

The impact of ESG ratings (ESG stands for Environmental, Social and Governance) on financing is becoming increasingly important. Large investment firms such as BlackRock are paying more attention to these ratings in their investment decisions. Those who score poorly receive less favorable financing terms or face difficulties covering their capital requirements.

It is surprising to see the amount of space companies devote to these causes in their annual reports, as well as how much concrete information they provide. The stances have also found their way into corporate mission statements and into the public statements of senior executives. Christof Bosch, the spokesman for the Bosch family,[15] has said that "it is our job as a business to help find answers to the great ecological questions."[16] From 2020 onward, "the 400 Bosch locations worldwide should no longer leave a carbon footprint" even though those efforts will cost an additional €1 billion.[17]

Of course, pronouncements on corporate values and missions serve as good advertising and brand messages as well. Adam Neumann, the founder of WeWork, wrote in a report that in the US start-up scene, it is proper to present oneself as someone out to improve the world. Companies in the tech sector in particular love to talk about how they are on a mission to serve mankind.[18] WeWork's mission statement claimed that its purpose will be to "elevate the world's consciousness."[19] Such statements might seem exaggerated, but that is part of the effort to attract attention. If the company

---

[14] IKEA-Homepage: "Ingka Holding B.V. and its controlled entities has an ownership structure that ensures independence and a long-term approach. Stichting Ingka Foundation in the Netherlands is our owner, and its funds can be used in only two ways: it can be reinvested in the Ingka Group or donated for charitable purposes through the Stichting IKEA Foundation."

[15] Bosch is the world's largest automotive supplier, with revenue of 78 billion euros and 402,000 employees.

[16] Interview with Christof Bosch, *Frankfurter Allgemeine Zeitung*, May 6, 2019, p. 22.

[17] "Bosch prescht beim Klima vor," *Handelsblatt*, May 10, 2019, p. 18.

[18] "Der exzentrische Vermiete,r" *Frankfurter Allgemeine Zeitung*, May 8, 2019, p. 20.

[19] Ibid.

can back up its mission to improve the world, then it is legitimate to use that in communications. In fact, most successful innovations do make a contribution to improving the world. That is the reason for their success, and that will be rewarded with profit. There is absolutely no reason why there must be a fundamental contradiction between the common good—for which marketing guru Philip Kotler pleads vehemently in his book *Advancing the Common Good*—and the long-term profit orientation of companies in a market economy.[20] Tyler Cowen, in fact, considers profit maximization to be the cause of such behavior, when he writes: "Profit maximization alone—not to mention the consciences of some CEOs—puts business these days on the side of inclusion and tolerance."[21] He also emphasizes that entrepreneurs and business leaders are less polarizing than politicians.

The critics of profit orientation—and especially profit maximization and the concept of shareholder value—claim that these corporate goals lead to worker exploitation, child labor, damage to the environment, price pressures on suppliers and customers, the exploitation of monopoly positions, usury, and similar distortions. I am not so naïve to believe that a profit orientation has no harmful side effects. Corruption, fraud, and extortion also occur. The Volkswagen "diesel scandal" or the Wells Fargo "account fraud scandal" are recent examples, and time and again such scandals shake people's trust in business leaders. Sometimes the corporate misbehavior triggers a hefty response from customers, partners, law enforcement authorities, or policy makers. They can even bring about the complete downfall of a company. Recall the Enron scandal in 2001, which not only brought down Enron itself, but also the world's leading accounting firm, Arthur Andersen, which once employed 85,000 people.

The Role of the Internet

The internet is playing an increasingly important role in the ethical behavior of companies. That is a two-way street, especially considering the ability of customers to punish companies for perceived offenses. Cowen comments: "With the rise of the internet and social media, corporations have an increasing incentive to behave honestly. This is because unscrupulous business behavior can result in high reputational damage."[22] Conversely, upstanding

---

[20] See Kotler [8].

[21] Cowen [9].

[22] Ibid., p. 39.

behavior can lead to positive feedback from consumers, although these reactions tend to be less pronounced. A study by Simon-Kucher & Partners with 6,400 respondents from 23 countries shows that consumer ratings were the third most important purchase criterion, and 71% of respondents said that the ratings are relevant for them.[23]

Entrepreneurs and managers are human beings, and thus there are upstanding ones and unscrupulous ones. I don't know whether the percentage of one or the other is higher than the average for the general population. But in the book I cited earlier, Zitelman provides convincing empirical evidence that the collateral damage caused by a market economy is less than that of other economic systems, especially less than under socialism.[24] That applies to corruption just as it does to environmental damage, poor quality, frequency of accidents, worker safety, and other such issues.

The real world always differs from the ideal world, and that applies to profit and to decency. How should one combine these two concepts? Wallace Brett Donham, the dean of Harvard Business School from 1919 to 1942, had a classic formulation to answer that question: "We want to educate leaders who make a decent profit decently."[25] Donham is not talking about maximum profit, but rather about a decent profit. But he neither specified nor quantified what "decent" means. But intuitively, everyone understands what he meant. A statement from Robert Bosch (1861–1942) goes in the same direction. "An upstanding style of management is the most profitable in the long run, and the business world holds that in higher esteem than one might believe."[26] Vasant Narasimhan, the CEO of the pharmaceutical giant Novartis, leaves no doubt about where ethics and profit rank. He said that "I want us to be measured against the highest ethical standards. And there is no profit or revenue goal that is worth turning our backs on those standards."[27]

I can only second that statement. Here I must say that I'm not the kind of person who will confront entrepreneurs and managers with ethical standards, never mind dictate them. In the article "Philosophy of Price" I examined many concepts, including the notion of a "just price", which dates back to Thomas Aquinas. This notion becomes acutely clear and relevant for many highly innovative pharmaceutical products (including some from Novartis),

---

[23] See Simon-Kucher Trend Radar—The Rating Economy, Bonn 2019.

[24] Zitelmann [1].

[25] "We want to educate leaders who make a decent profit decently." Speech by Nitin Nohria on June 27, 2016 at the Harvard Research Symposium in Munich. Harvard Business School (HBS) was founded in 1908. Wallace Brett Donham was the second dean of HBS.

[26] From Robert Bosch, "Lebenserinnerungen", excerpted in *Bosch-Zünder*, 9/1921, pp. 230–232 and 9/1931, pp. 194–198 as well as in *50 Jahre Bosch—1886–1936*, Stuttgart: Bosch Eigenverlag 1936.

[27] Paland [10].

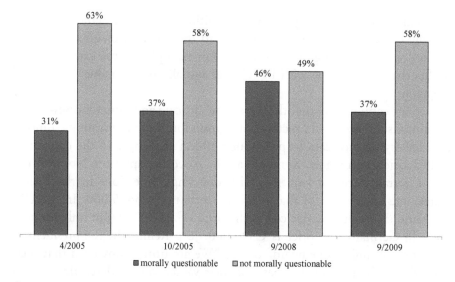

Fig. 4.1 Opinions on whether high profits are morally questionable

that can eradicate previously incurable diseases with one injection, but cost hundreds of thousands of dollars, if not millions, per application. I came to this conclusion: "The concept of just price, which dates back to Thomas Aquinas, is considered obsolete today, at least for competitive markets. But the problem remains in certain cases, such as monopolies or emergencies. We have no clue what is just in such situations."[28] This example illustrates that one should be careful with generalizations and blanket judgments when it comes to the relationship between profit and ethics.

Are Profits Morally Questionable?

Are high profits morally questionable? The German Banking Association posed that question in four surveys conducted from 2005 to 2009. Figure 4.1 shows the results.[29]

On average over the four surveys, some 38% of respondents held high profits to be morally questionable. But if we interpret that the other way around, it means that almost two thirds of the German population (62%) do not feel that high profits are morally questionable. I will let these data speak

---

[28] Simon [11].

[29] See http://www.spiegel.de/fotostrecke/umfrage-ergebnisse-deutschland-im-wahl-und-krisenjahr-fotost recke-48256-11.html.

for themselves and limit myself to one additional remark: whether profits are morally questionable comes down more to the question of how the profits are earned than how high the profits are. For example, are the extremely high profits that Apple earns with its iPhones morally questionable? I withhold judgment.

But one cannot deny that there are some delicate and difficult cases—from an ethical standpoint—in sectors with groundbreaking innovations. Innovative, life-saving medications pose tough ethical challenges to the companies and to society as a whole. Kymriah, a gene-based therapy from Novartis, can cure a certain form of leukemia with one single injection. In the United States, one application of that medicine costs up to $475,000. In the UK, the National Health Service covers the price of £220,000, but only for children. In Germany, the price is €320,000. Jörg Reinhardt, the president of Novartis's administrative board, argues: "We are firmly convinced that therapies should be paid on the basis of their value. We are determined to set our prices in accordance with that principle. In the future, the costs for gene therapies will be justified by their value to an individual patient."[30] Even higher prices have begun to emerge. The value of another revolutionary drug, a Novartis product against spinal muscular atrophy, was estimated by a British institute at $4 million.[31]

The firm Spark Therapeutics, acquired by Roche in 2019, is working on a new therapy for a genetic defect that causes blindness in children. It has announced that it plans to sell the therapy in the United States for $850,000 per patient, but will offer partial rebates if the patients do not meet their therapeutic goals.[32] How will society assess the value of these kinds of revolutionary products? Will it accept prices that high or will it try to limit profits? At the moment there are no clear answers to those questions.

Profit and Intellectuals

Criticism of profit orientation comes in large part from intellectuals, but by no means only from the political and intellectual left. One political philosopher asks: "Should entrepreneurs be allowed to earn profits?"[33] What a

---

[30] *Frankfurter Allgemeine Zeitung*, October 17, 2018, p. 22.
[31] "Was darf Leben kosten?" *Handelsblatt*, December 19, 2018, p. 1.
[32] "Roche Nears Deal to Buy Spark Therapeutics for Close to $5 Billion," *The Wall Street Journal online*, February 24, 2019.
[33] Höffe [12].

question! One former manager complains that "profit skimming ruins businesses and society."[34] When he was chairman of the German Episcopal Conference, Archbishop Robert Zollitsch claimed that profit maximization was responsible for the rise in food prices. Even Pope Francis has criticized "the autonomy of markets" and reiterated his critique of the capitalist system in his third Encyclical Letter in October 2020.[35]

We could continue the list of similar statements indefinitely. One can see that this is not only left-wing criticism—which would be expected—but rather criticism from people that one would consider moderate or centrist. Zitelmann remarks: "I have observed that in most intellectuals there is a little bit of anti-capitalism, even among those who would never declare themselves to be anti-capitalist. This stance apparently belongs to the identity of many intellectuals, even if they otherwise hold a wide range of political positions."[36] Zitelmann has conducted empirical studies in the US, Germany, England, and France on how people view the wealthy. These studies have backed his conclusions. In the book *Mind vs. Money: The War between Intellectuals and Capitalism,* Alan S. Kahan sheds light on the critical attitudes of intellectuals toward capitalism and profit and delivers an in-depth analysis of the root causes.[37]

I'll limit my conclusions here to saying that many intellectuals' view toward profit orientation, and profit maximization in particular, ranges from harsh criticism to outright rejection. For a deeper view of this topic, I refer to the previously mentioned works of Zitelmann and Kahan, from which I have cited only a few important insights.

What are the roots of these attitudes? The most important cause might simply by envy, combined with a feeling of injustice. Intellectuals generally think they are smarter than businesspeople. If one uses the intelligence quotient (IQ) as a metric, that self-perception may indeed be correct. So how can it be that intellectuals need to make do with relatively modest incomes, while businesspeople swim in money? Because the intellectual will rarely attribute that imbalance to their own capabilities (or lack thereof), the cause must lie in the "system." From there, it is only a small step to associate this perceived discrepancy with unethical behavior by businesspeople. Survey

---

[34]Manfred Hoefle, "Wie Abschöpfung Unternehmen und Gesellschaft ruiniert," Denkschrift Nr. 11, *Managerismus,* see also Hoefle [13].

[35]http://www.vatican.va/content/francesco/de/encyclicals/documents/papa-francesco_20201003_encicl ica-fratelli-tutti.html.

[36]Zitelmann [1].

[37]See Kahan [14].

respondents with higher educational levels agreed with the statement "Rich are good at earning money, but are not usually decent people" as follows:[38]

- 28% in the US
- 21% in Germany
- 14% in the UK and in France.

Noteworthy in this study is that younger Americans tend to be much more critical of capitalism and the profit motive than older Americans. Among the four countries surveyed, this age-based gap is the widest in the US.

Massive criticism of profit orientation comes not only from outside the economist community, but also from "insiders." One of the most prominent critics of profit orientation is Mariana Mazzucato, a professor at the London School of Economics. She writes: "Things are only getting worse. 'Rent seeking' refers to the attempt to generate income, not by producing anything, but by overcharging above the 'competitive price', and undercutting competition by exploiting particular advantages (including labor), or … block other companies from entering an industry, thereby retaining a monopoly advantage."[39] Joseph Stiglitz, a recipient of the Nobel Prize in economics, considers "weak regulation and monopolistic practices" to be the causes of "rent extraction."[40] In these statements, the terms "rent seeking" and "rent extraction" are essentially synonyms for profit maximization. The practices mentioned above—overcharging, exploiting particular advantages, undercutting competition, blocking other companies from entering an industry, or retaining a monopoly advantage—could be unethical and even illegal, but that is not necessarily true in every case.

The arguments of Mazzucato and Stiglitz should be taken seriously. The question of the ethics of profit orientation will not go away. Entrepreneurs and managers need to grapple with these questions and adapt to the changing values of society. But there are no simple, universal answers to the questions, nor will there ever be.

Taboos and Transparency

Profits are a delicate topic. It is not an exaggeration to speak of a taboo, although this does vary by culture. In Europe, hardly any entrepreneurs

---

[38]Zitelmann [15].
[39]Mazzucato [16].
[40]See Stiglitz [17].

willingly admit how much profit they earn, nor is it proper decorum to ask. Even in my days as a consultant, I was hesitant to ask about it at the beginning of projects. One prefers to talk instead about revenue, number of employees, and market share while sidestepping the question of profit. Closely held companies rarely provide profit numbers in their press releases. This is somewhat different in the United States and Asia, but still not widespread.

Treating profit numbers as taboo has some plausible reasons. Companies and individuals shy away from the topic when their profits are either relatively low or relatively high. If margins are low or negative, exposing that fact can cause business leaders to lose face, especially if they have previously highlighted their revenue figures. I have often experienced such situations. The question "And how does profit look?" draws either a lot of hemming and hawing or an embarrassed silence. Rarely does someone cite a concrete number. Conversely, if margins are high or very high, publicizing them could put the business leaders in a precarious position. If suppliers or customers catch wind of the high margins, they might demand a larger share of the pie. Margins are an extremely sensitive topic among suppliers in the automotive industry or in food and grocery retail. One business leader described the situation this way in a note to me: "In our year-end talks, I have been confronted many times with publicized 'rich lists.' My business partners insist that they must have a share of the 'riches.'"

A company with high margins needs to have a strong market position in order to resist the demands of large customers. But sometimes the demands of customers are not as aggressive as one might fear. When Hermann Kronseder, the founder of Krones AG, the world market leader for bottling machines, took his firm public, he feared that the greater transparency would intensify the price pressures from customers. But to his surprise, the opposite effect occurred. The history of very solid profits demonstrated to customers that the company did not live hand-to-mouth, making every negotiation a "must-win." In Kronseder's view, this information improved the company's negotiating position.[41]

The CEO of a Hidden Champion for specialized packaging machinery told me a similar story: "We have a high EBIT margin of around 20%. Because that piece of information is accessible in public databases, we decided to launch a communications offensive—with positive resonance so far. We inform people that while we do earn robust profits, they result from our high

---

[41]Krones went public in 1984. At that time, there was no profit-reporting requirement in Germany.

level of vertical integration. On average we regularly re-invest about half our profits back into the business."

A second fear among highly profitable business leaders and entrepreneurs arises in their private or social lives. That is the fear of envy. Wealth and riches derive primarily from business activity, and the wealthy are usually the target of choice when it comes to envy. Zitelmann has conducted empirical studies on this topic in Germany, France, the United States, and the UK. He defines an "envy index" based on the ratio of the envious to the non-envious in a population. France has the highest index value with 1.26, which means the number of envious people is 26% higher than the number of people who are not envious. Germany is next with an index value of 0.97, followed by the US and UK with much lower values of 0.42 and 0.37 respectively.[42]

Consistent with these findings, US entrepreneurs and business leaders speak much more openly about their profit situation. One CEO joked about the difference in attitudes between the US and Europe: "In the US, you're poor if you don't have at least 10% margins, in Europe you're a felon."[43] One English friend formulated the sentiment as "Americans love winners, Europeans love losers." One manager from the engineering sector wondered about the root causes: "It remains unclear to me why striving for profit in Germany is associated with a guilty conscience. It can't be the Christian influence, because then we would see the same situation in other European countries." Closely related to the desire to avoid envy is the fear that open communication about wealth and profit could make someone a target for criminals.

So all in all, there are good reasons why entrepreneurs and business-people tend to offer very little transparency about their earnings. More than a few make every effort to conceal their profit numbers. Their means include choosing a corporate form with limited or no reporting requirements, to shifting activities abroad, to paying fines for not publishing a financial report. But this effective lack of transparency around profit numbers can have several unintended consequences. When consumers overestimate actual profit margins by a factor of six or eight, concealing the true numbers could backfire and intensify the social envy.

My expectation is that in most countries, little will change regarding the taboos around profit numbers. Whether that represents a net advantage or disadvantage for companies and entrepreneurs remains an open question. But for society as a whole, the relative lack of transparency around profits is a disadvantage.

---

[42]Zitelmann [18].
[43]Karl-Heinz Johnen, *Handelsblatt*, October 7, 2013.

Is Profit Maximization Necessary?

The general answer to the question of whether profit maximization is necessary, or even a form of compulsion or obligation, is "no." In a free market economy, every business and every entrepreneur can decide for themselves whether to maximize profits or be satisfied with an amount below their maximum profit potential. I would like to add that, strictly speaking, profit maximization is a theoretical concept. In practice, it is rare for someone to know which behavior will lead to the highest possible profits, or how high their profits could actually be. That is true even more so for long-term profits.

But if we consider the profit realities described in great detail in Chap. 2, many businesses would be well advised to pursue a strategy of profit maximization. Why do I say that? Keep in mind that the average net profit margin for companies in OECD nations over an eight-year period came to just 5.71%.

This average itself still seems to be acceptable. But one should keep in mind that more than half of all companies have a margin below that average. Furthermore, companies in countries such as Germany (3.3%) or Japan (2.3%) have average margins that are well below the OECD average. I search regularly through corporate databases, and I'm often shocked at how low the earnings numbers are for companies that I assumed to be in relatively good shape. One must urgently advise these companies to shift their focus to profit maximization. When profit margins are consistently at plus-minus zero, companies are constantly teetering on the brink of bankruptcy. Only a significant improvement in profits can pull them away from the edge.

If we set the bar somewhat higher and demand economic profit instead of accounting profit, the severity of the profit situation of many companies worsens. In Chap. 1 we explained that economic profit represents the profit generated above the weighted average cost of capital (WACC). The OECD average of 5.71% is a net profit margin. If we assume capital turnover of 1, then Eq. (1.9) yields a return on total assets (after taxes) of 5.71%, the same as the net profit margin. If we assume that the corporate tax rate is 25%, then the pre-tax return on total assets is 7.61%. That value roughly corresponds to the WACC value for capital costs cited in Chap. 1. One can therefore assume that a considerable number of companies—probably more than half—generate no economic profit, i.e. they do not earn back their costs of capital.

In my decades of work with thousands of managers and entrepreneurs, I have seen that many are locked in a permanent struggle to keep their businesses afloat. When you are trying to keep your head above water, profit maximization sounds like a highly theoretical and foreign concept. Simply achieving an accounting profit alone is a success, never mind making an economic profit under those circumstances.

But what if a company posts a net profit margin of 10%, or is a Profit Star whose net margin exceeds 20%? One might think that such companies could be less consistent about their pursuit of profit maximization. But my impression is that profit maximization remains the most effective survival strategy even for such highly profitable companies. Jürgen Kluge, the former head of McKinsey in Germany, once posed an excellent question: "Is there such a thing as an optimal amount of profit, or is more always better?" Ultimately, every entrepreneur in a market economy needs to answer that question for herself or himself. I can only say two things. First, obviously, a significant positive profit number is better than zero and certainly preferable to a negative one. Second, when companies earn no economic profit, i.e. do not recover their cost of capital, they should seriously consider investing their money in something else.

Shareholder Value versus Stakeholder Value

In Chap. 3 we briefly described the concept of shareholder value, an idea that is highly controversial and also rejected by large swaths of society. In many ways, the term "shareholder value" has morphed into an expletive. Why is that? In my view, the primary reason is that many managers who claimed they were pursuing the shareholder-value concept were in reality doing just the opposite. Several prominent examples demonstrate this.

As the CEO of General Electric, Jack Welch became the poster child for shareholder value, presenting himself as one of its most evangelical proponents. And he did in fact turn GE into the world's most valuable corporation at one point. The company's market capitalization rose from $15 billion when he took over in 1981 to $592 billion by the year 2000. But was this increase sustainable in the spirit of shareholder value? The answer is "no." Since the year 2000, the market capitalization of GE has seen an ongoing steady decline, bottoming out at just under $48 billion in May 2020. Whether that decline is attributable to Welch or his successors is an open question. But for a long time, GE has no longer been synonymous with the idea of shareholder value.

We can cite Daimler as another blatant example of a contradiction between words and deeds. Jürgen Schrempp, who served as Daimler CEO from 1995 to 2005, maintained that he led the firm according to the concept of shareholder value. But between the day of the merger of Daimler-Benz and Chrysler on November 18, 1998 and the day Schrempp announced his resignation on July 27, 2005, Daimler's market capitalization fell from €66.5 billion to €36.8 billion. Almost half of the value of Daimler AG was destroyed during that period, while the German share index DAX declined by only 2.7% over the same period. Despite his declaration of a commitment to shareholder value, Schrempp created none, and in fact destroyed a considerable amount.

Nowadays shareholder value is often ridiculed. Even Jack Welch added his voice to the growing chorus of critics. After he stepped down as CEO of General Electric, he characterized shareholder value as "the dumbest idea in the world."[44] Fredmund Malik, a well-known consultant from Switzerland, has also criticized the concept: "Shareholder value kills its beneficiaries."[45] There seems to be no end to the criticisms. Witness the accusations against Wolfgang Reitzle, the chairman of Linde, after his company merged with Praxair to form the world's largest industrial gas company. He was called "a pioneer of an excessive shareholder-value culture" and someone who "pampers shareholders instead of investing in the future."[46] Reitzle has indeed created shareholder value. Between the merger in October 2018 and January 2021, Linde's market capitalization increased from $45 to $138 billion.

The stakeholder value concept has been proposed as an alternative to the shareholder value concept.[47] This alternative concept has a growing bandwagon of supporters. One of the first was Robert Coury, chairman of the drug maker Mylan, who declared: "This is a stakeholder company, not a shareholder company."[48] The influential American Business Roundtable attracted a lot of attention when it redefined stakeholder value in its "Statement on Purpose of a Corporation". The Business Roundtable includes 188 CEOs of large US companies, and 181 of them signed off on the new statement.[49] They included Jamie Dimon, CEO of JP Morgan Chase & Co., as well as the heads of the world's two largest investors, BlackRock and Vanguard Group. But a few prominent CEOs withheld their support,

---

[44] See *Financial Times*, March 12, 2009, see also *Business Week*, March 16, 2009, where Jack Welch qualified his statements in the *Financial Times*.

[45] Blog.malik-management.com, August 7, 2011.

[46] See https://www.germanboardnews.de/flops/2019/03/wolfgang-reitzle-wegbereiter-einer-exzessiven-shareholder-value-kultur/.

[47] For a more detailed treatment, see Blanpain et al. [19].

[48] *Wall Street Journal Europe*, July 28, 2015, p. 1.

[49] https://www.businessroundtable.org/business-roundtable-redefines-the-purpose-of-a-corporation-to-promote-an-economy-that-serves-all-americans.

including Stephen Schwarzman of the Blackstone Group and Larry Culp, CEO of General Electric.[50]

The statement makes the following declarations: "We share a fundamental commitment to all of our stakeholders. We commit to

- delivering value to our customers,
- investing in our employees,
- dealing fairly and ethically with our suppliers,
- supporting the community in which we work,
- generating long-term value for our shareholders."[51]

This prompted some journalists to speculate whether the statement represented the potential "end of capitalism as we know it" or "the swan song for shareholder capitalism."[52] What was my reaction to the Business Roundtable's pronouncements? My first reaction was that the statement is self-evident. Dimon, the chairman of the Business Roundtable, described the statement as "common sense corporate principles."[53] The Drucker Institute commented: "Today marks a historic return to commonsense principles."[54] The World Economic Forum issued a similar statement which it called the Davos Manifesto: "The purpose of a company is to engage all its stakeholders in shared and sustained value creation. In creating such value, a company serves not only its shareholders, but all its stakeholders—employees, customers, suppliers, local communities and society at large. The best way to understand and harmonize the divergent interests of all stakeholders is through a shared commitment to policies and decisions that strengthen the long-term prosperity of a company."[55]

Every company has been and remains well-advised to consider the interests of stakeholders. I do not see a fundamental contradiction between the shareholder and stakeholder value concepts, at least not in the stark form of the zero-sum game that some critics put forward. My experience has been different. When a company earns a solid profit, in most cases its employees, suppliers, banks, and its local and national governments benefit as well. In

---

[50]See "Move Over, Shareholders: Top CEOs Say Companies Have Obligations to Society," *The Wall Street Journal*, August 19, 2019.

[51]See https://opportunity.businessroundtable.org/ourcommitment/.

[52]Frankfurter Allgemeine Zeitung, August 21, 2019, p. 15 and Hans-Jürgen Jakobs, "Morning Briefing," *Handelsblatt*, August 20, 2019.

[53]See https://www.morningbrew.com/daily/stories/2019/08/19/business-roundtable-changes-course.

[54]Drucker.institute, E-Mail, August 20, 2019.

[55]https://www.weforum.org/agenda/2019/12/davos-manifesto-2020-the-universal-purpose-of-a-com pany-in-the-fourth-industrial-revolution.

December 2020, Texas Tech professor Alexander William Salter reaffirmed that sentiment in an opinion piece in *The Wall Street Journal*: "Since profits result from increasing revenue and cutting costs, businesses that put profits first have to work hard to give customers more while using less. In short, profits are an elegant and parsimonious way of promoting efficiency within a business as well as society at large."[56] Many others have cited similar causalitites. Robert Bosch once said: "I don't pay good wages because I have a lot of money. Rather, I have a lot of money because I pay good wages."[57] The converse also applies. If a company is not doing very well, then the staff, suppliers, banks, and governments suffer too. Peter Drucker expressed it this way: "A bankrupt business is not a desirable employer and is unlikely to be a good neighbor in a community."[58] There is plenty of evidence that companies that treat their employees well also achieve higher returns for their shareholders. In one US study, the difference in "total shareholder return" was two full percentage points over a span of five years. "What's good for employees appears to be good for shareholders," the study concluded.[59] In my many years of experience, I have witnessed hundreds of cases that confirm that same relationship, with only a small number of exceptions.

Is there a concrete and verifiable set of management objectives that one can derive from the Business Roundtable statement or the Davos Manifesto? I don't see one. Harvard Professor Michael Jensen wrote this about the topic: "It is logically impossible to maximize in more than one dimension. Purposeful behavior requires a single valued objective function. If there has to be just one objective of the corporation, maximizing shareholder value seems an obvious choice."[60]

The new statements introduce additional relevant aspects into the discussion. Some commentators from the investor and academic sides have raised the question of whether the shareholders, and not the CEOs, are responsible for fulfilling social obligations. This argument carries some weight, because the owners are spending their own money when they do something for the good of society. Managers, however, are custodians of money that is not theirs. Observers have also criticized that the Business Roundtable statement did not address the issue of inflated management salaries. Michael Bordo, a professor at Rutgers University, argues that the Purpose Statement burdens

---

[56] https://www.wsj.com/articles/profit-keeps-corporate-leaders-honest-11607449490?mod=opinion_l ead_pos8.
[57] Büttner [20].
[58] Drucker [21].
[59] Derousseau [22].
[60] Cited according to Fox and Lorsch [23].

companies with obligations that are the responsibility of governments and not private businesses.[61] Based on the discussions in the media, I have the impression that the essence of these statements is more about effecting a correction to short-term profit orientation and less about the shareholder value concept itself, which by definition embraces a long-term orientation. If the new resolutions change something in that regard, I would definitely welcome the change.

Profit in Good and Bad Times

A controversial question is how a company should deal with profit goals in "good" and in "bad" times. In a crisis, of course, a company must do everything possible to secure its profits, defend its revenues, and slash its costs. But in good times, can a company loosen up its pursuit of profitability?

My opinion is no.

One of the biggest and most common mistakes in boom times is to build up cost items (especially fixed cost items) that will become an albatross around the company's neck when the next crisis hits. Companies should remain resolute about their profit orientation in good times, in order to set aside a cushion for bad times. Independent of the current business situation, it is always the task of management to interject itself between revenue and costs. Those two variables apparently have a natural tendency to converge, but management needs to find ways to keep the distance between them as large as possible. Even in good times, profit orientation is a tried-and-tested means of survival.

Profit, Purpose, and Motivation

On one hand, profit has an economic dimension. On the other hand, for almost all entrepreneurs, profit is not the only purpose of their activities. Hermann Josef Abs, the famous CEO of Deutsche Bank after World War II, had an elegant way to describe this ambivalence. "Profit is as necessary as the air we breathe. But it would be terrible if we were only in business to make money, just as it would be terrible if the only reason we lived was to breathe." Profit is not what most entrepreneurs and managers live for. But there are, of course, diverging points of view, such as the following statement from the

---

[61]"Move Over, Shareholders: Top CEOs Say Companies Have Obligations to Society," *The Wall Street Journal*, August 19, 2019, p. 16.

founder of a Hidden Champion that employs more than 3,000 people. He wrote me that for him "profit is the meaning of life." No matter what, profit is an important performance indicator and is indispensable for entrepreneurial success. It is also a prerequisite for corporate survival and wealth creation.

Insufficient profits, or actual losses, have the opposite effects. They lead to frustration, self-doubt, demotivation, and in the case of insolvency, the destruction of assets. The statement of a young entrepreneur, who is the third-generation manager of his family's food industry business, is revealing in this regard: "I work like crazy, but in the end there's nothing left over. That's not any fun." His company has annual revenues of over $250 million. But the net profit in the last five years, which included one year with a loss, averaged just $200,000. That is a net profit margin of less than 0.1%. It is no wonder that the young entrepreneur does not enjoy walking that tightrope between profit and loss.

In my research I am surprised time and again by the sheer number of companies that generate losses. For some, that situation persists for years. Why do the banks remain quiet? One reason is that they are effectively held hostage by their own loans. If they call in a loan, the company could go bankrupt and in the worst case the loan would be a total loss for the bank.

The reasons behind these ongoing losses are numerous, but rarely are they due to a lack of effort on the part of the entrepreneur. Some struggle their entire lives and never earn a satisfactory margin. Profit not only has a financial side for entrepreneurs. It also provides personal validation, proof of their abilities, and fun at work. Those aspects contribute to profit as an important motivator.

In this context, how the entrepreneurs think and how they motivate themselves play an important role. Do they understand that profit is more important than revenue? Do they want to appear "big" to the outside world and become the center of attention, or keep to themselves and enjoy their profit? A favorite saying of a friend of mine gets straight to the point: "Revenue makes you proud, but profit makes you rich."

A Disappointing End

Some entrepreneurs experience a bitter disappointment at the end of their active careers. The cause is often the continual, long-term neglect of the profit motive. I will elaborate on this with two real-life examples. The first one involves a Hidden Champion that became world-class in mechanical engineering. The sole proprietor, an enthusiastic engineer, ran the company for

36 years. He is 70 years old, and has neither his own children nor a successor in his extended family. So he looks for an investor or another solution to keep the company going. The business is highly dependent on the economic cycle, and is thus very volatile. In good years, revenue tops €100 million, but in weaker years it might be only half that amount. Despite these fluctuations in utilization, the entrepreneur never laid off employees. Instead, he invested considerable sums in their capabilities and boasted a highly qualified team. The plant and equipment were state of the art. The company seemed to be in good shape.

But there was a catch. The company had posted a loss in four of the previous nine years, and in four others, it barely broke even. In the remaining year it achieved a net profit margin of 5%.

All previous attempts to find an investor had failed. The proprietor commissioned several appraisals to put a value on the real estate, the knowledge capital of the team, the modern plant and equipment, the brand, etc. He is extremely disappointed that he can't convince anyone to invest. He simply did not want to accept that the miserable profit history had reduced the company's value to such an extent that it might make a sale impossible. It finally became clear to him that he had failed to lead his company in a profit-oriented way.

I conclude this case with a remark from the proprietor, which I will let stand without further comment: "In my world, the primary motive behind business is not big financial results. For me, that is not the most important part of my activity. When a normal financial result covers basic needs, that is enough for me. Beyond that, there are other motives, such as the quest for perfection, the thrill of discovery, the passion for working with others, and the shared joy in our successes." The future of this firm remains uncertain.

The second case takes place in similar circumstances. This company offers complex technical services. It is a "high-tech" firm in the truest sense of the term. The founder, who holds a doctorate in physics, is Europe's leading expert in her field. Two thirds of her employees are academics, and many have doctorates in scientific fields. The founder is 66 years old and still runs the firm, working at least 60 hours a week. The reputation of the firm is strongly linked to her name. Key customers demand that she work with them personally.

As in the first case, this firm needs a new owner, and there are two options: either a takeover by an outside investor or by some of her most qualified employees. Cautious exploratory talks took place with candidates from each group, but neither had a strong interest in taking over the firm. When I asked about her firm's profit situation, the owner was hesitant to respond: "Actually we don't make any money. But we have always stayed afloat, we have always invested enough, and we are in good shape." When I looked at the numbers, I saw that in the last eight years, her firm had posted a slight profit in four years and had posted losses, though not dramatic ones, in the other four years. Each year the bottom line was essentially around zero. The owner stated her desired selling price for the firm, which struck me as a total fantasy based on the firm's profit history. She had also paid little attention to profit over the years. And now she is stuck in a difficult spot.

It makes me sad when I see entrepreneurs accomplish amazing things, but put their life's work at risk because they either didn't understand or didn't grasp the role of profit. The only way to ensure the long-term viability of an enterprise, and make it attractive for potential acquirers at an acceptable price, is to make money. That applies just as much to the ongoing business year to year as it does to the transfer of ownership to investors or the next generation of leaders.

Summary

Profit is a controversial and polarizing topic in society. But whether profit is the purpose, the consequence, or the essence of entrepreneurial activity is for me a completely academic question. Every entrepreneur must decide what profit means in his or her individual case. The hair-splitting distinctions among the concepts of profit maximization, profit optimization, and profit orientation are not very helpful.

Profit orientation remains a constituent element of capitalism. The superior performance of market economies relative to other systems ultimately derives from the profit motive. Private companies have a responsibility to society to earn a profit. That is the only way to secure jobs, make investments, and innovate. It is also the only way for a firm to meet its obligations to its employees and its business partners. Earning a profit must fall within the bounds of ethics and decency. But there is no doubt that in reality, sometimes these ethical boundaries are crossed. That is one of several reasons why so many intellectuals are critical of the profit motive.

Profit is a taboo topic in many countries. Objectively speaking, the level of transparency regarding profits is relatively high nowadays, thanks to databases, internet access, and government reporting requirements. Nonetheless, the general public is not well informed at all about the true profit situation in the business world. Entrepreneurs avoid discussing their profits, regardless of whether they are high or low, because they fear the potential consequences: price pressure, loss of face, envy, or threats.

Profit maximization in the strict sense is not absolutely necessary. But in light of the often poor profit situation, many companies would be well advised to do a better job of tapping their profit potential. The focus should be on long-term profit maximization, not short term. This corresponds to the concept of shareholder value, which is often interpreted incorrectly and subject to baseless criticism.

Profit is not the sole purpose or motivation for entrepreneurs and managers. But it is an indicator of performance and success, and is therefore an important motivator. In contrast, meager profits or losses lead to frustration and disappointment. Losses have brought down many companies, but no company ever went broke turning a profit.

References

1. Zitelmann, R. (2019). *The Power of Capitalism*, London: LID Publishing.
2. Plumpe, W. (2019). *Das kalte Herz. Kapitalismus: Die Geschichte einer andauernden Revolution*, Berlin: Rowohlt, 640.
3. Niehues, J. (2019). Ungleichheit zwischen Wunsch, Wahrnehmung und Wirklichkeit, *Frankfurter Allgemeine Zeitung*, 18.
4. Müller-Armack, A. (1947). *Wirtschaftslenkung und Marktwirtschaft*, Hamburg: Verlag für Wirtschaft und Sozialpolitik, 65.
5. Friedman, M. (1970). A Friedman Doctrine—The Social Responsibility Of Business Is to Increase Its Profits, *The New York Times Magazine*, 17.
6. Drucker, P. (1975). The Delusion of 'Profits', *The Wall Street Journal*, 10.
7. Emunds, B., & Hockerts, H. G. (eds.) (2015). *Den Kapitalismus bändigen. Oswald von Nell-Breunings Impulse für die Sozialpolitik*, Paderborn: Ferdinand Schöning.
8. Kotler, P. (2019). *Advancing the Common Good: Strategies for Businesses, Governments, and Nonprofits*, New York: Praeger ABC-CLIO.
9. Cowen.T. (2019). *Big Business: A Love Letter to an American Anti-Hero*, New York: St. Martin's Press, p. 6.
10. Paland, D. (2019). Der Goldjunge von Novartis, Manager Magazin, June, 42
11. Simon, H. (2019). Philosophie des Preises, *Marketing Review St. Gallen*, 5, pp. 12–21.
12. Höffe, O. (2016). Dürfen Unternehmer Gewinne machen? *Frankfurter Allgemeine Zeitung*, 20.
13. Hoefle, M. (2010). *Managerismus. Unternehmensführung in Not*, Weinheim: Wiley.

14. Kahan, A. S. (2010). *Mind vs. Money–The War between Intellectuals and Capitalism*, New York: Routledge.
15. Zitelmann, R. (2020). *The Rich in Public Opinion*, Washington: Cato-Institute, 273.
16. Mazzucato, M. (2018). *The Value of Everything: Making and Taking in the Global Economy*, London: Penguin Random House, 4.
17. Stiglitz, J. (2012). *The Price of Inequality: How Today's Divided Society Endangers our Future*, London: Allen Lane.
18. Zitelmann, R. (2018). *The Wealth Elite: A Groundbreaking Study of the Psychology of the Super Rich*, London: LID Publishing.
19. Blanpain, R., & Bromwich, W. (2011). Olga Rymkevich, and Iacopo Senatori (ed.), *Rethinking Corporate Governance: From Shareholder Value to Stakeholder Value*, New York: Wolters Kluwer.
20. Büttner, I. (2016). Reich, weil er gute Löhne zahlte, *Chrismon*, 3, 49.
21. Drucker, P. (2001). *The Essential Drucker*, New York: Harper-Business, 58.
22. Derousseau, R. When Workers and Investors Share the Wealth, *Fortune* pp. 22–23.
23. Fox, J. & Lorsch, J. W. (2012). What Good are Shareholders? *Harvard Business Review* pp. 48–57

5

Diagnosis and Therapy

In the previous chapters we strongly affirmed the idea of profit orientation, both from a purely economic perspective as well as an ethical one. At the same time, an analysis of the world's current profit situation revealed that a considerable portion of companies earn only modest profits. Many do not generate an economic profit, which means that they do not recover their costs of capital.

In this chapter we will endeavor to diagnose the potential causes of low profits and suggest possible "therapies." For now, we will restrict our diagnoses to factors related to the context of economic activity as well as its underlying foundations. In the subsequent chapters, we will look separately at each of the three drivers of profit: price, sales volume, and costs.

I do not want to raise exaggerated hopes and expectations for this chapter. On the surface, the explanations for high or low profits seem simple. But finding the root causes often proves difficult. We observe time and again that companies of similar size and market position show completely different profit trends.

Why does one company go under while an apparently similar firm not only survives, but prospers? Even academics find it hard to explain the origins and genesis of a firm's profit. Perhaps it is impossible to give a definitive explanation. If someone were to find a "secret recipe" for profitability, every firm would use it, and that would be the end of high margins. This "law" is well known on the world's stock exchanges.

© The Author(s), under exclusive license to Springer Nature
Switzerland AG 2021
H. Simon, *True Profit!*,
https://doi.org/10.1007/978-3-030-76702-0_5

One should also not expect any wonders or revelations regarding the solutions, which I refer to as "therapies" in this chapter. Sometimes it is clear what to do. But how one effectively implements a specific solution is often much less clear. When diagnosing the causes, there exists a sort of symmetry, in that one can use a certain lever or action parameter correctly or incorrectly. In both cases, the parameter is the same, such as goal setting. Because of this symmetry, I will not separate the therapies into "success strategies" and "failing strategies." Instead I'll treat each parameter holistically.

Wrong Goals

In Chap. 3 we took a general look at the role of goals and objectives. We concluded that revenue, volume, and market share goals serve as proxies for long-term profit orientation, but are not sufficient as stand-alone goals. So practically speaking, how do companies deal with goal setting? In my experience, only a few entrepreneurs and managers truly put the highest priority on profit. That certainly applies to their real behavior, though not necessarily to their official declarations during investor conferences or shareholder meetings. Key metrics such as margin, returns, or the absolute level of profit often get short shrift. The following statement from the board member of a major automaker is revealing: "If our market share falls by 0.1 percentage points, heads will roll. But if our profit falls by 20%, no one cares." That statement might belabor the point, but the board member made it to me several times and years apart. He is alluding to a widespread problem: in day-to-day business, the revenue, volume, or market share goals often dominate managerial thinking.

General Motors once provided a blatant example of this kind of orientation and its consequences. Roger More, a former professor at Harvard Business School, wrote that in the past, GM's key financial numbers focused more on market share and revenue than on profit. GM's managers lived out this philosophy. At a sales conference in 2002, all participating managers wore a lapel pin with the number "29." The market share of General Motors in the US had fallen steadily for decades, and was significantly below 29% at the time of the conference. The "29" symbolized the new target for market share, meaning that the company should claw back its old position. But outside the company, hardly anyone believed that GM could reverse the downward trend, never mind achieve that target. Even after subsequent market developments showed the "29" target to be a fantasy, GM stubbornly clung to it. Two years

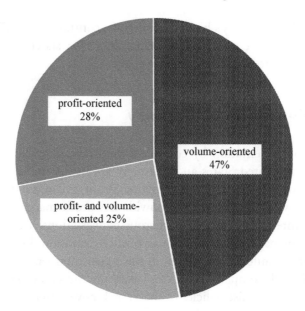

Fig. 5.1 Answers to the question "How is your industry oriented?"

later, Gary Cowger, the head of GM North America at the time, stated that "'29' will be there until we hit '29.' And then I will buy a pin with '30'."[1]

Such unadulterated and unrealistic market share goals are the fertile ground that breeds extreme discount activity. In that spirit, GM opened up its employee discount program to all customers in 2005. This unusual offer was initially a huge hit, as monthly unit sales rocketed ahead by 41% year-on-year. But the volume crash soon followed, leaving much damage in its wake. Within six months, GM's market capitalization fell from $20.9 billion to $12.5 billion. GM's market share likewise continued its decline, falling from 28 to 18.8% ahead of the company's bankruptcy filing in 2010. In 2020, the newly-formed General Motors had a market share of just 16.6% in the US market, which is roughly 40% below its market share at the turn of the century.

But that kind of goal-setting is by no means limited to the automotive industry. The Global Pricing Studies conducted by Simon-Kucher & Partners have repeatedly confirmed the dominance of volume and market-share orientations. Figure 5.1 shows the results of one such study with responses from 2,712 managers in 23 countries.[2] Only 28% of the respondents said

---

[1]"GM Is Still Studying the $100,000 Cadillac," *Automotive News*, May 17, 2004.
[2]Simon-Kucher & Partners, Global Pricing Study, Bonn 2012. A preliminary study from 2011 with 3,915 yielded similar results: 35% profit-oriented, 41% volume-oriented, and 24% balanced.

that profit is their industry's highest priority. In contrast, some 47% said that volume was their first priority. The remaining 25% stated their industries gave equal weight to profit and volume goals.

Profit Orientation by Country

A look at profit orientation by country is very revealing. Figure 5.2 shows these data. The United States and Germany are in the middle range, while France and Switzerland have the strongest profit orientations. Switzerland backs this up with an excellent nationwide net profit margin of 9.3%. But France is an interesting case. In numerous conversations, I have frequently heard French managers express a robust profit orientation, but that commitment does not manifest itself clearly in the actual numbers. The net margin number for French companies is 4.5%. I attribute this clash to high taxes and the strong interventionist policies of the French government.

The countries with the weakest profit orientations are Spain, China, and Japan. In China, the growth orientation predominates, confirming my own personal experience and impressions. The ultimate measure of success there seems to be the growth rate. That starts at the national level with the reporting of the gross domestic product (GDP) growth rates and filters down to individual Chinese companies. The situation seems to be different

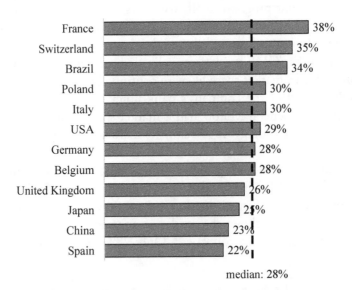

median: 28%

Fig. 5.2 Profit orientation by country: share of companies that say they are profit oriented

in Japan, where I have repeatedly encountered a pronounced orientation toward volume and market share. One occurrence at Sony was especially eye-opening. Despite its high worldwide brand reputation and its many innovations, the company had swung for years between losses and small annual profits. It was a long way from covering its cost of capital. I suggested that in order to get back to the profit zone, the company would need to finally extract a brand premium and end its suicidal discount policies. The global head of marketing spoke up and said "but then we lose market share." That was the end of the discussion. I had the sense that we had broached a subject that was taboo. At that time, it was unthinkable for Sony and many other Japanese companies to surrender any market share to the competition voluntarily.

Starting in 2015, a new CEO ended this flawed goal orientation and directed Sony's strategy toward premium products. The company's net profit margin was still below 2% in the business years 2015–2017, before a significant improvement to 6.4% in 2018. That improvement trend continued in 2019, when the company posted a net profit margin of 10.6%.[3] The change of goals played a key role in this turnaround.

Profit Orientation by Industry

The differences in profit orientation are greater by industry than they are by country. Figure 5.3 shows the results of the Simon-Kucher Global Pricing Study.

The pharma/biotech/medical technology industry reports the strongest profit orientation. This finding corresponds to my own experience. Automotive companies have the lowest profit orientation, with only 7% considering themselves as profit driven. More than half of the respondents from that industry (53%) considered themselves to be volume-driven. This orientation reflects not only the aforementioned case of General Motors, but also the frequently repeated mission of Volkswagen to overtake Toyota as the world's largest carmaker by volume. Volkswagen reached that volume goal in 2018 and 2019. In 2018, it sold 10.8 million cars, while Toyota sold 10.4 million. And in 2019 Volkswagen sold 10.97 cars and again beat Toyota, which sold 10.70 million cars. This made Volkswagen the world's number 1 in terms of volume, meaning it achieved its ambitious goal in 2018 and 2019. But how did the profit numbers look? Because annual profits can show significant fluctuations it is appropriate to take a longer-term look. In the five-year period

---

[3]Sony's fiscal year runs from April 1 to March 31.

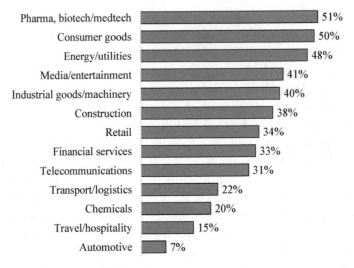

Fig. 5.3 Profit orientation by industry: share of companies that describe themselves as profit-driven

from 2014 to 2018, the two carmakers had virtually identical average annual revenues, with Volkswagen at $257 billion and Toyota at $259 billion. But the after-tax profit picture looked much different. Volkswagen netted $9.7 billion, which represented a net profit margin of 3.8%. Toyota, in contrast, earned an average net profit of $19.1 billion, for a net profit margin of 7.4%, almost twice as high as Volkswagen's. It is therefore no surprise that by February 2021, Toyota's market capitalization of $212 billion is almost twice as high as Volkswagen's of $115 billion. But Volkswagen has signaled a long-overdue reorientation: "The Volkswagen Group is focusing more than ever on the profitability of its business."[4]

Knowledge of Revenues and Profits

In order to get to the bottom of the goal conflict between revenue and profit, I conducted an ad-hoc survey with a "convenience sample" of managers and entrepreneurs. Instead of getting straight to the matter, I asked: "Off the top

---

[4] *Frankfurter Allgemeine Zeitung*, February 1, 2020, p. 22.

Question:Do you know your company's....		profit?		
		Yes	No	
revenue?	Yes	74%	16%	90%
	No	3%	7%	10%
		77%	23%	

Fig. 5.4 Knowledge of revenue and profit

of your head, do you know your revenue and your profit from your last business year?" I assumed that the knowledge of one or the other figure would serve as a proxy for the true orientation.[5] Figure 5.4 shows the results.

My *ex ante* hypothesis was that more respondents would know their revenue than their profit. I interpret the confirmation of that hypothesis to mean that revenue ranks above profit in the thinking of entrepreneurs and managers. Some 74% of respondents claimed that they knew both their revenue and their profit from the previous year. Altogether, 90% of respondents knew revenue, but only 77 knew their profit, confirming my hypothesis. The percentage of those who knew their revenue but did not know their profit (16%) was roughly five times as high as the percentage that knew their profit, but did not know their revenue. That is another indication that revenue orientation is likely to be more widespread and common than profit orientation.

My wide range of personal experience has also led me to believe that in practice, an orientation toward revenue, volume, or market share exerts a stronger influence than profit orientation. Many conversations over the years have confirmed this as well. To quote one consultant: "In my day-to-day work I often notice that my clients do not have profit numbers handy." The CEO of a very large food-and-grocery retailer told me: "Our revenue rose by 4% last year, which is a very good result. We give 1%, or a fourth of our growth, back to customers in the form of lower prices. That leaves our profit unchanged. We sell more, but we don't earn more money."

I found other orientations that can perhaps be instructive. In Beijing I asked the Asia–Pacific head of a large petroleum company about the revenues in his region and its most important countries. To my amazement, he could not cite the numbers. The next time we met, he told me he had thought about the conversation, because he himself was surprised that he did not

[5] 153 responses from 19 countries were received in this ad survey. I would likt to underscore that this survey makes no claim to be representative. I cannot rule out the potential bias that respondents were more inclined to answer when they knew both figures.

have the numbers top of mind. He said the reason was that revenues are rarely if ever discussed within his management team, because they place much greater emphasis on margin and profit. If I had asked instead about profits, he could have provided the numbers immediately. The reporting systems at his company are designed to manifest this profit commitment. Apparently, this company has a true profit orientation.

Despite my critical stance toward revenue, volume, or market share goals, I cannot ignore the fact that these goals—as demonstrated by the PIMS study and the experience curve (see Chap. 3)—are associated with some clearly positive aspects. The underlying motive behind a volume goal is often to maintain jobs. In Japan, that motive is very important, and helps explain why so many Japanese firms have a volume or market-share orientation. In Germany, the situation is somewhat similar. This came to the forefront in the Great Recession of 2008–2009. German firms used shorter workdays, paid leave, furloughs, flexible shifts, and pay cuts to avoid eliminating jobs entirely. These choices are hardly compatible with short-term profit maximization, but may have made a meaningful contribution to long-term profit maximization. Preserving jobs in a time of crisis brings two advantages. First, the company doesn't put its store of internal knowledge and social capital (know-how, competencies, customer relationships, identification, culture) at risk. Second, the company gets a quick head start on competitors when the crisis ends. That positive outcome actually did transpire for many companies after the Great Recession subsided in 2010.

In the United States, maintaining jobs is a secondary consideration. When volumes decline, American firms are quick to lay off employees or eliminate jobs outright, only to ramp up hiring when demand revives. The problem with that approach is that the companies do not always succeed in rehiring their experienced employees back and must therefore spend additional resources on training.

The importance of volume goals, the desire to maintain jobs, and the related effects on short- and long-term profit goals all vary significantly by country. As with everything else in life, volume goals have two sides to their story. A clear and consistent profit orientation is often lacking during crises. One investor who specializes in troubled firms wrote me the following: "In corporate restructurings I have often witnessed the problem that there was no profit orientation. It's as if there were inhibitions about turning a profit. By focusing instead on secondary metrics and priorities, management often ends up taking the wrong steps in a typical restructuring. The actions are well intended, but ineffective." This statement needs no further comment. A restructuring should have one goal and one goal only: to return a company to profitability.

A company's amount of equity investment can also affect the weighting of the goals. One entrepreneur from Austria commented: "A lower level of equity is what leads German companies to focus more on revenue, capacity, and employment goals than companies in other countries do." The reason is that the level of risk rises as the leverage (debt-to-equity-ratio) rises. In order to avoid insolvency, companies do whatever they can to keep their employment levels and their capacity utilization high.

Adjusting the Goals

Wrong goals or exaggerated one-dimensional goals are an important cause behind weak profitability. The therapy is clear. Companies should strive to develop a resolute focus on the profit goal. That is easier said than done, however, and can trigger a culture shock. I will outline several concrete steps here.

Reporting

A small entrepreneur with a six-person firm told me: "I learned from my father never to pay much attention to revenue, and instead focus on what's left over for profit. That's why I always look at the bottom line first."

In the same spirit, a very successful entrepreneur recommends a simple trick to make that step even easier. He literally turned the traditional profit-and-loss statement on its head by putting profit on the topline of his reports, and revenue at the bottom line. "Under my leadership, profit was indeed the first line of reporting. Doing it this way made the profit focus transparent for everyone."

In a typical profit-and-loss statement, revenue is on the first or top line. Profit appears far below. In other words, it may get lost somewhere on the tail end of the report. I wonder whether this positioning at the bottom robs profit of the attention it warrants. Before readers get to the profit number, they often need to absorb more than 20 lines of other data, unless they jump straight to the end. Simple tricks such as reversing the order of revenue and profit could be a helpful step towards a stronger profit orientation.

Communication

One indispensable tool is effective and repeated communication by top management regarding the profit orientation. Unfortunately that is often taboo, especially in closely held or family companies. It is easier to talk about revenue or market share than profit, especially about profit in absolute terms. Talking about margins or returns is somewhat less touchy. One communications consultant expressed the idea this way: "Important questions are whether and how a company succeeds in getting its people to talk openly, without reservation, about the pursuit of profit and naming the incentives accordingly." One entrepreneur, who built a billion-dollar frozen foods business on a direct sales model, wrote me this: "Revenue is the least important piece of data in the company. I avoid talking about it, and instead talk about profit goals. Profit is the distillate remaining after costs, interest, and taxes. That's what it's all about, and that's what I communicate."

Time Periods and Profit

When management sets goals, what time period should they apply and how should that be communicated to the team? Is it best to set goals for a month, quarter, year, or even for a longer term? One entrepreneur described his experiences and offered some recommendations: "Practice has demonstrated that profit goals should be defined and communicated on a quarterly basis. Annual goals are much less effective. When an organization misses a quarterly goal, it gets a chance to earn back its bonuses in the next quarter. Such a model creates a totally new dynamic, and everyone from the factory worker to the office assistant is thinking about ways that the organization can make more money." Getting the time period right may indeed have a strong effect on profit orientation.

Chief Profit Officer

One company appointed a Chief Profit Officer. This manager's mission was not only to think day and night above the company's own profit, but also how to help customers increase their profits. The entrepreneur reported that this concept was well received by customers. But this is more of an original and clever trick than a sustainable concept to improve profits. In my opinion, companies already have a Chief Profit Officer in place. It's their CEO.

Function	Profit	Revenue	Market share
Chief Executive Officer	1	3	2
Chief Financial Officer	2	1	3
Head of Sales	1	2	3
Head of Marketing	2	3	1
Product Manager	3	1	2

Fig. 5.5 Conflicting or contradictory goals among senior managers. Priorities ranked from high (1) to low (3)

Goal Conflicts

In Chap. 3 we discussed the problem of goal conflicts in general terms. The consultants at Simon-Kucher & Partners regularly encounter goal conflicts in their projects. These can arise between many different parties in the client organization. The most common conflicts occur between finance and sales, but in other cases, marketing and sales are not aligned either. The goals of regional offices often diverge from the goals the headquarters pursues.

Figure 5.5 shows a real-life example of such conflicts. The goal priorities of the various managers are not aligned. While the CEO and the head of sales put the highest priority on profit orientation, the CFO's primary goal is revenue. The head of marketing prioritized market share.

It is clear that such goal conflicts make a consistent profit orientation difficult, if not impossible. The solution lies in aligning the managers' goals, and there are many ways to do that: formal agreements, incentives that align with the goals, joint workshops, the use of moderators or external consultants, and organizational restructuring. As a last resort, the company may have to replace some of the senior leaders.

Wrong Incentives

Incentives are the most important means to align the goals of investors and hired managers. Having the wrong incentives is a common cause behind unsatisfactory company performance (from an investor standpoint). One of the most egregious examples is the high bonuses paid to investment bankers even though companies lose money. Some stock-option programs—such as the one Daimler AG instituted under the regime of CEO Jürgen Schrempp—also fall into this category. How could the enormous destruction of capital have been prevented or at least limited?

Apparently, the various stock-option programs offered to top managers didn't help. Heading off that disaster would have required a far simpler but much more effective approach. Instead of offering clever, complicated, and ineffective option programs burdened by goal conflicts, the company could have required CEO Jürgen Schrempp to invest €10 million or €20 million of his own money in Daimler shares which he would need to hold until the end of his tenure. Other C-level executives would participate in a similar way. Had such a program existed, I'm convinced that Daimler's market capitalization would not have fallen by half.

Shares Instead of Options

There is a fundamental difference between stock options and stock purchases. The share option is akin to a lottery ticket, while the stock purchase means the manager has real skin in the game. The point is that the investors want to ensure that they and the managers share the same goals. What are the goals of shareholders? Of course they want the share price to go up, but in some cases the more important goal is ensuring that the value of the shares does not decrease! Share options, in contrast, are almost always designed around an increase in value.

What happens when value is destroyed instead? Stock options do not put their holders on the hook for the losses. While their upside opportunity can be substantial, their downside risk stops at zero. Their only risk is that their options are under water. The shareholders, in contrast, have downside risk and not only upside opportunity.

We can illustrate this idea with a simple and intentionally exaggerated example. Imagine an option program that entitles managers to 10% of the increase in market capitalization, but managers do not participate in declines. There is also a choice between two kinds of actions, A and B. Action A has a 50% chance of seeing a total market capitalization increase of $5 billion and an equal chance of a decline of $10 billion. Action B has a 50/50 chance of either a value increase of $1.5 billion or a decline of $500 million. Under Action A, the expected gain for management is $250 million (10% of 0.5 × $5 billion). But the shareholders face an expected collective loss of $2.625 billion (0.5 × $5 billion—0.5 × $10 billion—0.5 × $250 million for management). Action B offers the opposite outcome. A positive outcome means $75 million for management (10% of 0.5 × $1.5 billion), while share-holders get an expected value of $462.5 million (0.5 × $1.5 billion—0.5 × $500 million—0.5 × $75 million for management). It should be clear what alternative management would choose, assuming they choose based on expected value: Action A! If the equity holders allow such incentives, they shouldn't wonder about the results. Management acted in an economically consistent and decisive manner. The mistake was in the option model.

A critical point in these models is the extent to which the managers' investment is significant. The amount that managers invest needs to "hurt." Depending on the form of investment, this could be several hundred thou-sand or several million dollars. This level of investment forces the managers to bear risk and puts them in the same boat as the shareholders. And that's the whole point. Siemens AG has implemented such a system. It requires senior executives "to maintain an equity investment in the company equiva-lent to a multiple of their base pay."[6] The factor for the CEO is three. With a base pay of €2.13 million, this means the CEO needs to maintain an invest-ment of more than €6 million. The factor for the other senior executives is 2, meaning they need to invest at least twice their base pay. In some cases that means individual investments of over €2 million. Those levels are probably high enough for some of the senior executives to "feel the pain."

An important aspect of such systems is the duration of the holding period. If one wants to sustain the orientation of management over the longest possible term, the duration of the incentive period should reflect that, even extending for a certain time beyond the time that the senior executive is active in the firm. That would support the long-term orientation and thus the thinking in terms of shareholder value very effectively.

How salespeople are compensated can also have a strong influence on profit. The most common incentive is a sales commission. If a company awards salespeople a commission and grants them control over the price nego-tiation, in all probability this will have a negative effect on profit. Salespeople will try to maximize revenue and thus maximize their own income. The most effective way to accomplish this is through comparatively low prices. This hurts profitability, because the revenue-maximizing price is always lower than the profit-maximizing price, assuming marginal costs are not zero. This cannot be in the firm's interest. Companies should instead put together an incentive system for salespeople that conforms with the company's own goals. That is not easy to do in practice, because companies generally shy away from revealing their contribution margins to salespeople. To get around that

---

[6]Siemens annual report, 2017.

sensitive issue, companies can adopt proxy indicators for profit such as point systems, anti-discount incentives, or similar measures. Our diverse experience with such systems proves that in most cases they have a significant and long-lasting positive effect on profits.

Wrong Industry

The choice of industry is one factor that influences how much profit a company can earn. If one is active in an industry or sector where earning money is difficult, the chances of turning an acceptable profit are low, even with good management. In game theory, one speaks of an "empty core." The core of a market is represented by a constellation that allows all competitors to operate profitably. If this core is empty, then there is no money to earn in that market. The airline industry is a typical empty-core sector: "The air transport sector has never been consistently profitable," one expert notes.[7] In its roughly 100-year history, the cumulative profit of the air transport sector is essentially zero. That does not preclude some operators—such as Southwest Airlines in the US or Ryanair in Europe—from making a profit thanks to their lower operating costs. This begs the question of what determines whether companies can operate profitably in a sector.

Five Forces

Harvard Professor Michael Porter developed an intelligent model to help answer that question. The five forces that determine the extent of profit potential are shown in Fig. 5.6.[8]

This analysis tool is so widely known that a brief overview will suffice here. Rivalry between companies puts pressure on profits. The supply-and-demand balance of power between customers and suppliers along the value chain also plays a role in determining profit levels. If a company depends heavily on a powerful supplier that can command high prices and make them stick, chances are slim that this company will achieve a high margin. The situation is similar downstream. Customers with a high level of buying power can drive down prices and margins. Examples of companies that face customers with high buying power are the suppliers to automotive OEMs

---

[7]Kenneth Button, "Empty Cores in Airlines Markets," Speech at Hamburg Aviation Conference, February 14–15, 2002.
[8]See Michael E. Porter [1].

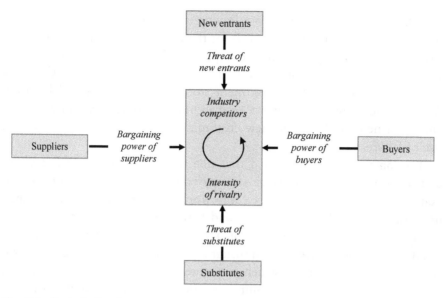

Fig. 5.6 Porter's five forces

and grocery retailers. Even the world's largest food-and-beverage company (Nestlé) is confronted with margin pressure from European retail giants such as Edeka. Edeka has delisted Nestlé products in order to extract lower prices, presumably with success. Customers with a high level of buying power will often force their suppliers to reveal their costs, the so-called "open book policy". The powerful customer will then refuse to allow the supplier to earn a high margin. Only strong suppliers can refuse to open their books. I have witnessed suppliers who have rejected such demands, and have withstood the pressure thanks to the strength of their technology, quality, or brand. Other forces which can suppress profit margins are substitutes and the threat of new entrants.

If one finds the causes of margin pressure within the Five Forces, the therapy should be self-evident. Whether the company can make the therapy successful is another story. In the worst case, one draws the conclusion that several if not all of the Five Forces are harming profit margins, meaning that there is essentially no money to earn in the industry, because it has an empty core. There is no shortage of industries where this discouraging diagnosis applies. The conclusion to draw is that the company should shut down the business or switch industries.

Interestingly, many companies that have survived for a long period have made such industry shifts, and some have done it multiple times. Examples include Haniel and Nokia. On the other hand, exit barriers might be so high that they prevent a company from leaving its current industry behind. One common solution to that problem is for the company to merge with a similarly positioned competitor, in the hope that the combined firm will have greater power, in the spirit of the Porter model. One example in Germany is the merger between the department store chains Karstadt and Kaufhof. Another alternative is to enter a new industry through diversification, by taking on new products and new customers. But such moves carry a high risk of failure.

If a company has determined that one or more of the Five Forces are destroying profits, an avoidance strategy could lead to higher profits. For example, if the profit pressures come from a rivalry between established firms that are caught in price wars and battles for market share, a sensible therapy would be differentiation or a re-focusing on niches instead. The Hidden Champions have enjoyed sustained success with that strategy. The so-called Blue Ocean Strategy, which recommends that companies concentrate on market segments with less competitive intensity, is a similar approach.[9]

If the profit pressures come from the supplier side, the company should attempt to find alternative vendors or develop new sources of supply. But the trend toward multi-sourcing can run counter to economies of scale which are easier to achieve with single sourcing. The same applies to the customer side. If a company is too dependent on one customer, the only solution is to acquire more customers and open new markets. One European food supplier improved its profit situation significantly when it entered Asian markets and reduced its dependence on European customers from 65% of volume to under 40%. In the fight against margin pressures caused by substitutes and new competitors, the only antidote is innovation, in some cases going so far as changing the business model.

These therapies as such are rather obvious and not big discoveries. The difficulty lies in the implementation. Can the company find a buyer for an unprofitable business? How does a company succeed in entering a new market? How can a company create or extend its differentiation over the competition? How does a company improve its balance of power with respect to key suppliers or customers? How does a company develop the innovations that will safeguard it against new competitors and against substitutes? The answers to these questions, which result from the diagnoses based on Porter's Five Forces, are anything but trivial and represent enormous challenges to companies that are weak in terms of profit.

---

[9]See W. Chan Kim und Renée A. Mauborgne [2].

Overcapacity

Overcapacity means that the production capacity of an industry exceeds the demand. It is one of the most drastic destroyers of profit, as I have witnessed first-hand in many projects over the years. Even growth industries such as wind energy face this problem: "The capacity in the windmill sector exceeds the global demand by a factor of two," the manager of an industry association told me.[10]

One sees overcapacity almost everywhere. In one project in the construction industry, the topic kept managers busier than any other. The steel industry moans all the time about having too much capacity, and overcapacity seems like a constant concern in the automotive industry. In the year 2017, the world's auto factories churned out 99 million vehicles, so we assume that overall capacity is at least that high. But production fell to 91 million units in 2018 and 89 million in 2019. That indicates overcapacity of at least 10 million vehicles. The actual number is probably higher, because several new plants were built in those years.

The existence of overcapacity is a typical sign that a market is starting to mature, as players overestimate growth rates. It can also be an indication of an unanticipated market downturn. High amounts of capacity can come online quickly, even in emerging markets. "Overcapacity is not only a problem for the mature markets in Europe. Sooner or later, the rapid build-up of capacity in emerging markets—especially China—will become a problem for carmakers," one expert said.[11]

The CEO of a large engineering firm succinctly described the detrimental effect that overcapacity can have on profits: "In our industry no one can earn any money. All suppliers suffer from overcapacity. Every time a project comes to market, someone needs the business and offers suicidal prices. Sometimes it's this firm, sometimes it's that one. Despite the fact that four key suppliers control 80% of the world market, no one makes money." It didn't take long for me to respond: "As long as the overcapacity persists, not much will change." The Great Recession forced one of the suppliers out of the market, and the remaining competitors managed to cut their capacity. What happened as a result? The industry quickly became profitable.

After that engineering firm's share price had bobbed along for years, it rose by a factor of eight over a four-year period once the problem of overcapacity disappeared. An individual competitor, acting alone, could not have ended

---

[10] See *Frankfurter Allgemeine Zeitung*, January 31, 2013, p. 11.
[11] *Produktion*, April 23, 2012.

the misery of capacity. It took reductions by several competitors before prices reached a level that allowed some profitability.

The fact that overcapacity exists doesn't seem to deter investors from building more. One story on luxury hotels noted that "today's overcapacity is ruining the prices for rooms at top hotels" and "the higher the standard, the lower the margins."[12] Despite this miserable price environment, heavy investments continued to pour into the luxury hotel sector, threatening to make the overcapacity problem worse. In many companies and industries I have witnessed countless discussions and attempts—some lasting years—to earn a reasonable return. But whenever overcapacity pressures a market, these attempts will not be effective. One must address the capacity problem first.

Lack of Focus

I consider focus itself to be a profit driver. The Hidden Champions offer convincing proof for this claim. Conversely, I feel that fragmentation, or lack of focus, is a major destroyer of profits, and it comes in many forms. One of the most common examples is the company that carries along an unprofitable business year after year without resolving the situation. When I ask the management why they do that, the typical answers range from tradition to alleged synergies to the need to have certain products in the assortment. But in my view, the real reason in most cases is that companies simply lack the will to jettison an unprofitable business unit.

"Diversification" is a fancy nickname for a lack of focus. The following example illustrates why this is a problem. The well-established company in question is family-owned with traditional business activities in many sectors, including materials, services, media, and retail. The company had around 70 companies on its balance sheet, and held stakes in more than 100 others. With revenues of €2.5 billion, the group isn't exactly small, but its annual growth rate since 2010 has been a modest 1%. The group's net profit margin is a mere 2.5%, dragged down by a huge heap of unprofitable businesses that offset the performance of the two business units that are strong internationally and very profitable.[13] The company does not earn back its cost of capital. Of course the owners have the freedom to invest their money as they see fit and accept that performance. They aren't starving. But I find such situations unsatisfactory.

---

[12]"Unter einem schlechten Stern," *Handelsblatt*, March 20, 2013, p. 20.
[13]Average of the years 2010 to 2017.

On the other hand, there are companies that aggressively prune unprofitable businesses. One example is Griesson-de Beukelaer, Europe's leader in baked goods. One of its guiding principles is "no business without profit." Griesson-de Beukelaer began in the gingerbread business. Several years ago, the company realized that that business could not turn a sustainable profit because of the brief selling season and tough price competition. It decided to close it down, even though it accounted for 30% of total revenue. That decision freed up resources that it could use more effectively in other areas, and the company continues to post solid profitable growth.

Bosch, the world's leading automotive supplier, is also committed to shutting down poor performing business lines. For example, management chose to exit the solar industry completely, even though the group had invested more than €2 billion in what was once a very promising sector. Family spokesman Christof Bosch said that the sector saw extremely painful losses and enduring them over time would erode the company's ability to act.[14] The losses were rumored to be €3.7 billion. Even wiser is the decision to avoid getting into a "hot" sector to begin with, when the risk-reward profile seems dubious. Bosch took that approach with battery cells. Sometimes the best alternative is not to get into a business in the first place. Microsoft founder Bill Gates notes that when it comes to a good strategy, it is just as important to know what one doesn't want as to know what one wants. In general, the rigorous elimination of businesses that are a drag on profits is a good recommendation. Ultimately this applies to businesses that earn no economic profit. The capital tied up in those businesses is better invested elsewhere.

The tendency of entrepreneurs to get bogged down often has its roots in their personalities. I have observed on numerous occasions that entrepreneurs who have enjoyed success in one area harbor the illusion that they can replicate that success in just about any other market. One engineer founded his first company, an electronics firm, while still in college. Within 12 years, the company grew to become the European market leader in its field, and the founder sold the firm to an American company for a nine-figure sum. He used those proceeds to start several new businesses and to take majority stakes in others, in a wide range of industries. But instead of serving as a passive investor, he took an active role and even served as CEO of some of the companies. Although a few businesses earned a meager profit, overall the losses piled up. The group as a whole does not generate an economic profit.

A second example comes from the machinery industry. A core business earns a modest return, but it is rather dull and doesn't fully tap the creative

---

[14]Interview with Christof Bosch, *Frankfurter Allgemeine Zeitung*, May 6, 2019, p. 22.

juices of the entrepreneur. So he rides nearly every new trend, from new energy sources to biotech, from internet and software to health and leisure. Eventually his portfolio swells to 27 firms, and he has the final say in each and every one. The managers enjoy only limited power. The group's revenue fluctuates around €750 million, but the annual average net profit margin has remained around 1.5% since 2010. This includes losses in some years and a peak net margin of 3.1%.

Both entrepreneurs are extremely competent. Their workloads, as well as the amount of information they retain, are almost unimaginable for a normal person. One wonders what they could have achieved with a more singular focus. I'm confident that either of them could have built a world market leader with very high profits if they had followed the Hidden Champion strategy of combining focus with globalization. Instead they spread themselves very thin and certainly do not generate an economic profit.

A lack of focus is most pronounced in emerging markets. South Korea, China, and Turkey are home to many conglomerates with activities in a multitude of businesses. The driving forces are similar to the ones that inspired the entrepreneurs in the examples above. They see many opportunities in these up-and-coming economies and they seize them. Some of these groups—such as the Korean "chaebols" Samsung and Hyundai—do succeed in achieving world-class status in some areas. But most of these conglomerates remain trapped in the home markets, where they often have a strong position but do not develop into international leaders.

When a lack of focus results in lower returns, the therapy is clear: more focus and less diversification. Of course, this recommendation has two sides, because it leads to changes in the risk profile. But it is not automatically the case that more focus causes the overall level of risk to increase.[15]

Overemphasis on Long-Term Orientation

Can an overemphasis on long-term orientation be a cause for weak profit performance? I'm not going to answer that question with a clear-cut "yes" or "no". Instead I will shed some light on the pros and cons. There is a serious discussion around whether short-term profit orientation—as long as it is not exaggerated—is indeed harmful for long-term profit goals. The following quote from the *Harvard Business Review* addresses that question: "On the one

---

[15] Regarding the risks of focus versus the risks of diversification, see Hermann Simon, *Hidden Champions des 21. Jahrhunderts. Die Erfolgsstrategien unbekannter Weltmarktführer*, Frankfurt/Main: Campus 2007, Chap. 3.

hand, there's a consensus that too many companies are sacrificing long-term growth on the altar of smooth, reliable short-term earnings. On the other hand, most large sample studies in the accounting literature show something different: firms that manage their short-term earnings perform better than firms that don't (and not just in the short term)."[16]

Long-term orientation requires continuity. Hermut Kormann, the former CEO of Voith, the world market leader in machines for the paper industry, says: "The long-term nature of the strategy results from the continuity of the strategy bearers and their term of office."[17] But continuity on its own is neither good nor bad. If a weak senior executive remains in office for a long time, that is obviously not advantageous. But a competent business leader who stays at the helm for a long time is a blessing.

Surprisingly, research on the topic of continuity is rare in the management literature. One exception is the work of Collins and Porras. In their book *Built to Last* they compare the tenures of the CEOs of successful companies with those in a control group of less successful companies.[18] The companies that enjoy long-term success—the authors call them the "best of the best"—have an average CEO tenure of 17.4 years, compared to only 11.7 years in the control group. My own findings about the Hidden Champions, whose CEOs stay in office for 20 years on average, offer further support for the value of continuity. On the other hand there is the viewpoint that permanent short-term pressure to earn profits can lead to higher returns over time. At minimum, such pressure will ensure that the company doesn't keep delaying or postponing necessary measures to improve the business.

Overextended continuity, a pronounced awareness and respect for tradition, and a high comfort level can lead to diminished profit orientation. The following comment on traditional farmers speaks volumes: "At the end of the day, the highest priority for most farmers is to keep the farm going, not to achieve the highest profit. The goal of the average farmer is security for his family and for future generations. Everything else is secondary."[19] Perhaps there is no inherent contradiction in that statement, but merely a very sharp difference in time horizons. The traditional farmer thought in terms of generations, while the modern businessperson considers a period of three to five years as long term. In sectors such as the internet, such views might be perfectly appropriate. But in the end, the best options lie in avoiding

---

[16] Sarah Cliffe [3].

[17] Hermut Kormann, "Gibt es so etwas wie typisch mittelständische Strategien?," Discussion Paper Nr. 54, University of Leipzig, Economics Faculty, November 2006.

[18] See Jim Collins und Jerry I. Porras [4].

[19] Geert Mak [5].

extremes. Overemphasis on continuity is likely just as bad for profits as an overemphasis on the short term.

Country-Specific Determinants of Profit

The opportunities to earn a certain level of profit also depend on country-specific factors such as the tax burden, the strength of unions, market size, industry structure, the banking system, management styles, and culture.

Dominance of Mature Industries

In some countries, mature industries dominate. These sectors show less volatility but also have a narrower range of profits. In Japan, these industries include automotive and consumer electronics. Most European countries also depend heavily on classic sectors such as automotive, engineering, and consumer goods. In contrast, Europe has only a few leading internet companies.

The situation is much different in the United States. In a short period, companies such as Microsoft, Apple, Amazon, Google, and Facebook have achieved profit levels and market capitalizations that rival the gross domestic product (GDP) of some countries. The total net profit of Apple, Microsoft, Alphabet, and Facebook totaled $137 billion in 2019, and thus exceeded the total profits of the 30 companies that comprise Germany's leading stock index DAX as well as the total profits of the 250 least profitable companies among the Fortune Global 500, which together earned $83 billion.

Weaknesses in Scaling Up

The start-up intensity varies by country. One explanation is the availability of venture capital. Even larger are the differences in scaling-up, meaning the ability of new companies to reach a significant size. In this aspect, China and the United States rank far above other countries. Figure 5.7 shows the number of unicorns by country. A unicorn is a young company with a valuation of at least $1 billion. The figure covers 494 unicorns from 24 countries, and 409 or 83% of them come from either China or the United States.[20]

---

[20]See https://de.statista.com/statistik/daten/studie/1062432/umfrage/ranking-der-laender-mit-den-mei sten-unicorn-unternehmen/.

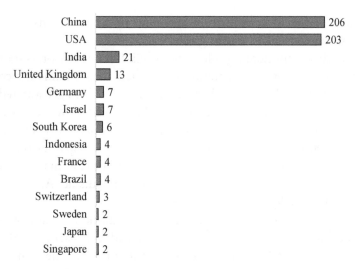

Fig. 5.7 Number of unicorns by country

The supply of capital in the phase of strong growth is an important prerequisite for achieving unicorn status. China and the US have an advantage thanks to their well-developed venture capital markets, although state intervention is important in China. The size of those nations' domestic markets also plays a decisive role. A strategy successfully pursued in a smaller country would potentially achieve a much smaller size than in China or the US in the same amount of time, and thus realize economies of scale and reach the profit zone more slowly. Start-ups from smaller countries are slower and less successful, even with a global rollout, than American start-ups. Facebook was founded in 2004 and achieved a net profit of $18.5 billion in 2019. Uber, founded in 2009, had a valuation of $75 billion when it went public in May 2019. Such scale-up successes are almost inconceivable in smaller countries.

Individual versus Team Responsibility

Responsibilities within a management team are treated differently from country to country. These responsibilities have an influence both on profit orientation and actual profit levels. In the United States, the CEO carries the sole responsibility, similar to the PDG (Président Directeur Général) in France. The regulations are much different in Germany. According to German law, the board of directors bears joint responsibility. The roles of chairman and CEO are also strictly separated. In Japan, decisions emerge after a long period of coordination and tend to reflect a consensus, which means that the team plays a strong role.

I suspect that consolidating sole responsibility in one person is more likely to lead to a stricter profit orientation than when a team holds the collective responsibility. In the latter case, it is easier for the goals to get watered down. This is especially true amidst the goal conflicts cited above. Such conflicts are the rule rather than the exception when groups need to make decisions. These views mirror my experience that owner-run companies often have a stronger profit orientation. An owner who is CEO or chairman naturally has a stronger position than a manager hired from the outside. And he or she is directly and personally affected by losses.

Professor Erich Frese points to a potential additional cause within the context of leadership positions.[21] He compared the backgrounds of top managers in US and German companies. Traditionally, one is more likely to find an engineer or a scientist in the highest ranks of German companies. Frese thinks that this difference has an effect on the company's profit orientation. German managers place greater weight on technical goals. Even when an American manager has a degree in a technical or scientific field, he or she is likely to have supplemented that with an MBA, which raises their awareness about the role of profit.

The Power of Labor

The power of labor and the role of labor unions likewise varies significantly across countries. Unions used to be extremely strong in the UK, but that power was broken during the tenure of Prime Minister Margaret Thatcher and has continued to wane. Unions are also much weaker today in the United States. But in France, unions continue to play a politically strong and active role. And Germany is a unique case with respect to unions, thanks to its laws around co-determination (*Mitbestimmung* in German). In companies with more than 2,000 employees, shareholders and labor must have an equal number of seats on the corporate board. This balance could be confrontational, but it is also empowering because labor now shares the entrepreneurial responsibility. This usually fosters a culture of management by consensus, which can yield numerous benefits. The company loses fewer days to strikes, and in some cases finds it easier to implement restructuring measures that would be highly controversial in other contexts. Finally, the social peace

---

[21] See Erich Frese, "German Managers' Organizational Know-how in the Interwar Period 1918–1939," *Vierteljahresschrift für Sozial- und Wirtschaftsgeschichte*, 2/2016, pp. 145–177.

within the company can have a positive effect on productivity. Having said that, it seems likely that the power and influence of labor damps a company's profit orientation.

The Role of Banks

A further sharp difference across countries is the nature of the banking system. In Switzerland, the three largest banks have a combined market share of 80%, while the same concentration is 41% in France, 31% in Germany, and only 18% in the United States.[22] One study noted: "A higher concentration in the banking sector goes hand in hand with the market power of the individual banks."[23] One would assume that a higher market concentration leads to the banks' not only setting more rigorous standards for the profitability of the projects they finance, but also being able to enforce them.

Germany is an interesting case in this regard. Savings banks and cooperative banks comprise two thirds of the market. Because of their regional roots, these banks establish close relationships with companies, who often refer to their "house bank." These relationships are particularly close with small and mid-sized businesses. I have often wondered what drives banks to finance certain projects which in my view have little or no chance of success (and more often than not do fail). The most probable reason is that regional and local banks are more lax in their profit requirements than the more powerful large banks. If a bank has a big book of outstanding loans with a particular company, it is difficult for the bank to withdraw when a crisis hits and let the company go under. In the worst case, the company could default on the loans entirely. That often leaves the banks with no other options than to extend lines of credit, even if the projected returns and profits do not justify them. I suspect that these effects are even more pronounced in countries such as China where the government-run banks play a dominant role. In my view, banks should apply more pressure with respect to profit orientation. Banks generally have considerable leverage to push for such improvements.

Taxes

It is obvious that high corporate tax rates reduce net profits. After all, we defined the ultimate relevant profit metric as Earnings after Taxes

---

[22] https://www.diw.de/documents/publikationen/73/diw_01.c.417892.de/13-13-1.pdf.
[23] https://www.econstor.eu/bitstream/10419/203677/1/1676920420.pdf.

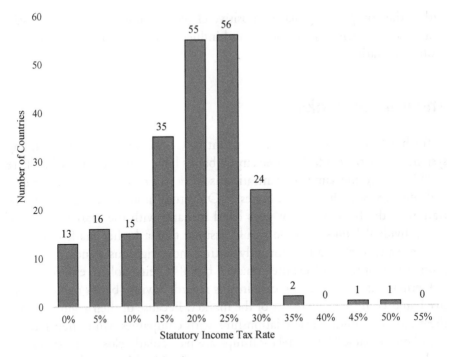

Fig. 5.8 Distribution of worldwide corporate tax rates

(EAT). Figure 5.8 shows the enormous differences in corporate tax rates by country.[24]

Most large countries have tax rates between 20 and 30%, including the US (21%), China (25%), and Germany (30%). At the higher end of the range are Japan at 31 and France at 33%. Smaller countries often have lower taxes, such as Switzerland (18%), Singapore (17%), and Ireland (12.5%). This spread explains some of the differences in net profits by country. If a company has revenue of 100 and a pre-tax profit of 10, its net margin would be 8.75% in Ireland but only 6.7% in France.

But there is another effect that an entrepreneur from Hong Kong pointed out to me: "In high-tax countries, companies generate more costs without giving them much thought, because they know that the government effectively has a stake in those costs. This line of thinking does not exist in countries with low tax rates. In those countries, the government's participation in the costs doesn't come into the calculations. The entrepreneur bears

---

[24]OECD, Table II.1. Statutory corporate income tax rate; KPMG, Corporate tax rates table; some jurisdictions researched individually.

the brunt of those costs. This strengthens the commitment to a profit orientation." Perhaps this behavior explains why companies in high-tax countries tend to have lower margins. One can express the situation this way: high tax rates reduce the incentive to maximize profit. On the one hand, the tax rates by definition reduce the amount that remains for the equity owners. On the other hand, the government has a bigger stake in the company's costs.

Negative Connotation

The connotations of terms and phrases such as profit and profit maximization also differ by country. One remark captures the prevailing sentiment in the United States: "Profit is an attitude and attitudes are the foundation for long-term profitability."[25] But while the United States has generally held a positive view of profit,[26] the connotation of the word tends to be negative in other nations. A German manager at IBM told me: "Time and again, I have observed that statements regarding the need for profit orientation do not manifest themselves in the daily actions of top managers. In some countries the negative connotation of the word 'profit' was inescapable and that prompted me to use the word all the time. Among my colleagues I was known for the saying 'You can't live from revenue.' I hope that I've had some effect with that statement. Of course, I made sure that the incentive system in my group was built around profit, not revenue."

My suspicion is that the negative connotation of the word 'profit' correlates with the envy I described in Chap. 4.[27] The fact that profit is negatively loaded, and in some cases even taboo, is most certainly detrimental to the pursuit of a profit orientation. Conversely, countries where profit enjoys a positive connotation are better suited for making a commitment to profit orientation.

In the end, there are many open questions with respect to the diagnosis and therapies for profit weaknesses. Why are net profit margins in Switzerland three times higher than in Germany and 50% higher than in the United States? Differences in tax rates cannot be the sole explanation for these enormous discrepancies. In contrast to the United States, Switzerland lacks the economies of scale that often lead to higher profits. I attribute the higher margins simply to the dedicated profit orientation of Swiss entrepreneurs and

---

[25] https://www.concreteconstruction.net/producers/profit-is-an-attitude_o.

[26] A 2019 survey showed that young Americans hold a much more critical view toward profit and wealth than older Americans; see Rainer Zitelmann [6].

[27] See Rainer Zitelmann, *The Rich in Public Opinion*, Washington: Cato-Institute 2020.

managers. How does one explain that net margins in France are one third higher than Germany's, even though France has higher tax rates and a greater degree of government intervention in the economy? Again, the difference lies in the stricter profit orientation of French managers, something I have witnessed myself first-hand. I believe that country-specific cultural factors have a significant influence on profits.

Summary

In this chapter we examined the causes behind differences in profitability. We focused on aspects that have an overarching character and are not directly attributable to the three profit drivers: price, sales volume, and costs. It is not easy to draw direct lines of cause-and-effect behind weak profits. Even academics are at a loss to diagnose the causes. So one should not embark on that exploration with unrealistic hopes for therapies and cures for poor profit performance. Nonetheless, we can draw several conclusions on causes and cures.

Having the wrong goals is probably the most important cause behind low profits. Numerous studies and empirical observations indicate that in practice, companies tend to emphasize revenue, sales volume, and market share goals more strongly than profit goals. When profit is in fact the primary goal, the focus often ends up being too short-term, and thus not in line with the long-term orientation of the shareholder value concept. My own personal experience has shown me that the goals that dominate managers' thinking are often neither focused on nor derived from profit. Goal conflicts, an all-too-common occurrence, make the problem worse, because departments of the same firm pull in different directions and work against each other.

The opportunities to earn a sustainable profit, or better yet, earn an economic profit depend not only the company itself, but also the industry it operates in. Porter's Five Forces concept offers a useful tool to diagnose the profit opportunities in a sector. There are sectors in which making money is difficult and earning an economic profit is hardly possible, thanks to the constellation of competitors, suppliers, and customers. If the possibility arises and exit barriers aren't prohibitive, the best course of action in that situation is to switch sectors. Other alternatives include differentiation, a more precise market segmentation, or a so-called Blue Ocean strategy.

A lack of focus is another cause behind poor profits. Many companies keep unprofitable business units instead of pruning them. Entrepreneurs who have been successful in one area sometimes feel that their expertise is directly transferable to other sectors, although that often proves to be an illusion. Diversification may reduce the overall level of risk, because the company is not putting all its chips on one card, but it also tends to water down profits. A therapy for the lack of focus is the Hidden Champion strategy, which combines focus with globalization.

In addition to these general factors, there are a whole host of country-specific factors that influence a company's ability to earn a profit. These include tax burdens, labor costs and regulations, and the strength of unions. Other country-specific root causes of profit weakness are less apparent at first glance. They include the dominance of mature industries, which reduce volatility but at the same time limit profit opportunities. In many countries, we also see weaknesses in scaling up new companies, due to the presence of a small domestic market, a lack of venture capital, and an inability to globalize quickly. China and the United States seem to offer the best conditions for scaling-up. More than 80% of the unicorns come from those two countries.

A country's typical management structure, banking system, and attitude toward the word "profit" also affect profitability. It is likely that profit opportunities are lower when responsibility is shared by a management team rather than concentrated in one person (the CEO). A decentralized banking system with many small banks probably applies less profit pressure on its customers than a concentrated system led by a few powerful large banks. Cultures that treat profit as a negatively loaded word are not conducive to a profit orientation.

Nonetheless, our diagnoses and therapies leave many causes for hope. Companies have numerous concrete starting points for profit improvement, some general and some country-specific. In the next three chapters, we will turn our attention back to the three profit drivers—price, volume, and costs—to find more opportunities for profit improvement.

References

1. Porter. M. E. (1985). *Competitive Advantage–Creating and Sustaining Superior Performance*, New York: The Free Press.
2. Kim, W. C., & Mauborgne, R. A. (2015). *Blue Ocean Strategy, Expanded Edition: How to Create Uncontested Market Space and Make the Competition Irrelevant*, Boston: Harvard Business Press.
3. Cliffe, S. (2015). A Partial Defense of Our Obsession with Short-Term Earnings, *Harvard Business Review*, May 7, https://hbr.org/2015/05/a-partial-defense-of-our-obsession-with-short-term-earnings

4. Collins, J., & Porras, J. I. (2004) *Built to Last: Successful Habits of Visionary Companies*, 3rd edition, New York: Harper Collins.
5. Mak, G. (2014). *Wie Gott verschwand aus Jorwerd. Der Untergang des Dorfes in Europa*, München: Pantheon, 50.
6. Zitelmann, R. (2020). *The Rich in Public Opinion*, Washington: Cato-Institute.

6

Profit Driver: Price

There are only three profit drivers: price, sales volume, and costs. Revenue is the product of price and sales volume. Subtract the costs—which consist of variable and fixed costs—and the result is the profit. The principle relationships, therefore, are very simple. But the reality of price management is complex for a number of reasons.

Special Features of Price as a Profit Driver

As a profit driver, price has some interesting features in terms of management, controllability, and effects. The first question to ask is who is affected by price measures. First and foremost, these are the customers. They ultimately determine the effect that a price action has on volume and profit. The customers decide how they will react to price changes, i.e. whether they will buy less when prices increase or buy more when prices decline. But price measures also affect the sales force of a supplier, because salespeople need to justify price actions to customers. When the price action is a price increase, justifying it can be a difficult and unpopular task, especially in negotiations. I have experienced cases where the sales force has outright sabotaged price increases decided by the management board. When prices are lowered, salespeople have an easier time with the customer. In any case, it is important that the sales team stands behind a price measure. Otherwise it can easily become a flop.

© The Author(s), under exclusive license to Springer Nature
Switzerland AG 2021
H. Simon, *True Profit!*,
https://doi.org/10.1007/978-3-030-76702-0_6

Price has a very strong influence on profit. Price affects profit directly by determining the contribution margin, and indirectly by influencing the sales volume. For consumer products, the price elasticity—the effect of price on sales volume—is between 10 and 20 times as high as the advertising elasticity and roughly 8 times as high as the sales force elasticity.[1] In other words, a price change of 1% has between 10 and 20 times the effect of a 1% change in the advertising budget and 8 times the effect of a 1% change in the sales budget. Sethuraman et al. have found that a company would need to increase its advertising budget by 30% to produce the same volume uplift as a price decrease of 1%.[2]

Rapid Deployability and Response Time

Price is a versatile and responsive instrument that a company can deploy quickly. It takes time to plan and implement changes to products (via innovation, research, and development), to advertising campaigns, or to a company's cost structure, and these changes also require time to take hold. In contrast, prices can be adjusted quickly as business situations change. The exception is when the prices are locked in because of binding contracts or printed catalogs. The internet has increased this speed and responsiveness further. Prices can be changed in seconds by the push of a button. The concept of dynamic pricing uses this speed in order to adjust prices continually to reflect the prevailing supply-and-demand situation.

The effect of price on customers also manifests itself quickly as well. If a gas station changes its prices and its local competitors do not follow, market shares can shift dramatically in a matter of minutes. The same applies to the internet, which has created unprecedented price transparency. Information about the real-time prices of the most diverse range of suppliers is just a click away, and the customer can decide which offer to choose without any additional research. A consumer can scan the bar code of a product in a store and find out how much the same product costs online or in nearby stores. When a company makes changes in other marketing levers—a new advertising campaign, a new product introduction—customer demand takes time to respond, and the time lag can be considerable.

The flipside of this speed of implementation and response is that competitors can respond quickly with their own price changes. Such price reactions tend to be swift and sharp, and it is not unusual for a profit-sapping price

---

[1] See Albers [1].
[2] Sethuraman et al. [2].

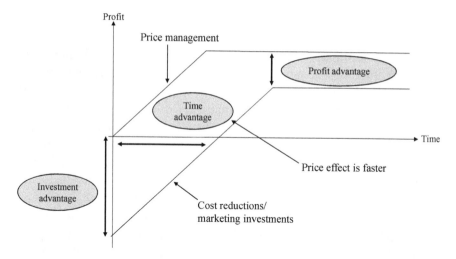

Fig. 6.1 Advantages of price as a profit driver, compared to cost reductions or marketing investments

war to develop. According to one of the Global Pricing Studies conducted by Simon-Kucher, some 57% of the 1,643 companies that responded said they were engaged in a price war.[3] Because of how quickly companies can respond to each other's price changes, such price measures rarely produce competitive advantages on their own. In addition, one would need to have a sustainable cost advantage or greater financial power to prevent competitors from keeping up. That applies more than ever in the internet era.

Price is also the only marketing instrument that does not require any advance investment or expenditure. That means that a company can set an optimal price even amid financial constraints, a typical situation faced by start-ups or new product launches. With marketing instruments such as advertising, sales, or research and development, the time lag between current expenditures and the resulting future cash flows means that an optimal level is often not feasible due to a lack of financing. If one takes a comprehensive look at the special characteristics of price, relative to cost reductions or marketing investments, the advantages shown in Fig. 6.1 come to light.

The investment advantage means that price optimization requires less upfront capital than cost cutting or marketing investments. The time advantage means that the positive effects that price has on profit happen sooner. Finally, the leverage effect means that among all marketing instruments, price has the strongest effect on profit.

---

[3] See Simon-Kucher & Partners, Global Pricing Survey 2019, London 2019.

Attention Paid to Price

Given its extraordinary role as a profit driver and its unusual effectiveness as a marketing instrument, one would expect that entrepreneurs and top managers pay a lot of attention to price. But in practice, that is often not the case. Instead, cost is what preoccupies managers' thinking and consumes most of their energy. Volume—driven by marketing instruments such as advertising and sales—also tends to attract more management attention than price. Many companies do not treat price with the professionalism and seriousness it warrants.

Symptomatic of this situation is a statement heard in an engineering company. When asked how the firm determines prices, a senior executive gave the following answer: "Essentially we calculate our price by multiplying our manufacturing costs by a factor of 2.5. The rest is up to sales." Such a process is not necessarily wrong. But in this company, a closer examination revealed that it was leaving a lot of money on the table. A statement by a senior executive at a large bank is also very revealing: "This bank is 125 years old, and to the best of my knowledge, this project marks the first time we have approached pricing in a professional way."

The Complexity of Price Systems

One factor that contributes to the complexity of price management is the structure of the product and service portfolio. Companies with one product and one price essentially do not exist. Almost every company sells many products or variants and thus needs to set a corresponding number of prices. The assortments of grocery stores, home improvement stores, pharmacies, industrial manufacturers, and spare-parts suppliers often include tens or even hundreds of thousands of articles, and each item needs a price. Banks, hotels, restaurants, and similar service providers can easily have price lists with several hundred line items.

The price that ultimately determines profit often comprises more than one parameter and appears in multiple forms. In addition to the base price, there are discounts, rebates, bonuses, and other special offers, and sets of terms and conditions. There are also customer-based price differentiation, multidimensional prices, bundling, and multi-tiered distribution with graduated prices, to name only a few of the most important forms.

The internet unleashed a massive wave of pricing innovations. These include flat rates, dynamic pricing, freemium, pre-paid systems, pay per use,

An improvement of 5% .... increases profit by

	Profit driver		Profit			
	old	new	old	new		
Price	$100	$105	$10m	$15m		50%
Sales volume	1.0m	1.05m	$10m	$12m		20%

Fig. 6.2 Effects on profit from a higher price or higher volume

and name your own price. Systems using artificial intelligence set prices autonomously. Airlines change their prices several million times over the course of a single year.

One should also not forget that many prices are negotiated rather than set autonomously by the seller. That applies to most B2B transactions, as well as to many larger B2C purchases such as cars and furniture.

All of these peculiarities and complexities make price management a high-stakes, high-risk task. It offers enormous opportunities for profit improvement, but also carries major risks of profit deterioration. Companies need to make decisions about each individual price component. The role of price as a profit driver is too complex to cover completely in this book. Therefore, I will limit the discussion to the most important aspects. For a more comprehensive treatment, I refer you to my book *Price Management*.[4]

Price versus Volume

The first area of price management to explore is the relative effects that price changes and volume changes have on profit. Let's consider the case of a power tool. The company currently sells 1 million units per year at a price of $100. The variable unit costs are $60 and the fixed costs are $30 million. The total revenue is $100 million, and the profit is $10 million after deducting the total variable costs ($60 million) and the fixed costs ($30 million). The pre-tax return on sales is therefore 10%.[5] The business is profitable. What happens if we improve price or volume by 5% in isolation? Figure 6.2 shows the results.

---

[4]See Simon and Fassnacht [3]. See also Simon [4].
[5]This corresponds to the pre-tax return on sales. For simplicity's sake, we leave taxes out of the calculation, because they do not have any effect on the relative advantages or disadvantages.

A decline of 5%...   ... reduces profit by

	Profit driver		Profit			
	old	new	old	new		
Price	$100	$95	$10m	$5m	-50%	
Sales volume	1m	0.95m	$10m	$8m		-20%

Fig. 6.3 Profit effects resulting from a price cut or a volume cut

If we raise the price by 5%, revenue rises to $105 million. Costs remain unchanged at $90 million, because the volume hasn't changed. This means that profit rises by 50% to $15 million. The picture looks much different if instead we increase volume by 5% to 1.05 million units. The revenue rises to the same amount of $105 million, but the higher volume means that variable costs also increase, in this case to $63 million. The total costs (variable plus fixed) thus rise to $93 million. This leaves a net profit of $12 million, which represents only a 20% increase.

Under the assumption that we raise either the price or the volume by 5%[6], the revenue growth generated by the price increase is significantly more profitable than the identical revenue growth generated by the volume increase. This holds true when marginal costs are positive. If marginal costs are zero—as can be the case for software or digital products—there is no difference between the higher profit from a price increase and the higher profit from a volume increase of the same magnitude.

What happens if we do the opposite, namely, we cut either the price or the volume by 5%? Figure 6.3 shows the effects on profit.

The reductions in profit are mirror images of the previous case. If the price declines by 5% (at constant volume), profit plunges by 50%. If volume drops by 5% (at constant prices), the decline in profit is only 20%, because the variable costs fall by $3 million and total costs as a result decline from $90 to $87 million.

Nonetheless, the practical profit implications from the two cases are asymmetric. In the case of growth, it is more profitable to grow via price than via sales volume. If a market is shrinking, it is better to accept a drop in sales volume rather than a drop in price. These recommendations could not be

---

[6]This is the *ceteris paribus* condition, which is "all else being equal."

clearer from the standpoint of a strict profit orientation. But other goals can come into conflict with these recommendations. Accepting lower volumes can have consequences on employment and could lead to job cuts. In the case of growth, pure price growth does not create more jobs, because volume remains constant.

Profit Elasticity of Price

The relationship between a percent change in one variable and the percentage change of a causal variable is called an elasticity. The profit elasticity of price expresses the percentage change in profit when price changes by 1%. In the examples shown in Figs. 6.2 and 6.3, the profit elasticity of price is 10 (50% divided by 5%), while the profit elasticity of volume is 4 (20% divided by 5%). What do such profit elasticities look like in real life? How would a price increase of 1% change the profits of selected companies in the Fortune Global 500? As with the previous examples, we assume only a price change of 1% and hold all other parameters constant.[7]

Figure 6.4 shows the answers for 25 companies from nine countries.[8] To facilitate intuitive understanding, we express the change in profit in percentage terms.

A price increase of 1% is relatively small, but its effects on profits vary dramatically. If Bosch, the world's largest automotive supplier, were able to raise prices by 1% without losing volume, its profit would rise by 34.2%. Profits at Walmart, the world's largest retailer, would jump by 24.6%, while Amazon would see profits rise by 16.9% and General Motors by 14.3%.

Even for highly profitable internet companies such as Apple, Alphabet, and Alibaba, the small price increase if 1% would boost profits by around 3%. In absolute terms, that means an additional $1.82 billion for Apple, $1.13 billion for Alphabet, and $515 million for Alibaba.

Is the *ceteris paribus* assumption in these cases realistic? Would sales volume really remain stable when prices change? Of course volume would change. But the assumption of only a weak volume response to a slight price increase of 1% is not far from the truth. Furthermore, the volume effect depends very heavily on how the company implements the price increase. We have

---

[7]We have assumed a corporate tax rate of 30% for this calculation. The actual tax rates vary by country, and range between 20 and 33 % for the selected countries.

[8]The basis for the revenue and profit data is the Fortune Global 500 List, *Fortune*, August/September 2020, pp. F1-F22. The profit increase is calculated by assuming a corporate tax of 30%. This means that of 1% price increase 0.7% are net profit. The profit increase is calculated as follows: profit increase in percent = 0.7%/net margin in % × 100. For Walmart 0.7%/2.84% × 100 = 24.6%.

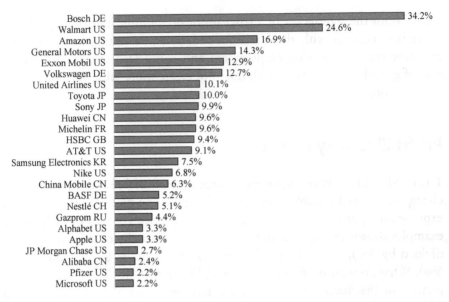

Fig. 6.4 Percentage change in profit for selected Fortune Global 500 companies when price increases by 1%

experienced this in hundreds of projects at Simon-Kucher. In one project for an industrial supplier we recommended an "anti-discount" incentive. When salespeople granted smaller discounts, their commissions would rise. The new system worked quickly and effectively. Within three months, the average discount granted by salespeople declined by 2% points, without any losses in volume or customers. That is the equivalent of a price increase of 2% with no volume decline. The resulting profit increase was 16%, which corresponds to a profit elasticity of price of 8. In absolute terms the profit increase was more than $100 million. Price is an extremely effective profit driver. That makes optimizing price worthwhile.

Profit-Maximizing Price

In general, the profit-maximizing price results from an elasticity-dependent markup on the marginal cost:

$$\text{profit-maximizing price} = \text{price plasticity} \times \text{marginal cost}/(1 + \text{price elasticity})$$
$$(6.1)$$

In other words, there are two factors that determine the profit-maximizing price: the marginal cost and the price elasticity. The price elasticity measures the percentage change in volume caused by a 1% change in price. Because the volume declines when price rises (and vice versa) the price elasticity is negative. The smaller the price elasticity is (in absolute terms), the higher the markup to marginal cost will be. If the price elasticity is −3, the markup on marginal cost is 50%. If the price elasticity is −2, the markup is 100%. Typical values for the price elasticity lie between −1.5 and −4. One should notice that Eq. (6.1) is not identical to cost-plus pricing, but rather represents a general optimality condition. The price elasticity generally changes with the price level, meaning that it is not a constant. The same can be true for marginal cost.

The optimal price always lies in a range for which the price elasticity (in absolute terms) is greater than 1. If it is lower in absolute terms, then the positive effect of a price increase on the unit contribution margin more than compensates for the negative profit effect of the decline in sales. Because the price elasticity at the revenue-maximizing price is equal to −1, the profit-maximizing price is always higher than the revenue-maximizing price.

A very important insight from Eq. (6.1) is that fixed costs have no bearing on the profit-maximizing price. Fixed costs do not appear in the optimal price equation.

When the price response and cost functions are linear, the profit-maximizing price lies exactly at the midpoint between the maximum price, where volume is zero, and the variable unit costs, which in the linear case are identical to the marginal costs. The profit curve is symmetrical. That means that upward deviations from the optimal price have exactly the same negative effect on profit as downward deviations. Contrary to conventional wisdom, prices that are too high are just as damaging to profit as prices that are too low.

Another consequence for linear cost and price-response functions is that when variable unit cost changes—whether up or down—only half of that change should be reflected in the profit-maximizing price. Thus, cost increases should be only partially passed on in the price. The same applies to customs duties and exchange rate variations. The theory confirms the rule of thumb that a supplier should share any changes in its cost position (good or bad) fairly with its customers. Companies actually apply this rule. When the discount grocery chain Aldi experienced a purchasing price increase of 10 cents on milk, it passed only 7 cents on to customers. The same applies to reductions in the purchasing price. Aldi promises to pass savings on to customers. In a similar vein, Michael O'Leary, CEO of Ryanair, promises that "almost all, if not all" cost savings will be passed on to customers.[9]

So let's summarize:

- The profit-maximizing price results from an elasticity-based markup on marginal cost.
- Fixed costs have no influence on the profit-maximizing price. For that reason, any price setting on a full-cost basis makes no sense.
- The profit-maximizing price is always higher than the revenue-maximizing price. That means that revenue maximization is not a sensible goal.
- Deviations above the profit-maximizing price are just as harmful to profits as deviations below it.
- When the price response and cost functions are linear, the profit-maximizing price lies at the midpoint between the variable unit cost and the maximum price.

Marxist Prices

If I ask the question "Are you a Marxist?" almost all managers would emphatically answer "no." Then I follow up by asking "If you aren't a Marxist, why do you set your prices in a Marxist way?" While Marx' labor theory is totally rejected today, it has survived in pricing. What a strange phenomenon! Let me explain why that is the case.

The most important contribution of Karl Marx (1818–1883) was his labor theory of value, according to which only labor creates value. In 1865 he wrote that the "prices of goods are determined by wages."[10] Marx allows for differences in productivity and qualifications of workers, and thus for different values per unit of time. But the core of his theory is that only labor creates value. Labor costs, therefore, are the sole basis for price calculations.

In modern terminology we call this method "cost-plus pricing." Based on my decades of observations around the world, I would claim that 80% of all prices in today's economies are primarily determined on the basis of costs. And all costs are labor costs. Lawyers, consultants, and most other service providers charge prices for their time (hourly, daily, monthly rates). If an automotive company buys parts from a supplier, these parts carry labor costs up the value chain.

---

[9]"Die Luft wird dünner," *General-Anzeiger Bonn*, February 9, 2015, p. 7.
[10]Marx [5].

In essence, even the costs of raw materials comprise labor costs. If the price of a product is then based on a markup on the respective costs, one can justifiably speak of "Marxist" pricing. Karl Marx's labor value theory is considered completely obsolete. Nevertheless, cost-plus pricing, which is nothing but Marxist pricing, not only lives on, but predominates. If one doesn't believe in Marxism, one should get rid of Marxist pricing. That would certainly be beneficial from a profit standpoint.

Price Differentiation and Profit

Until now we have assumed uniform pricing: one product offered at only one price. When a company charges only one price, it leaves a large amount of its profit potential untapped.

Figure 6.5 illustrates this assertion. If the price-response and cost functions are linear, the large shaded triangle represents the total profit potential. A uniform price extracts only the amount shown by the lighter shaded rectangle. In other words, in this configuration the uniform price extracts only half of the potential profit. If the functions are non-linear, the situation looks slightly different at the detailed level, but the overall message is the same. If customers' willingness to pay is heterogeneous, charging a uniform price will invariably capture only a portion of the available profit potential.

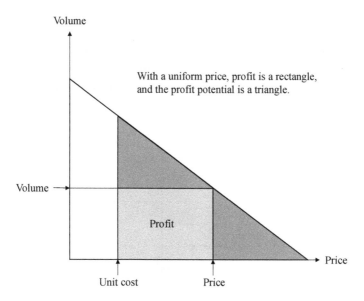

Fig. 6.5 Profit derived from a uniform price

In order to get the largest possible amount of profit from the triangle shown in Fig. 6.5, a company needs differentiated prices. The forms of differentiation are numerous and diverse. Individual price negotiation is common at bazaars, car dealers, and for industrial transactions. Auctions have the goal of exploiting the individual willingness to pay of the highest bidder. Beyond that, we witness price differentiation by:

- Person: seniors, students, children, club members, categories of workers and professionals
- Multiple people: families, groups, associations
- Purchase volume: volume discounts, rebates in kind, bonuses, and non-linear price systems
- Time: seasonal prices, weekend prices, evening rates for electricity
- Place: foreign vs. domestic; urban and suburban/rural; local vs. national,
- Channel: local shops, supermarket, train stations, airports, wholesale, internet

Other forms include multidimensional price systems. e.g. a base price and a price for usage. Such forms include credit cards, phone and data plans, Amazon Prime, and the BahnCard offered by the German railroad. Companies can also offer bundles, which give customers a discount when they buy several products together. Well-known bundles include fast-food menus (burger, fries, drink) and Microsoft Office (Word, PowerPoint, Excel, and Access).

Figure 6.6 shows the profit improvement potential from price differentiation, using selected examples. These results all assume that a company can actually group and separate customers according to the willingness to pay.

The internet introduced and popularized new forms of price differentiation:

Methods of price differentiation	Possible profit increase
Two prices instead of one	33%
Three prices instead of one	50%
Non-linear price cinema	36%
Multi-person price tourism	17%
Price bundling consumer goods	22%
Price bundling extra features car	21%

Fig. 6.6 Examples of profit improvements from price differentiation

- Flatrates: The usage or consumption is not limited (e.g. Spotify, Netflix)
- Freemium: A basic version is offered for free, but the customer must pay for the premium version (e.g. LinkedIn, Xing, Spotify)
- Name-your-own-Price: The customer proposes a price, and the supplier decides whether to accept it (e.g. Priceline)
- Pay-what-you-want: The customer pays a price and the supplier delivers the goods or services at that price (e.g. certain zoos, the rock group Radiohead, some restaurants and hotels)
- Pay-per-use: The customer pays for actual usage or consumption (e.g. jet engines according to thrust; tires based on miles driven; bikes or scooters based on time). Automated measurement using sensors plays an important role for pay-per-use models.

The ultimate goal of price differentiation is to go from the rectangle in Fig. 6.5 to the much larger triangle, which represents the full profit potential. Successful implementation of price differentiation can lead to considerable gains in profit. But price differentiation also carries risks. If the company cannot segment its customers according to willingness to pay, the attempts at price differentiation can backfire. Customers with a higher willingness to pay end up buying at low prices that were never aimed at them. Without effective "fences" between customer groups, the price differentiation can yield a lower level of profit than what the company would have achieved with a uniform price.

We summarize price differentiation as follows:

- Profit potential, graphically speaking, generally resembles a triangle.[11] Uniform pricing only carves out a rectangle within that triangle, leaving a large amount of potential profit untapped.
- The challenge lies in expanding one's profit to cover as much of the triangle as possible. This requires price differentiation, which comes in many forms.
- The key prerequisite is the ability to separate or "fence" customers according to their willingness to pay. Companies need to manage their different offers in such a way that customers with higher willingness to pay actually do pay higher prices rather than taking advantage of lower prices.
- The internet pioneered numerous price differentiation models which have become popular. Sensors and low transaction costs play an important role in their successful implementation.

---

[11]The concrete form of profit potential depends on the price-response and cost functions.

Price differentiation, and especially its implementation, is a complex task from an organizational standpoint, but relative to uniform prices, it promises the reward of strong profit improvement.

Psychology of Price

The psychological aspects of price have attracted considerable attention in recent years, beyond the pure economic and quantitative profit effects. Behavioral economics research has revealed numerous price phenomena that can have a massive effect on profits. Some of the corresponding behaviors of consumers are seen as irrational.[12] Whether they are truly irrational or merely simplified rules for decision-making is a question I will leave open.

Some of these psychological effects have been known for a long time:

- Price as an indicator of quality: Consumers perceive a high price as an indicator of high quality
- Snob or "Veblen" effect: The perceived utility of a product rises with its price, because it signals higher social status.

Due to these two phenomena, some portions of the price-response curve may have a positive slope. In other words, a price increase would lead to higher volumes. The so-called Giffen Paradox can cause the same effect, but it is most likely to apply only to poverty situations.

In addition to these classic effects, the new research has revealed other phenomena that apparently contradict economic rationality:

- Anchor price effects: Consumers seek reference points in order to judge how favorably priced a product or service is. To do so, they make comparisons or use information that does not necessarily have a factual basis.
- "Magic of the middle": When information is limited or lacking, consumers tend to select a mid-priced product. For my farm, I needed a padlock, a rarely purchased item. At the home improvement store, the prices for the relevant size ranged from $4 to $12. I selected one at a price of $8.
- Expanding a price range: If a restaurant normally sells wine in a price range of $20–$30 and adds a $50 bottle to the menu, the share of wine sold at $30 will increase, even when no one ever buys the $50 bottle.

---

[12]See Ariely [6], and Trevisan [7].

- Creating scarcity: If the impression arises that the supply of a product is low or restricted, the willingness to pay more or to buy more can increase.
- More alternatives: For banking products, the average price shifts upward when more alternatives are offered.
- Prospect theory: According to this theory, positive and negative marginal utility are asymmetric. Applied to car insurance, for example, this means that it could be advantageous to book the insurance premium in one annual payment, but pay refunds or reimbursements in several small installments. But one should be careful with such models. A study for a fitness center revealed that it is better to collect the annual fee in 12 installments rather than in one lump-sum payment. Monthly payments led to more intensive usage of the studio and also increased customer loyalty.[13]

The profit effects that come from the application of these insights into price psychology are often enormous. But one should proceed with caution, because they may lead to unintended consequences that can leave customers feeling duped ... and willing to express their bad feelings online.

Premium Strategy

Modern markets are increasingly segmented. They range from luxury to ultra-low priced. In between, one finds the premium and low-price positions. The ultra-low price segments exists almost exclusively in emerging and developing markets. The luxury segment is generally very small, but highly profitable. Here we will consider two large segments: premium and low-price.

Examples of companies that consistently practice premium pricing include Apple, Gillette, Porsche, Miele, and hotel chains such as Four Seasons and Ritz Carlton. Industrial goods can also have companies with premium prices, such as Enercon in wind turbines or Rational in professional cooking appliances. Premium pricing is only sustainable when a company consistently delivers superior value-to-customer. The critical competitive advantage lies in an appropriate price-value relationship, in contrast to the luxury segment, where competitive advantages derive from prestige. Generally speaking, innovation is the foundation that enables successful, sustainable premium pricing. This includes not only breakthrough innovations, but also continuous improvement, as captured in the motto of Miele: "forever better."

---

[13] See Gourville and Soman [8].

Successful premium offerings are characterized by a high, consistent level of product quality. Their services must also live up to that standard.

Premium pricers usually have strong brands. One function of a brand is to transform technological advantages, which are often temporary, into permanent advantages in terms of image. Premium firms invest considerable amounts of money into communication, in order to make the value and the advantages of their products apparent and understandable. What ultimately matters is perceived value, not objective value. They are more reserved, however, with respect to discounts and promotions, because overuse of those instruments can jeopardize their premium positions.

The key challenge in premium pricing lies in striking the balance between value and costs. These firms emphasize high customer value, which comprises not only the core product itself, but also a comprehensive spectrum of services. At the same time, costs must remain at acceptable levels.

Low-Price Strategy

The success factors for a low-price strategy are very different. Companies with sustained success with low-price strategies—including Aldi, Zara, IKEA, Primark, Uniqlo, Southwest Airlines, and Ryanair—have focused on low prices and high volumes from the very beginning. These kinds of companies have often created radical new business models. None of them transformed themselves from a higher-price position to become low-price suppliers. They also operate with the highest process efficiency and have rapid inventory turnover. These capabilities allow these companies to earn adequate margins and profits, even with low prices.

They guarantee an acceptable and consistent level of quality. Poor or inconsistent quality will not lead to long-term success, despite low prices. Low-price suppliers place a very strong focus on their core product and leave out anything that is tangential or unnecessary. Thus, they keep costs low without harming the core customer value. They pursue strategies of strong growth and high market share. That allows them to exploit economies of scale and experience curve effects to the greatest possible degree.

Their procurement strategies are tough and firm, but not unfair. They also eschew bank financing, preferring instead to self-finance or rely on credit from their suppliers, especially in retail. At the same time, they exert tight control over the entire value chain. From a marketing standpoint, they strongly prefer their own private label brands. When they advertise, they focus almost exclusively on price (Aldi, Ryanair). They usually practice Every

Day Low Pricing (EDLP), which means that discounts or promotions are rare. In most markets, there is only room for very few "low price, high profit" companies, often only one or two.

In short, it is possible to earn sustainably high profits with low prices. But only a few companies succeed with that strategy. The most important prerequisite is that costs remain significantly lower over time. The necessary capabilities to achieve that must be locked into the corporate culture right from the start. It seems questionable that companies with other traditions can transform themselves to meet that challenge.

The low-price category requires a special breed of entrepreneur and manager. Only those who are ready to be modest, frugal, or even stingy on a day-to-day basis should consider plunging into the world of low prices. The other prerequisite for success in this category is the establishment of an acceptable, but not bare-bones, level of value-to-customer. This depends heavily on how well the core product performs and whether the firm can maintain that level of performance and extreme cost efficiency at the same time.

Internet, Price, and Profit

The internet radically changed the environment and conditions for pricing, with correspondingly significant effects on profits. In e-commerce, it is easier to change prices, technically speaking. Many companies seize that opportunity. In general prices change more frequently than they did in the pre-internet world. One study found that within a three-month period, an online pharmacy changed 87% of its prices, and other sectors such as electronics (67%), fashion (50%) and auto parts (40%) also saw frequent prices changes.[14]

Dynamic pricing offers opportunities, but also carries considerable risks. One of the biggest is the increased frequency of price wars, which almost invariably destroy profits. On Amazon, 10 million products were tracked over a 10-month period. There were 60,000 price wars per day, but most of them lasted less than six hours.[15]

A very important and common effect of the internet is the massive increase in price transparency. This gives low-price suppliers an advantage and makes price cuts more effective. But it also puts premium suppliers at a disadvantage and makes price increases more difficult.

---

[14] See *Frankfurter Allgemeine Zeitung*, August 7, 2018, p. 7.
[15] Ibid.

The internet also increases value transparency. But this trend is in its early stages and still lags the developments in price transparency. Value transparency has an asymmetric effect on price elasticity. Positive customer feedback is becoming increasingly important for pricing and profit. When a company receives predominantly negative reviews online, even aggressive price cuts can't offset the damage. The price elasticity declines. The negative reviews and comments essentially defuse price as a weapon of attack. Price increases would invite disaster, because the price elasticity in that area rises.

Companies that receive mostly positive reviews experience the opposite effects. They sell more at constant prices, and can implement price increases with less volume loss, because the price elasticity declines. For price cuts, though the price elasticity rises, meaning that the cuts have a greater impact on volume. All of these responses can have strong profit effects.

New Price Metrics

An innovative path to improving profit is to change the measurement basis for the price. This is often called the price metric. One example from building materials illustrates the potential. A company that sells cinder blocks for wall construction could charge by weight (price per ton), by space (price per cubic meter), by surface area (price per square meter), or for the complete installation (price per square meter of finished wall). For each metric, the company could charge very different prices and face a very different competitive landscape. For example, with one new type of cinder block, a top manufacturer's price was 40% more expensive than the competitors' when using tons or cubic meters as the price metric. But the price difference was only about 10% with square meters as the metric. Because the new blocks weighed less and allowed a team to build the walls faster, the price per square meter for a finished wall conferred a price advantage of 12%. This makes it clear that the manufacturer should try to switch the price metric for these new blocks to square meters of finished wall.

Companies such as Hilti, the global leader for high-performance electric power tools, used to sell products to customers, which meant that the price metric was price per tool. Hilti broke that mold by introducing a "fleet management" model for its tools: the customer pays a fixed monthly price for its "fleet" of Hilti tools. Hilti ensures that the customer gets the optimal set of tools for its jobs, offers comprehensive service, and also takes care of everything from repairs to battery exchanges. This program has two advantages for the customers. They can count on a predictable, fixed monthly price for tools, and they can focus on their core competencies of executing the job instead of procuring tools.

Dürr, the world market leader for painting systems, has cooperated with BASF for several years to offer paint services to auto manufacturers at a fixed price per vehicle. EnviroFalk, a specialist for industrial water treatment, makes its equipment available to customers for free, then charges them based on the cubic meters of water treated. Winterhalter, the world market leader in washing systems for restaurants, offers a "pay per wash" program. The company claims that the program is "no investment, no risk, no fixed costs, fully flexible, and all-inclusive."[16] In 2020, the world market leader in laser machines, Trumpf, founded a financing joint venture with the world's largest re-insurer, Munich Re. Under the new financing model, Trumpf customers no longer purchase their machines outright. Instead, they pay a fixed price per finished part. This kind of "pay per use" model is similar to how Michelin charges for truck tires. Customers pay according to the miles driven.

Customers benefit from such models, because they can calculate their costs better and have a lower capital burden. The supplier, in turn, has a more predictable cash flow and can allocate resources optimally. These models can also create competitive advantages, because only companies with a strong capital position or strong partners can afford to offer them.

The adoption of cloud computing is turning several new price metrics into standard practice. Software is no longer sold on a license basis and then installed on-premise. Instead, it is offered online and on-demand for a fee. This model is known as Software as a Service (SaaS). Microsoft's Office 365 suite is no longer sold in the traditional way, but rather under a SaaS model with a monthly or a discounted annual subscription. In Europe, the Office 365 Home Premium costs €10 Euros per month or €99 Euros per year. In return the customer receives immediate online access to the latest versions and a range of additional services.

Adobe is a compelling example of the transition from a product-based sales model to a subscription model. Adobe traditionally sold its software on discs with a perpetual license. The model was profitable, with Adobe achieving a net profit margin of 19%. But this inflexible business model also had disadvantages. It did not enable permanent customer relationships, nor did it permit software updates. For these reasons it impeded Adobe's ability to offer customers a continuous stream of innovative improvements. The solution was a radical shift to "Adobe Creative Cloud," a cloud-based subscription model that superseded the old disc-and-license model. Supported by a

---

[16]http://www.pay-per-wash.biz/de_de/, called up on November 10, 2020.

massive communication effort, the shift turned out to be extremely successful. Adobe's market capitalization stood at $22.5 billion when it launched the new model in 2013. By autumn 2020, it had risen to more than $200 billion.[17]

The price metric for car-sharing services is not new in principle, but its precision far exceeds what traditional car rental models offer. Many of these services charge by the minute. The basic rates include a block of free miles, after which the customer must pay per mile. Digital technologies enable the tracking down to the exact minute and mile, without placing any additional burden on the customer.

The car industry must start thinking in depth about new business models, so that it can continue to earn adequate profits. Andreas Herrmann and Walter Brenner commented on this topic: "A carmaker earns around $2,800 on the average car, which stays on the road for 150,000 miles. That translates into less than two cents per mile driven, which makes the following recommendation imperative: a business model based on profit per car must be replaced by a philosophy of profit per trip."[18] Low transaction costs and low monitoring and controlling costs are vitally important for such models, especially for low-value shared vehicles such as bicycles or electric scooters.

The price system for Google AdWords also relies on a new price metric. Traditional media has long used circulation as its price metric, even though the degree to which circulation impacts sales volume or the image of the advertised brand has always been uncertain. Google adopted a pay-per-click model for advertising. This established a tighter perceived link between cause-and-effect and price, and apparently advertisers appreciate the new model. For several years running, Google has claimed an increasing share of the advertising pie.

Enercon, the global technology leader in wind energy, uses an innovative price model. Its Enercon Partner Concept offers customers the following benefits:

- technical availability guaranteed at 97%
- reimbursement of yield loss if guaranteed technical availability is not met
- repair and spare parts guarantee
- no additional costs for spare parts or main components
- complete coverage against unforeseeable events with Enercon's additional or conventional insurance
- regular maintenance

---

[17]On November 4, 2020 the market capitalization of Adobe was $233.72 billion.
[18]Herrmann et al. [9].

- central monitoring and 24/7 remote monitoring via SCADA (Supervisory Control and Data Acquisition), a system developed by Enercon
- local point of contact and prompt reaction due to decentralized service network
- performance-oriented payment
- calculable costs based on yield.[19]

The most important aspect of this arrangement is that Enercon shares the business risks with its customers.

New price models are also making headway in the insurance industry. New technologies allow more reliable estimates of risks, which in turn enable the insurance providers to perform better cost-based price calculations. One car insurance company that operates in several countries installs a black box in a customer's car, connecting it with the insurer's GPS. The customer then pays a rate per mile based on the distance driven, the time of day, and the accident risk along the chosen route. Because these new risk parameters better reflect the actual causes of accidents, they are replacing traditional but less precise risk parameters such as how old a customer is and where he or she lives. The insurer thus no longer needs to cross-subsidize different risk profiles, because it has detailed knowledge of its customers and their driving behaviors.[20] In the United States, this model already has a market share of 10%.[21]

Similar approaches exist in health insurance. Companies could incentivize certain healthy activities through lower insurance premiums. There are many potential ways to deploy new price metrics in the health field. Smart watches, sensors in armbands, and other forms of remote diagnosis make it easier to track and measure key health parameters. The British health insurer AIG Direct uses Body Mass Index (BMI) as the basis for determining monthly rates. Exemptions are made in specials cases, such as for people whose muscle mass—thanks to heavy sports activities—can skew a BMI calculation.[22]

The theater Teatreneu in Barcelona introduced a futuristic price metric. It outfitted the seats with sensors that can analyze facial expressions. The theatergoer agrees to pay €0.30 for each laugh recognized by the sensor, up to a maximum of €24 (or 80 laughs). The payment is made via smartphone. The revenue has reportedly risen by €6 per person.[23] This example may seem rather exotic and may not become the standard model for theaters in the

---

[19]https://www.enercon.de/en/dienstleistungsportfolio/service/.
[20]Friemel and Malcher [10].
[21]Siedenbiedel [11].
[22]Zuboff [12].
[23]Morozov [13].

future. But it demonstrates what technology can make possible. After all, it does make sense to pay more for an enjoyable theater performance than a boring one, right?

One could in fact call most conventional price metrics into question. Hotels (one day), package tours (one week), public transportation (one month), museums (one year), or craftsmen (one hour) all use time-based price metrics. Restaurants, however, normally charge by meal, hair salons charge on a case-by-case basis, and taxis charge on the basis of distance. But one could imagine that restaurants, hair salons, and taxis could also use time as their price metric. If the bottleneck at a restaurant is availability of tables, it could make more sense to charge patrons by time in order to achieve the highest possible turnover.

Airlines traditionally price travel per person, with differentiation by age, status, or similar criteria. But in 2013, the airline Samoa Air Ltd. came up with a totally different price metric: charging passengers according to their body weight. The price for a flight from Samoa to American Samoa costs $0.92 per kilogram. Such a price metric seems compelling, because Samoa has the world's third highest level of overweight people, far ahead of the United States. Despite initial protests, CEO Chris Langton wants to stick to the plan: "It's a pay by weight system and it's here to stay", he said. [24] The logic speaks for such a system, because the weight of passengers is a legitimate cost driver for an airline, not age or status. Why should the transport of freight be charged by weight, but not the transport of people? Some US airlines have started to demand that extremely large passengers buy two tickets on a full flight.

New technologies will make performance-based price metrics increasingly possible. Health care companies could use sensors to measure the effects of pharmaceuticals, medical treatments, or other services and set prices depending on the actual efficacy. In general, new price metrics create opportunities for companies to overcome the limitations of old metrics and do a better job of extracting value. In their book *The Ends Game*, Marco Bertini und Oded Koenigsberg offer a detailed discussion of innovative price models based on the value customers derive.[25]

---

[24]Craymer [14].
[25]See Bertini and Koenigsberg [15].

Price and Shareholder Value

Profit and growth are the drivers of shareholder value. Price is an essential determinant of shareholder value, because it exerts a powerful influence on both profit and growth. Managers are waking up to the importance of this connection, and have started to incorporate it into their strategic planning as well as into their communication to capital markets.[26] Pricing comes up more and more frequently in roadshows, analysts calls, and shareholder meetings. The claim of Warren Buffett—that "the single most important decision in evaluating a business is pricing power"—has reinforced this trend.[27] The successful Silicon Valley investor Peter Thiel also emphasizes the influence of price on shareholder value, making a firm case for building market positions with strong pricing power.[28]

The so-called EVP model, developed by Simon-Kucher, gives executives and managers a way to make the relationship between price and shareholder value operational.[29] EVP, which stands for Enterprise Value of Price, is the ratio of two values: the additional shareholder value generated by a 1% price increase, and the growth expectations of analysts for the next 12 months. The model makes a similar assumption to the one we used in Figs. 6.2 and 6.3, namely, that the 1% price increase changes neither the sales volume nor the cost. The revenue increase induced by the price increase is therefore pure profit. Expressed mathematically, the Enterprise Value of Price is defined in Eq. (6.2):

$$EVP = VP/VEG. \qquad (6.2)$$

where VP = Value of Price and VEG = Value of Expected Growth. These values are defined as follows:

$$VP = R(1 - s) \times 0.01/(WACC - g) \qquad (6.3)$$

$$VEG = \text{enterprise value in period } 1 - \text{enterprise value in period } 0. \qquad (6.4)$$

---

[26] See Srinivasan et al. [16].

[27] Excerpted from an interview with Warren Buffett before the Financial Crisis Inquiry Commission (FCIC) on May 26, 2010.

[28] See Thiel [17].

[29] The EVP concept is registered as a brand number 174368295 at the INPI (Institut National de la Propriété Intellectuelle), Paris.

R is the revenue, s is the corporate tax rate, WACC is the Weighted Average Cost of Capital according to Eq. (1.12) und g is the growth rate of the free cash flow.[30] One observes that the Eq. (6.3) only makes sense when the denominator is positive, i.e. WACC must be greater than the growth rate g. Company-specific values for WACC, the growth rate g, and the Enterprise Value can be retrieved from databases such as Thomson Reuters. In other words, the EVP metric can be calculated using publicly available information.

An EVP value of 0.6 means that a one-percent price increase would contribute 60% to the expected growth in shareholder value in the coming 12 months. If analysts expect an increase of $3 billion in shareholder value, a price increase of 1% would account for $1.8 billion of that amount. The higher the EVP is in absolute terms, the greater the influence of a price increase will be, and the more it makes sense to invest in a stronger price position. In the words of Warren Buffett, that is an investment in pricing power.

Pricing Process

So far in this chapter we have dealt with the profit-boosting topic of "price optimization." No less important is the "pricing process." Ultimately, price cannot make its full contribution to profit unless a company succeeds in implementing profit-maximizing prices. Practical experience shows that that is a difficult task. In a study conducted in the United States, some 58% of the companies responding said they attempted to raise prices, but only 19% of companies (roughly one third of those who tried) actually succeeded in implementing higher prices.[31] According to the Global Pricing Study of Simon-Kucher, only one third of all planned price increases actually get implemented.[32] Even then, companies realized only 37% of the planned amounts on average. In other words, a planned price increase of 10% yielded on average an increase of only 3.7%.

Pricing processes encompass all aspects, ranging from strategy to implementation to monitoring. The effective management of a pricing process can typically improve return on sales by between 2 and 4, sometimes even 6 percentage points. When one considers that the average net return on sales of companies is around 5% (see Chap. 2), the addition of 2 to 4% points

---

[30] For the definition of free cash flow, see Chap. 1.

[31] "Wall Street braced for 'earnings recession' as margins fall, US companies struggle to pass on rising labour, transportation and raw material costs," *Financial Times*, March 26, 2019.

[32] See Simon-Kucher & Partners, Global Pricing Study 2014, Bonn 2014.

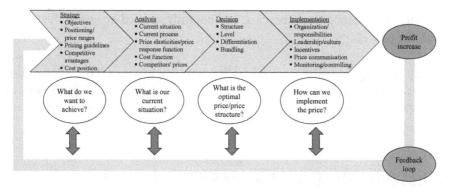

Fig. 6.7 Generic pricing process

would represent a massive improvement. But achieving this level of improvement requires deep immersion into the specific characteristics and nuances of a business.

To set up a pricing process, we recommend the generic four-phase approach shown in Fig. 6.7. The process—from strategy to monitoring—corresponds to phases many businesses already follow in some form.

But this representation is not sufficient for a specific case. Our experience shows that a price management process depends heavily on aspects peculiar to an industry or even to the company itself. Nonetheless, the generic view provides a starting point for a crisper and deeper definition of the individual tasks.

We have the following recommendations for organizing the pricing process:

- The company needs to assign responsibilities for the various tasks. The individual steps in the process and the organizational units should be tailored as much as possible to fit the company's business model.
- It is generally advisable to place the price decision-making power relatively high up in the hierarchy. Securing cooperation and a smooth flow of information between the market side and the internal functions is indispensable.
- The role of the CEO in price management is critically important. The CEO must ensure that goals are met, processes are established in an optimal way, and a profit-oriented culture with respect to price takes hold.
- Effective price controlling and monitoring is absolutely essential, and in most companies, this is only possible with a requisite amount of information technology. Ideally, price controlling should be integrated into the

entire price management process, and not only applied *ex post* to the results of the process.

Any strategy is only as good as its implementation. This saying also applies to price as a profit driver. In the course of the professionalization of price management, senior leaders need to focus more of their attention on implementation.

What Benefits Does Better Pricing Bring?

To wrap up the chapter, we will look at selected case examples which show the profit improvements that professional pricing can generate. Figure 6.8 lists cases from various industries. The last column shows the respective increase in the net return on sales in basis points. The wholesaler (last row), for example, saw its net return on sales rise from 4 to 6%, which is a difference of 2% points or 200 basis points.

The column "Primary Levers" illustrates just how diverse the profit-driving price measures can be. One of the special characteristics of price measures is that the profit improvements come quickly, and definitely faster than the profit improvements a company could achieve through rationalization, innovation, or reorganization.

Industry	Primary levers	Increase in return on sales in basis points*
Banking	▪ Better exploitation of brand equity ▪ Enhancing the pricing competence of the customer representatives	160
Tourism	▪ More strongly differentiated price structure ▪ Indicator- supported identification of opportunities with profit potential	160
Automotive supplier	▪ Introduction of new elements to the price structure ▪ Invoicing of additional services	150
Software	▪ Reorganization of the selling process and guidelines ▪ Stronger centralization	800
Machinery	▪ Reduction of overengineering through target valuing/target costing ▪ Standardisation of processes, especially for limited/small run series	250
Electronics	▪ For innovations: Using value-pricing instead of cost-plus ▪ Better forecasting of cost developments for long-term contracts	220
Consumer goods	▪ Value-to-customer based price setting ▪ Systematic estimation/determination of price elasticity	110
Engineering	▪ Systematic quantification of value-to-customer ▪ More comprehensive and reliable competitive intelligence	80
Wholesaler	▪ Classifying customer and product groups based on price elasticities ▪ Anti-discount incentives for the sales force	200

*100 basis points equal 1 percentage point

Fig. 6.8 Profit improvement through professional pricing in various industries

Summary

Price is a more effective profit driver than sales volume, but the reality is that price optimization is complex. If marginal cost is positive, a price increase yields higher profits than a volume increase of the same percentage magnitude. Conversely, a price decrease will have a more pronounced negative effect on profits than a volume decline of the same magnitude. The profit elasticity of price is normally high, which means that a 1% change in price has a significantly stronger percentage effect on profit.

The profit-maximizing price does not depend on fixed costs. If the price-response and cost functions are linear, the profit-maximizing price lies at the midpoint between the variable unit cost and the maximum price. The profit-maximizing price can be expressed as an elasticity-dependent markup on marginal costs. In contrast to a uniform price, differentiated prices offer opportunities for much higher profits. In geometric terms, it means going from "rectangle to triangle." There are many useful methods for price differentiation.

In addition to the purely economic effects, psychological phenomena play a major role in pricing. Classic effects include the "snob" or Veblen effect as well as the role of price as an indicator of quality. More recently, behavioral economics has uncovered a wide range of phenomena, such as anchor price effects, the "magic of the middle", the effects of a higher number of alternatives, and prospect theory, which points out the asymmetry between positive and negative utility.

Premium and low-price strategies require different competencies. That applies even more for luxury goods and for ultra-low-price products. It is definitely possible to earn high profits with low prices. But only a few companies succeed with that strategy, because one needs very pronounced economies of scale to achieve and sustain the requisite low costs.

The internet has changed the conditions for pricing and thus for profit as well. The frequency of price changes and price wars is increasing. Price transparency and thus price elasticity are also changing, mostly increasing. This creates advantages for low-price suppliers. At the same time, value is becoming more transparent, which can work in favor of premium suppliers with strong brand reputations.

Price is a very important determinant of shareholder value. The metric EVP, derived from publicly available data, indicates the extent to which a 1% change in price can contribute to the growth in shareholder value that analysts expect in the coming year. EVP clarifies when it is worthwhile to invest in pricing power.

A process perspective is necessary for the implementation of price measures. A typical pricing process encompasses strategy, analysis, decision-making, and implementation. When implemented professionally, price measures can boost net return on sales by between 200 and 600 basis points.

References

1. Albers, S., Mantrala, M. K., & Sridhar, S. (2010). Personal Selling Elasticities: A Meta-Analysis, *Journal of Marketing Research*, 5, pp. 840–853.
2. Sethuraman, R., Tellis, G. J., & Briesch, R. A. (2011). How Well Does Advertising Work? Generalizations from Meta-Analysis of Brand Advertising Elasticities, *Journal of Marketing Research*, 48(3), pp. 457–471.
3. Simon, H., & Fassnacht, M. (2019). *Price Management - Strategy, Analysis, Decision, Implementation*, New York: Springer Nature.
4. Simon, H. (2015). *Confessions of the Pricing Man*, New York: Springer.
5. Marx, K. (1951). Wages, Prices, and Profits, *Marx Engels Selected Works*, I, Progress Publishers, Moscow, p. 28.
6. Ariely, D. (2010). *Predictably Irrational: The Hidden Forces that Shape Our Decisions*, New York: Harper Perennial.
7. Trevisan, E. (2013). *The Irrational Consumer: Applying Behavioural Economics to Your Business Strategy*, London: Routledge.
8. Gourville, J. T., & Soman, D. (1998). Payment Depreciation: The Behavioral Effects of Temporally Separating Payments from Consumption, *Journal of Consumer Research*, 25(2), pp. 160–174.
9. Herrmann, A., Brenner, W., & Stadler, R. (2018) *Autonomous Driving: How the Driverless Revolution Will Change the World*, London: Emerald Publishing, p. 29.
10. Friemel, K., & Malcher, I. (2006). Gewusst wie, *McKinsey Wissen*, 18, pp. 18–25.
11. Siedenbiedel, C. (2014). Revolution der KfZ-Versicherung, *FAZnet*, January 13.
12. Zuboff, S. (2015). Die Vorteile der Nachzügler, *Frankfurter Allgemeine Zeitung*, March 23, p. 15.
13. Morozov, E. (2013). Unser Leben wird umgekrempelt, *Frankfurter Allgemeine Zeitung*, November 2, p. 14.
14. Craymer, L. (2013). Weigh More, Pay More on Samoa Air, *Wall Street Journal Online*, April.
15. Bertini, M., & Koenigsberg, O. (2020) *The Ends Game – How Smart Companies Stop Selling Products and Start Delivering Value*, Cambridge: MIT Press.
16. Srinivasan, S., Pauwels, K., Silva-Risso, J., & Hanssens, D. M. (2009). Product Innovations, Advertising, and Stock Returns, *Journal of Marketing*, 73 (January), pp. 24–43.
17. Thiel, P. (2014). *Zero to One. Notes on Startups or How to Build the Future*, New York: Crown Publishing Group.

7

Profit Driver: Sales Volume

Management of sales volume—one of the three profit drivers—is about steering the volume in such a way that profit is maximized, or at least improved relative to a starting situation. Another goal can be to minimize the effects of a potential profit downturn. Higher volumes only make sense when they drive higher profits. When a volume decline brings about an increase in profit, the company should accept that decline.

Special Features of Volume as a Profit Driver

Similar to price, volume has special features with respect to its role as a profit driver. We touched on some of them when we introduced Fig. 6.1.

Who is affected by volume measures? As with price, the customers' actions are what matters, because customers decide whether to buy more or less of a product or service. The exceptions are periods of scarcity, when the seller allocates volume.

The sales force is also affected by volume measures, because sales policies are typically linked to volume targets. It is common in the automotive industry, for example, to specify the number of vehicles to be sold in a given country or region. Incentives are also often tied to the achievement of volume targets. Sales sometimes uses questionable methods in order to meet its volume targets. These can include sales via gray channels or going against company policy to export volume to other countries at reduced prices.

© The Author(s), under exclusive license to Springer Nature Switzerland AG 2021
H. Simon, *True Profit!*,
https://doi.org/10.1007/978-3-030-76702-0_7

Functions such as production and logistics are also affected by volume measures. These departments produce and physically distribute products. Production and logistics managers have often told me that marketing's decisions on sales and volume policies can unleash chaos upstream along the value chain when those decisions lead to massive increases in volume. The opposite situation can also occur. If the volume actions fall short of expectations, it can leave warehouses full and, in some cases, force the company to temporarily shut down production or get rid of the unsold merchandise at deep discounts.

The lesson from these experiences is that the upstream value chain must be included in the planning and implementation of any actions to change volumes.

In contrast to price, a supplier cannot increase its sales volume at will. The supplier cannot command customers to buy more, because the purchase decision is the customers' domain. While the supplier can change price directly and unilaterally, it can only indirectly influence volume through instruments such as advertising, sales, distribution, promotions, and discounts. The supplier can, however, act on its own to reduce or limit volumes. It can cap the individual purchase volumes for retail promotions, for example, at "normal household levels."

Similar to price, volume has a double-barreled impact on profit. The direct effect is on revenue, the top line. The indirect effect on profit comes via variable cost. How strong that second influence is depends on the cost structure and the cost function. If marginal costs are zero, volume affects only the top line.

Efforts to increase volume generally require time to take hold, because they depend on intensified efforts in advertising, sales, production, and distribution or on the launch of innovations. The adjustment of production lines generally requires some lead time. In short, there is a time lag between implementation of volume-increase measures and the onset of their effects. Volume cuts, in contrast, can have a more immediate impact because the supplier simply produces less or arbitrarily sells less.

Generally speaking, advance investments in the abovementioned instruments are a prerequisite for volume increases. If a company faces financial bottlenecks, it might not be possible for the chosen instruments to reach a profit-optimal level, and thus make the achievement of the volume increase target impossible. This situation is typical for start-ups as well as for rapidly growing or financially constrained companies.

Autonomous versus Price-Induced Volume Growth

An important difference revolves around the question of whether volume increases occur on their own or whether they are induced by price cuts. The autonomous growth takes place without significant prices changes or at constant prices. Volume and revenue both grow at the same or similar percentage rates. For volume growth induced by price cuts, however, the revenue does not grow as rapidly as the volume. Let's assume a starting situation with a price of $100 and a sales volume of 100 units, which results in revenue of $10,000. If volume grows by 20% with no change in price, revenue increases to $12,000. The growth rates in volume and revenue are identical. But if the company cuts the price by 10% to $90 and the volume grows by 20% to 120 units (which corresponds to a realistic price elasticity of -2), the revenue rises only to $10,800. That is a growth rate of 8%.

It is obvious that the profit effects of autonomous volume growth are vastly different from those of price-induced growth. If we assume that variable unit costs are $60 and ignore fixed costs for now, the profit rises to $4,800 from $4,000 under autonomous growth. Price-induced growth, in contrast actually leads to a profit decline to $3,600, despite the 20% increase in volume. Beyond this simple calculation, let's now assume that changes in volume also have an effect on costs. If the variable unit costs drop to $54 thanks to economies of scale, the profit would rise to $4,200 from $4,000 in the price-induced growth case. These simple calculations show that the relationship between volume and profit varies and can lead to significantly different outcomes. Companies should therefore always be very careful when lowering prices in an effort to boost volumes. The following real-life examples illustrate the wide range of effects that sales volume can have on profit.

More Volume, Less Profit

"Tax free" days are a common and popular gimmick in retail. In some US states, customers can make purchases without paying sales tax. In European countries, the retailer "forgives" the value-added tax (VAT). To look at the effects these promotions can have, we will examine how one large European retailer with revenue of more than $20 billion offered to waive the 19% value-added sales tax for its customers on one weekend.

"The traffic we generated was incredible," one of their top executives told me. "We had 40% more customers in our stores over the weekend!"

But what happened to the profit?

Figure 7.1 compares the situations with and without the VAT. For the situation with VAT, we set the sales volume at 100 units and set the price at $119 to reflect the tax charge. We assume that the retailer earns a gross margin of 30%, so that the variable unit costs are $70. For simplicity's sake, we will assume that fixed costs are zero. This base case leaves the retailer with a profit of $3,000. The two columns "without VAT" shows what happens if we hold volume or profit constant.

If volume is the same when the price does not include VAT, the profit falls by more than half. In order to achieve the same profit, volume would need to increase by 113%, i.e. it would have to more than double. Customer traffic may have increased by 40%, as the executive celebrated, but that increase falls far short of the level needed to keep profits constant, even if some customers buy more than they otherwise would. It is extremely unlikely that the increased volume from this promotion led to higher profits.

In Chap. 5, we referred to a promotion action of General Motors under which the automaker opened up its employee discounts program to all customers. In the first month of the promotion, GM sold 41.1% more cars than it did in the year-ago month, a spectacular achievement. Sales volume then rose by another 19.8% in the next month. The success from a volume standpoint was indisputable.

But what happened to the profit?

For the full business year, the company posted a loss of $10.5 billion. Within four months, GM's market capitalization fell by more than 40%. A few months later, GM Chairman Bob Lutz commented: "Selling five million

	Initial situation with price including VAT	Price without VAT	
		same sales volume	same profit
Sales volume (units sold)	100	100	213
Price ($)	119	100	100
Revenue incl. VAT ($)	11,900	10,000	21,300
Unit costs ($)	7,000	7,000	14,900
VAT ($)	1,900	1,597	3,400
Profit ($)	3,000	1,403	3,000

Fig. 7.1 Sales volume and profit from a "tax free" retail promotion

vehicles at zero profit isn't as good a proposition as selling four million vehicles at a profit."[1]

With premium products, the temptation can arise to increase volume by extending the brand to more price-conscious segments. But such a move carries the risk that a product loses its premium status and becomes a mass product. One example is the automotive brand Opel, which had belonged to General Motors since 1929, before the French automaker PSA (now Stellantis) acquired it in 2017. In the 1950's and 1960's, Opel was known for legendary premium cars and trendy iconic models such as Diplomat, Admiral, and Senator. But in the ensuing decades, the company lost its way, plagued by quality and image problems in its attempts to build smaller cars. Despite massive increases in unit sales volume, the company posted huge losses.

The Lacoste brand suffered a similar fate. In 1933, the French professional tennis player René Lacoste founded a firm to sell shirts he designed. The crocodile emblem adorning the shirts stood for exclusive prestige, turning Lacoste into a high-price, high-margin business. US President Dwight Eisenhower and other famous people wore the shirts in public. Up until the start of the 1980's, the brand remained associated with high social status and held a premium position. But Lacoste wanted to get bigger, and over time the brand became a mass product. The prices fell, and with them the profits as well.

Less Volume, More Profit

A mid-sized supplier had a large customer that accounted for 10% of its sales volume. This key account not only applied massive pressure on prices. It also demanded a slate of services—including consulting, stocking, and shipping—that was so comprehensive that the supplier hardly earned any money from that customer at all. The supplier's management became convinced that they could invest those resources more profitably elsewhere, so they "fired" that customer. The consequence was an immediate decline of 10% in sales volume. But within a year, the supplier acquired new customers that applied less aggressive price pressure than the former key account and placed more reasonable demands for service. The new business did not fully offset the lost volume, but the supplier increased its margins by a full percentage point despite the lower volume.

---

[1] *Chicago Tribune*, January 9, 2007, see also "GM's Employee-Discount Offer on New Autos Pays Off," *USA Today*, June 29, 2005.

Political considerations can also cause a company to lose significant volume. Before sanctions were imposed on Russia for its annexation of Crimea in 2014–15, a European meat processor shipped a quarter of its volume to Russia. When the sanctions took effect, this business dried up almost overnight. The company immediately turned its attention to opening up the Chinese market. It not only succeeded, but also achieved higher prices in China than it had in Europe. The business in China did not fully make up for the volume shortfall, but the company's profit improved significantly due to the higher prices.

Stepping back from the "more is better" mindset can support a company's efforts to boost its profitability. After David Bradley bought the magazine *The Atlantic Monthly*, the annual loss increased to $8 million even though circulation and advertising pages increased and the magazine's prestige—based on the awards it won—also grew. To re-establish profitability, Bradley undertook some radical steps. He cut the print run from 450,000 to 325,000 and adjusted advertising rates accordingly. He also reduced the number of editions from 12 to 10 per year. The annual subscription price rose from $16 to $30. Despite the lower volumes, the magazine returned to profitability.

These examples show that lower sales volumes can lead to higher profits. But normally, of course, the reverse is true and higher sales volumes generate higher profits. In a global survey, 63% of respondents said that sales and revenue growth are their most important means to increase their profits.[2]

Profit Elasticity of Sales Volume

The profit elasticity of sales volume is the percentage change in profit that results when sales volume changes by 1%. In the illustrative numerical example in Chap. 6, the profit elasticity of sales volume was 4, meaning that profit rose by 4% when sales volume changed by 1%. This value is much lower than the profit elasticity of price, which is 10 in our working example. Calculating the profit elasticity of volume for a company with multiple products is more complicated or even impossible, because it does not make sense to simply add up the unit volumes of different products. The costs will also be different from product to product. For these reasons, one cannot make generalized statements about the magnitude of the profit elasticity of volume. The examples from the previous section demonstrate this. More volume can lead to higher or lower profits. The same applies to less volume.

---

[2]See Simon-Kucher & Partners, Global Pricing Survey 2019, London 2019.

The most important reason why the elasticity is hard or impossible to determine is the cost function. In contrast to price changes, any change in volume results in a change in costs, unless marginal costs are zero. Thus, the effects on profits could be completely different, depending on whether higher volumes result in constant, higher, or lower marginal cost. If marginal cost remains constant, i.e. the cost function is linear, each additional unit of volume increases absolute profit by the contribution margin. If marginal cost declines and price remains constant, this effect is even stronger, and correspondingly weaker if marginal cost increases. If marginal costs are zero and the price is positive, higher unit sales will always lead to higher profits. If the price stays constant, then sales volume maximization is the equivalent of profit maximization. But that applies only in the case of zero marginal cost and only within certain boundaries determined by either production capacity or by how much volume the market can absorb at a given price.

The Profit-Maximizing Sales Volume

It is easy to describe the conditions under which more volume leads to higher profits. The general optimality condition for profit-maximizing volume is:

$$\text{marginal revenue (with respect to volume)}$$
$$= \text{marginal cost (with respect to volume)} \qquad (7.1)$$

An increase in volume results in higher profits when the marginal revenue exceeds the marginal cost. If the price p and the marginal cost c are constant, and the unit contribution (p–c) is positive, then every incremental unit sold generates additional profit. The maxim then is: the more we sell, the better.

Of course, that holds true only as long as neither capacity nor demand reaches its limits. But if higher volumes are achievable only with lower prices or rising unit costs, the profit will rise only to its optimum and then will decline as the sales volume grows. In that case, the motto of "the more we sell, the better" is only true until the maximum level of profit is reached. Every unit sold after that reduces profit. If costs are degressive, i.e. the costs decline with increasing volume due to economies of scale or experience curve effects, then the point at which sales maximize profits is pushed further out. But even in that case, the volume that maximizes profits is not infinite. At some point, demand or willingness to pay is exhausted, or sufficient resources are no longer available.

Revenue growth, especially in early market phases, depends typically on volume growth. In the next section we will focus on the most important strategies for increasing volumes.

Market Penetration

Market penetration refers to volume growth in an existing market that a company already serves. One determinant of profit is whether the market is growing, stagnant, or declining. In a growing market with constant market shares, sales volume grows automatically. Because unit costs often decline when volume increases, profits will rise, assuming constant prices. In a stagnant market, a company can increase its sales volume only by increasing its market share. Competitors will almost certainly resist such actions, because market share shifts are a zero-sum game in a stagnant market. The chances increase that a price war erupts. The alternative to boost profit is to cut costs.

In a declining market, achieving an increase in volume or profit is more difficult thanks to intensified competition, declining prices, and rising costs. You might recall our discussion of Porter's Five Forces in Chap. 5 and how they can help a company determine whether a particular sector or industry is worth competing in. When a company is in a stagnant or declining industry, the idea of higher returns is an illusion. One potential evasive maneuver is to enter other market segments. But the success chances of that strategy are limited. Most industries have established competitors already, and they will make it hard for newcomers to gain a foothold.

More Effective Sales Activities

My decades-long experience tells me that sales ranks among the less efficient and less effective functions in most companies. Perhaps that is inevitable, because there is a participant in the sales process that cannot be controlled like a machine: the customer. Sales efficiency means that the best possible sales result is achieved with the available resources. Effectiveness means that sales does the right thing. The "right thing" is ultimately the achievement of profit, which depends on sales volume and price. Sales also influences costs, directly through its own expenses and also through obligations that sales agrees to in the negotiations.

In our projects we see over and over that sales teams have many levers they can pull to achieve higher volumes and generate higher profits. That long list starts with increasing the effective time that the salespeople spend with customers. That often accounts only for 15% of their time. The list also includes administrative tasks that are often done by hand instead of with modern information technology. Another bottleneck is improving the skills of the salespeople so that they can sell on the basis of value communication, not through price concessions. Many companies, if not most, incentivize their sales teams to achieve revenue, not profit. When this incentive structure applies to teams with price negotiation authority, one can assume that the team will maximize revenue, and probably sales volume, but will almost certainly not achieve the highest possible profit.

Profit-oriented leadership of the sales function brings complex challenges with respect to talent selection, training, motivation, incentives, and organization. In general, sales departments have considerable latent profit potential, but admittedly it is difficult to tap that potential quickly.

Reducing Overcapacity

In Chap. 5 we discussed how overcapacity can destroy profits. If any industry's production capacity is too high relative to demand, one should make every effort to reduce the capacity. Under such circumstances, it usually does not make sense to increase sales pressure and offer aggressive prices to boost capacity utilization. Such actions typically lead to cutthroat competition and price wars that destroy profits.

But a company can put itself in a precarious position when it cuts capacity, and competitors either do not respond in kind or actually boost their own capacity in response. The company loses market share and over time can endanger its market position. What can a company do when competitors respond that way, or when they see others' capacity reductions as an opportunity to increase their own market shares?

In game theory, this situation is known as the Prisoner's Dilemma. The option "do not follow the capacity reductions" corresponds to the option "betrayal" in the dilemma's classic form. The option "follow" corresponds to the classic option "silence."[3] These potential interactions make it indispensable for a company that wants to reduce capacity to observe the competition very closely and do what it can—within legal boundaries—to get the industry as a whole to reduce capacity.

---

[3]See Hermann Simon and Martin Fassnacht [1].

Of course I say "within legal boundaries," because collusion—whether tacit or contractually arranged—is forbidden under anti-trust and competition laws. Signaling, however, is permissible. In this case, it means publicly announcing one's own intentions to reduce capacity. As part of the signaling effort, the company could also state that it will defend its market share, or be more specific and state that it will strike back if a competitor tries to take advantage of the planned capacity reduction. In any event, companies should use signaling in a systematic way when they plan to reduce capacity. Effective signaling, however, hinges on credibility. It is very important for the company to make sure that its statements and actions are consistent. To preserve that credibility, the company needs to follow through on its capacity reductions in line with its announcements, and in parallel needs to ensure that its sales force stays within the new constraints. If the company announces a supply reduction, but allows its sales force to continue pursuing large deals at aggressively low prices, they instigate the competitors to fight back, to the detriment of the entire industry.

In a time of crisis, the chances are more favorable that competitors will appreciate the overall circumstances and respond with their own capacity reductions. Overall production capacity did indeed shrink in many industries between 2008 and 2010 during the Great Recession. The leading tour operator TUI cut its capacity sharply during that time.[4] Many airlines reduced or eliminated flights on less frequented routes. During the Covid 19 crisis, such capacity reductions were much more extreme due to a collapse of demand. The future will show whether these reductions are temporary or permanent.

Overcapacity is one of the main causes of weak profit performance. As long as the root cause remains, addressing the symptoms will have little effect. Restoring a reasonable level of profits requires the reduction of capacity and the willingness to accept lower sales volumes.

Digitalization

The digitalization of communication and distribution creates enormous growth opportunities. In one international study, some 74% of respondents said they have invested in digitalization with those goals in mind. Roughly half of these firms (49%) reported a noticeable positive impact of digitalization on volume and revenue. The industries showing the strongest growth

---

[4]See Klaus Meitinger, "Wege aus der Krise, " *Private Wealth*, March 2009, pp. 26–31.

effects were software (81%), electronics (67%), e-commerce (66%), and automotive with 61%.[5]

The following case of a furniture retailer shows that the volume uplifts from digitalization are by no means limited to typical internet-oriented businesses. This traditional brick-and-mortar retailer traditionally achieved an annual sales revenue of around $5 million. Management recognized the potential of the internet at a very early stage and reserved a domain name which conveyed—with no further explanation—that their offerings sell at very attractive prices. When the company launched its e-commerce business in the early 2000's, most experts believed that the online channel would remain irrelevant for the furniture sector. Yet the company now has annual online revenue of $50 million, ten times more than its previous revenue from the brick-and-mortar store. And the profit margin is also higher.

How does that profit calculation work? After the consumer orders online, a contract shipping service picks up the merchandise directly from the manufacturer and delivers it to the consumer's door. The retailer saves on costs for floor space, warehousing, and personnel, and passes some of those savings along to customers. Nonetheless, the margins are still higher than in the brick-and-mortar business. By increasing revenue by a factor of 10 and earning higher margins, the company clearly showed the opportunities that digitalization can create.

New Products

Innovations and the introduction of new products are the most effective ways to achieve higher sales volumes and profits. A common characteristic of companies with strong growth is that innovations make up a high proportion of their assortments. But this does not necessarily translate into higher profits. One of the Global Pricing Studies by Simon-Kucher uncovered some contradictions in this regard. On the one hand, companies tend to view innovation as the most important means to strengthen market positions, pricing power, and margins. But on the other hand, managers report that 72% of their newly launched products fell short of profit expectations.[6] Innovations per se do not guarantee higher profits. It comes down to whether they offer clearly superior value-to-customer that generates a level of willingness to pay well above the variable unit costs. That is how innovations lead to higher profits.

---

[5] Ibid.
[6] See Simon-Kucher & Partners, Global Pricing Study 2014, Bonn 2014.

Less Expensive Alternatives

When a company faces increased competition, or when a new low-price segment opens in the market, should a company respond by launching a so-called less expensive alternative (LEA)? If so, should the LEA run under the flagship brand name or under its own separate brand? In most cases, companies establish a second brand in order to distinguish the LEA clearly from the primary brand and to avoid cannibalization.

An LEA strategy generally has a net positive effect on sales volume, but should be deployed carefully. If the LEA cannibalizes the flagship brand's sales, the result can be higher sales volumes with lower profits. But in the case below, the LEA strategy was successful.

A world market leader saw that its unique specialty-chemical products were losing their competitive edge. Low-price imitators now posed a major threat. Instead of cutting the prices for its lead brand, the market leader met the threat by introducing an LEA with a price position around 20% below the lead brand's. The LEA included only minimal service, no customization, and was shipped only by full tank car. Customers would need to wait between 7 and 20 days for delivery, so that the firm could produce the product as excess capacity became available.

After introducing the LEA, the company experienced strong double-digit growth. Its revenue rose from $2.3 billion to $6.4 billion within four years, and the company swung from an annual loss of $27 million to a profit of $475 million. The LEA became the company's growth engine, in part because cannibalization of the lead brand was minimal.

Internationalization

Over the last several decades, globalization—or at least international expansion—has emerged as one of the most important methods for increasing volume. The strategy has led to tremendous successes, especially for the Hidden Champions, who in many cases have increased their sales volumes by a factor of 10 over the last two decades. One vital characteristic of these lesser-known world market leaders is their focus, which is a prerequisite for world-class performance. The focus—accompanied by a specialization in terms of product and know-how—has one major disadvantage, namely, a small market in terms of volume. That's why the second pillar, globalization, comes into play. At least for small and mid-sized businesses, globalization makes almost any market sufficiently large. One success factor of the Hidden

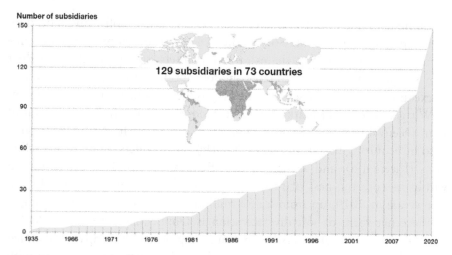

Fig. 7.2 How international expansion drove sales volume growth (Kärcher)

Champions is that they do not use third parties to enter foreign markets. Instead of relying on agents, importers, or distributors, they establish their own subsidiaries. Figure 7.2 illustrates this strategy of Kärcher, the world market leader for high-pressure cleaners.

Global expansion of the servable market basis in this manner makes sustained volume growth achievable. One reason is that many markets—especially emerging and developing markets—are far from saturated. This international expansion helped Kärcher boost its revenue from €633 million in 1995 to €2.58 billion in 2019. In the last five years, profit rose by 89%, much more than the revenue increase of 23%. International expansion proved to be very profitable.

Diversification

When a company's market is no longer growing and higher market shares are only possible with the tradeoff of lower profits, the only way to achieve more volume growth is to diversify. Strictly speaking, diversification means that both the products and the customers are new to the company. It is therefore no surprise that most diversification efforts either do not meet profit expectations or fail outright. Generally speaking, true diversification requires tremendous investment, but the sought-after volume growth often does not materialize.

Companies have better chances for success with "soft" diversification, which means going after only one of the two new dimensions. Hidden Champions, whose large market shares in core markets can eventually limit their growth opportunities, tend to favor the soft option: either sell a new product to existing customers, or sell an existing product to a new customer segment.

Wirtgen, the world market leader in road-milling machines and a unit of John Deere since 2017, took the first of those routes. It expanded its portfolio by acquiring brands of pavers (Vögele), steamrollers (Hamm), recycling units (Kleemann), and asphalt mixers (Benninghoven). This diversification within its core business of road construction led to more than €3 billion in revenue in 2019, up from €250 million in the mid-1990's. An example of the other form of soft diversification is Doppelmayr, the world market leader for lifts and cable cars for mountain regions. The company expanded the market for its products to include cities and airports, two segments with strong growth potential. This strategy has helped Doppelmayr to more than double its revenue in the last 15 years to €935 million.

Yield Management

Capacity utilization represents an extremely important determinant of profit in many industries, especially those with high fixed costs. Yield management, also known as revenue management, is the dynamic steering of available (and often fixed) capacity in a profit-maximizing way. Capacity is assigned different prices at certain times or under certain conditions. When marginal costs are low, the typical goal of yield management is revenue maximization, which is identical to profit maximization if marginal costs are zero.

Yield management is a comprehensive marketing and competitive instrument. Companies that practice it report significant increases in revenue and profit.[7] Yield management is commonly associated with airlines, but is not limited to that industry. Hotels, cruise lines, car rental companies, and online service firms also use this instrument. It is increasingly expanding into other areas such as made-to-order manufacturing. The fixed capacity of airlines, hotels, factories, etc. means that the marginal costs are low, but the opportunity costs for an unsold unit are high. A vacant hotel room on a given night is a revenue opportunity lost for good. Yield management optimizes the type of capacity (such as the aircraft), incorporates the distribution system,

---

[7]Robert L. Phillips [2], as well as Peter O'Connor and Jamie Murphy [3].

and communicates in a targeted way with potential customers. Because these services are perishable, time and speed play an important role.

The key consideration in yield management is whether a unit of capacity (a seat on a flight, a hotel room, a production window) should be offered earlier at a lower price or should be held back for a customer who books on short notice at a higher price. Ultimately it comes down to the classic question in the hotel business: "Should I rent a room right now at a lower price to avoid the risk that it remains empty, or should I wait in the hope that a customer comes later and pays a higher price?" The ability to answer that question has improved tremendously, thanks to the combination of modern information technology and sophisticated analytical methods. It is now possible to make such decisions on an empirical and quantitative basis that takes experience and data into account.

Despite the prevalence of yield management, there are many sectors that hardly use it all. One example is parking garages, especially at airports and train stations where finding a parking space can be critically important. With yield management, there are neither fixed capacities nor fixed prices for each time unit (e.g. hour or day). Instead, capacities and prices vary according to how many parking spaces are still available. Heathrow Airport in London has such a system. Capacities and prices are managed in a way that someone can always find a parking space, even if it means that space is very expensive.

For a deeper treatment of the complex methods of yield management and the problems it addresses, we refer to the specialized literature.[8] But it is clear that yield management offers considerable potential for revenue, sales, and profit growth in many service sectors.

Service Expansion

Services are not the exclusive domain of service companies. Many manufacturers derive a significant amount of their revenues from services. For a typical industrial goods company, services and spare parts often make up 20% of total revenue and a significantly higher share of the profits. That is because services generally have higher margins than products. Figure 7.3 shows the results of a study of 76 machinery manufacturers.[9]

In boom times, the potential offered by the service business is often neglected in favor of new products. This is not surprising. When a company has production bottlenecks and faces deadline pressure to fulfill orders,

---

[8]See Robert Klein and Claudius Steinhardt [4] as well as Robert G. Cross [5].
[9]Study of 76 machinery manufacturing companies, conducted by Simon-Kucher & Partners.

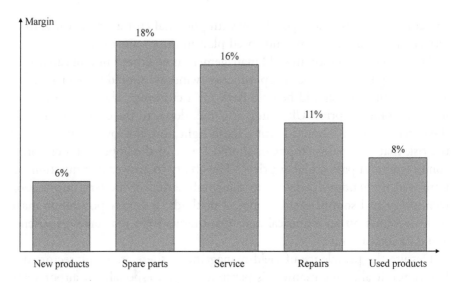

Fig. 7.3 Margins earned by machinery manufacturers, by business area

management focuses its full attention on production and logistics. In a seller's market, service tends to move into the background. Its volume and profit potential go untapped. But when a company has a large installed base, the service business and the associated parts business are less vulnerable to crises and other macroeconomic changes than the new-product business.

Manufacturers often offer a limited range of services, meaning that they do not take full advantage of the services they could offer. One large manufacturer of pre-fabricated homes with an installed base of thousands of homes responds to customer requests, but does not actively offer services. There is no service strategy worthy of the name. It is not unusual for manufacturers to see services as a burdensome obligation or necessary evil, in part because a service department requires a different organizational and management system than a factory. This mindset means they overlook volume and profit opportunities.

On the other hand, there are manufacturers who offer a comprehensive range of services and generate not only high, but also very profitable revenues. This is how the wind turbine manufacturer Enercon—within the framework of its Enercon Partner Concept (EPC)—guarantees its customers a high level of uptime for the first 12 years. One master contract covers the customer's maintenance, security services, repairs, and other eventualities. Customers love the concept, and over 90% sign a 12-year agreement. The large installed base offers Enercon a safeguard against the shocks of economic cycles and crises.

Some companies extend the value chain by offering customer training, which is becoming an increasingly important part of service. The reasons are twofold. First, products are becoming more complex. Second, companies are penetrating into countries in which the education level of employees is relatively low. Some companies operate their training as a stand-alone business. Festo, the world market leader for pneumatics in industrial automation, formed the firm Festo Didactic, which describes itself as "the world-leading provider of equipment and solutions for technical education." It offers courses in more than 100 countries.[10] The content covers a wide range of topics and is not limited to Festo products. It is also aimed at non-customers. Festo Didactic has 950 employees.

A strong sales push can significantly increase the share of customers under service contracts. The example of a crane manufacturer illustrates this. By attracting new service customers, the company raised service's share of total revenue from 18.4 to 26.8% within three years. This translated into highly profitable incremental sales of almost €147 million. Cisco, the leading global manufacturer of equipment to manage data flows, followed a similar path. During a crisis period, Cisco switched its emphasis to services in order to grow and to stabilize its financial situation. Order inflows for products fell by 20%, but revenues from services rose by 10%.

Unbundling of Services

One way to generate additional revenue is to charge separately for services that are normally covered in the overall price. This is known as unbundling. Industrial firms often offer extra services that are not charged separately. If they succeed in carving out these services from the offering and billing separately for them, the change can have a considerable positive effect on revenue and profit. But one should proceed carefully with this tactic. Some industries have a long tradition of performing services as part of the overall package. If customers find out that they need to pay extra for those services, they may react negatively. At the same time, we have seen in our project work that customers generally do not object to the separate billing when it is coupled with special or premium services or when the customers perceive that the company is going the extra mile. Examples include surcharges for express delivery, odd lots, specialized training, extraordinary guarantees, or the assumption of risk.

---

[10]https://www.festo-didactic.com/int-en/.

From Product Offering to Systems Offering

Another promising route to volume and profit growth lies in the transformation from a company that sells products to one that offers systems. That is how Groz-Beckert, the world market leader in needles, went from a pure manufacturer of needles for sewing and knitting machines to an important system supplier of precision parts. Primarily via acquisitions, the company advanced step by step into needles for many other applications and supplemented these businesses with accessories for sewing and weaving machines.

The firm Hako, one of the world market leaders for professional cleaning machines, generates only a small portion of its revenue through the sale of machines. The vast majority of its revenues comes from a package of services that encompasses leasing, installation planning, consulting, and other services. Hako offers its customers programs that calculate costs for a project or an installation, and then shares in the business risk by guaranteeing those cost estimates. This transformation took Hako from an industrial manufacturer to a "service provider for service providers." Its net return on sales has risen from 6.7 to 9.8% over the last five years.

Lantal, the world market leader for the outfitting of commercial aircraft cabins, offers airlines a comprehensive system that includes design of the entire interior—based on the customer specifications—as well as the production of seat coverings, curtains, cabin bulkheads, head rests, and carpeting.[11] Then Lantal expanded its systems offering even further. Knowing that the materials used in aircraft cabins are subject to extremely high safety standards, Lantal has received the authorization from the Federal Aviation Administration (FAA) and the European Aviation Safety Agency (EASA) to certify carpeting and other materials. Every customer prefers to cooperate with a sole supplier for questions of certification and liability.

The Australian company Orica, the world market leader in commercial explosives, offers rock quarry companies a complete solution. Orica supplies not only the explosives, but also analyzes the stone formations and does the drilling and blasting itself. Orica then provides the customer with blasted rock and charges by the ton on that basis. Because each Orica solution is customer-specific, the prices are less transparent and thus more difficult for customers to compare. For Orica, revenue per customer, efficiency, and safety all increase, as does the level of repeat business that drives a continuous revenue stream. The customer doesn't have to take care of the blasting anymore. The nature

---

[11] See "Wohnlichkeit in der Flugzeugkabine," *Neue Zürcher Zeitung*, February 5, 2007, p. 7.

of this relationship increases customer loyalty. It has proven many times that customers who buy multiple products or system solutions from a supplier are less likely to switch than customers who buy an individual product.

Discounts in Kind

In negotiations it is typical for customers to ask for concessions in the form of price discounts. But discounts in kind—which means the customer receives additional volume at no charge—are more advantageous for the supplier. One prerequisite for discounts in kind, however, is that production capacity is not fully utilized and the additional units can actually be delivered. Discounts in kind have three advantages:

- They increase unit volumes and therefore keep staff busy.
- They are generally less harmful to profits than price discounts of the same percentage.
- The nominal price level remains intact.

In lieu of price discounts, a manufacturer of playground equipment that costs around $10,000 per unit offered resellers a special deal: buy five and get the sixth unit for free. This represents an effective discount of 16.7%, because the reseller receives six units but only pays for five. The profit calculations show the effect of a discount in kind versus a straight-up discount. At a price of $10,000 with one unit for free, the manufacturer gets revenue of $50,000, has a volume of six units, and earns a contribution of $14,000. But if the manufacturer had offered the flat discount of 16.7% instead, it would get a price of $8,330 per unit (reflecting the discount of 16.7%). The manufacturer gets $41,650 in revenue, has a volume of five units, and earns a contribution of $11,650.

The discount in kind increased volume, kept the employees busy, and increased profits. If a company uses this tactic in the short run to fill capacity or avoid layoffs, it is easier to retract than a price discount, which may have a lasting detrimental effect on the list price.

A manufacturer of designer furniture has also fared well with discounts in kind. This leading brand valued its price consistency and continuity. Whenever customers argue for a price discount—which they do frequently and sometimes relentlessly—any concession would involve an additional piece of furniture rather than a price discount. In most cases, the customers were satisfied with this offer. The tactic resulted in higher capacity utilization and also in a higher contribution than a price discount would have achieved. The manufacturer and the customer perceive the value of the additional furniture differently. The customer perceives the value of the additional furniture based on its retail price, while the manufacturer looks at the variable cost. In other words, the manufacturer can offer a "gift" that has a value of $100 in the eyes of the customer, but costs the manufacturer only $60. In the case of a direct price discount, the manufacturer needs to give up the actual $100 in order to give the customer a "gift" of the same value.

The same principle applies to renting. In general, it is more advantageous for a lessor to offer a new tenant several months rent-free instead of offering a discounted price per square foot for the duration of the lease. The valuation of a building depends on a multiple of the rent, and banks use a similar metric when they make lending decisions. This gives a lessor an incentive to have a high nominal rent, even if that rent will be zero for a few months. Tenants also place a high perceived value on the free rent, because they may have other pressing expenses—moving costs, new furniture purchases—during the initial months of the lease.

Volume and Shareholder Value

We have demonstrated that growth and profit are the key drivers of shareholder value. In the early stages of a company and a market life cycle, growth in terms of volume and the number of customers can have a greater influence on shareholder value than profit. The examples of Amazon and Salesforce.com, which we highlighted in earlier chapters, provide convincing proof of that point. It is not necessarily irrational for investors and capital markets to base their corporate valuations on volume. At the same time, higher customer and volume numbers do not automatically translate into higher valuations. Valuations ultimately depend on a variety of factors.

The most important question for the long term is: how large is the profit contribution a customer will deliver? This is what is referred to as monetization.[12] In this respect, the measure of success is not the profit contribution, but rather the average revenue per user, or ARPU. When marginal costs are zero—which is the case for some digital products—APRU is an appropriate metric, because revenue optimization and profit optimization are essentially the same goal. In many businesses, however, the monetization question either remains unresolved or gets pushed further and further into the future.

---

[12]See Madhavan Ramanujam, Georg Tacke [6].

Under freemium models, for example, companies only earn money from premium customers. Profits will remain low if the companies do not succeed in converting enough free customers into premium customers.

A second success factor is customer loyalty, which ultimately determines a customer's lifetime value. There is no benefit to acquiring a lot of customers who jump ship a short time later. High churn rates can have a catastrophic effect when customer acquisition costs are high.

The third key success factor is marginal costs. It makes a fundamental difference whether these are positive and significant or whether they are zero. If they are positive, every additional customer, or every unit of volume growth, can have a negative effect on profit. This happens, for example, when prices are lower than marginal costs. This condition is more easily fulfilled when some customers do not pay, as is the case with the freemium model. The situation is completely different when marginal costs are zero. When customers do not pay, the effect of cost on profit is neutral.

The development of these success indicators is inevitably subject to a high degree of uncertainty in the early stages of a company or a market. Nevertheless, these relationships between customer numbers, sales volumes, profits and shareholder value should be borne in mind in order to arrive at a reasonably sober judgment and not be carried away by market euphoria.

Summary

In this chapter, we looked at how to manage sales volume as a profit driver in such a way as to maximize profit and shareholder value. It is by no means the case that more sales always mean more profit. Under certain circumstances, lower volumes can lead to higher profit. One important difference is whether the growth happened on its own or whether it was induced with lower prices. If a company uses price discounts to drive higher volumes, the profits effects can be less advantageous and could even be negative.

The theoretical optimality condition for sales volume—"marginal revenue = marginal cost"—offers some rough insights into how changes in volume affect profit. If marginal revenue exceeds marginal cost, volume growth leads to higher profit. There are numerous ways under that condition to achieve volume and profit growth. They include improved sales performance, market penetration, the introduction of new products, entry into previously unserved market segments, internationalization, diversification, yield management, the use of new sales channels (especially e-commerce), expansion of the range of service, systems solutions, and discounts in kind.

The service business of industrial firms often has higher margins than the product business. Growing the service business therefore not only brings higher volume and revenue, but also higher profit. By transforming a product business into a systems business—which usually includes a significant service component—companies can expand their revenues and increase customer loyalty at the same time. All these methods involve profit risks because of the price and cost implications associated with them. In this respect, careful consideration and caution are indicated when implementing them.

Sales volume growth can be the decisive driver of shareholder value in the early stages of a company or a market. Whether this is justified depends on three factors: effective monetization, high customer loyalty, and low marginal costs. If these conditions are met, then sales and sales growth become very effective drivers of shareholder value.

References

1. Simon, H., & Fassnacht, M. (2019). *Price Management*, New York: Springer Nature, p. 201.
2. Phillips, R. L. (2005). *Pricing and Revenue Optimization*, Stanford: Stanford University Press.
3. O'Connor, P., & Murphy, J. (2008). Hotel Yield Management Practices Across Multiple Electronic Distribution Channels, *Information Technology & Tourism*, 10(2), pp. 161–172.
4. Klein, R., & Steinhardt, C. (2008) *Revenue Management*, Berlin: Springer.
5. Cross, R. G. (1997). *Revenue Management*, New York: Broadway Books.
6. Ramanujam, M., & Tacke, G. (2016). *Monetizing Innovation: How Smart Companies Design the Product around the Price*, Hoboken: Wiley.

8

Profit Driver: Cost

Price and volume, the profit drivers that we discussed in detail in the previous two chapters, affect revenue, i.e. the top line. In contrast, the third profit driver—cost—directly affects "only" the bottom line, which is the ultimate relevant level of profit. Price and volume do have an indirect effect on the bottom line as well via variable cost. Higher volumes result in higher variable cost, except in cases when marginal cost is zero. A price cut that results in higher volume leads indirectly to the same effect. Price, volume, and costs thus interact in complex ways, as expressed by the price-response and cost functions.

Special Features of Costs as a Profit Driver

Much like price and volume, costs also have special features in their role as a profit driver. Generally speaking, cost measures and actions are synonymous with cost-cutting initiatives. Whom do those measures affect? Primarily they affect two groups: employees and suppliers. They also involve all of a company's operations, as one author calls out explicitly: "Cost management should be an established practice among decision makers across all hierarchical levels."[1]

---

[1] Himme [1].

© The Author(s), under exclusive license to Springer Nature Switzerland AG 2021
H. Simon, *True Profit!*,
https://doi.org/10.1007/978-3-030-76702-0_8

The more value a company creates, the greater its potential is to save labor costs. In contrast to price and volume measures, cost reductions often inflict social hardships such as layoffs or wage reductions. Management has more control over cost measures than it does over price and volume, because in the latter two cases it is ultimately the customer who determines the outcomes. The power of management over labor is not unlimited, thanks to government regulations and the influence of labor unions. But it tends to be higher than the power towards the customers.

The higher the value of inputs, the greater the cost-savings potential on the supplier side, and thus the greater the pressure put on them. The relative balance of power between suppliers and their customers plays the decisive role. Grocery retail and the automotive industry are rife with examples about what happens when buyers not only have a powerful position over their suppliers, but actually take advantage of it.

This feeling of having more power over labor and suppliers than over customers is one major reason why cost-cutting actions are the first levers managers pull when they face pressure to shore up profits. Second on their list, generally speaking, are measures to increase volumes. Among the three profit drivers, price comes in third, and thus last, on the priority list. Private equity investors usually follow the same priority list when they acquire a company that is a turnaround candidate.

But I warn against considering cost measures in isolation. Such measures are only justified when they will not have a detrimental effect on price and volume. But that is more of an ideal than reality, because cost-cutting measures often have a negative effect on price and volume. For example, if a company switches to cheaper materials in order to save costs, the change can affect customers' perceptions of quality and of the value they derive from the product. This can lower their willingness to pay and also reduce sales volume. The automotive industry has experienced that, with the history of General Motors and Opel serving as one of many cautionary tales. One should always keep in mind the effects that cost-cutting can have on willingness to pay and on sales volumes.

In contrast to price measures, cost measures require more time to implement. In fact, a considerable amount of time can elapse before their full effects take hold. We mentioned this phenomenon in Fig. 6.1. When Schuler, the world market leader for stamping presses in the automotive industry, announced in July 2019 that it would cut 500 jobs due to weak demand, it said that it "expects total one-off costs … of around €85 million in 2019" and that it will see "initial savings effects as of the second half of 2020."[2] Another example for the delayed profit effects of cost-cutting programs is the closing of branch offices. Such programs are effective only after the existing rental contracts expire.[3] In general, time plays a critical role in cost management.

Cost-cutting measures often require additional short-term expenditures or investments. This fact imposes an additional burden on liquidity before the profit improvements kick in. Such examples include severance payments for long-term staff or investments in new machines that will ultimately lower the production costs.

The effects that cost measures have on profit and liquidity can vary significantly, depending on how the company produces its products or services. If depreciation is increased or reduced, this can affect costs on an accounting basis, but will not directly affect liquidity.[4] But these changes can also have tax consequences. Selling an asset, such as a building, and then leasing it back, will leave the profit level unchanged, assuming that the leasing costs are the same as the former depreciation and capital costs. But liquidity will change significantly. The sale of the asset leads to a one-time influx of cash, subsequently offset by periodic cash outflows for the leasing payments.

Profit Elasticity of Costs

For given levels of price and volume, i.e. at constant revenue, the impact of cost changes falls directly and fully to the bottom line. This statement applies, however, only to cost changes in absolute terms, not percentage terms. To demonstrate this, let's apply the numbers used in the illustrative example in Figs. 6.2 and 6.3. We set the price at $100, the sales volume at 1 million units, the variable unit costs at $60, and the fixed costs at $30 million. This resulted in revenue of $100 million, total costs of $90 million, and therefore a profit of $10 million. Figures 6.2 and 6.3 show the profit effects of a 5% change in price or volume, assuming all other profit drivers remain changed (*ceteris paribus* condition).

But what happens when we change the variable or fixed costs *ceteris paribus* by 5%? When we reduce the variable costs from $60 to $57 million, profit

---

[2]"Schuler strengthens international sites and reduces capacities in Germany," press release, July 29, 2019.

[3]Unless one can sub-lease the space, which is usually successful for attractive locations, or the lessor allows the lessee out of the contract, which can be likely when rents are increasing.

[4]The liquidity can be impacted in such situations, however, due to tax effects.

increases by 30%. The profit improvement in percentage terms is six times the percentage change in variable costs. The profit elasticity of variable costs is therefore 6.[5] If we reduce the fixed costs by 5% from $30 to $28.5 million, the profit rises by 15%, yielding a profit elasticity of fixed costs of 3.[6] Based on that same set of numbers, the profit elasticity of price is 10 and the profit elasticity of volume is 4.

To summarize, the respective profit elasticities are:

- Price—10
- Variable costs—6
- Volume—4
- Fixed costs—3

Under these conditions, variable cost is the second most effective profit driver, behind price. The same percentage change in fixed costs has the least effect on profit. While these statements apply only to this particular constellation, this breakdown is typical for an industrial company. If we flipped the ratio of fixed and variable costs, which is 60 to 30 in our example, then changes to fixed costs would be a more effective profit driver.

Data from profit-and-loss statements allow the calculation of profit elasticities for various cost categories. One line on US statements is "cost of goods sold," which comprises the direct expenditures for the production of products and services. It encompasses material and labor costs. The second broad category of costs is what we could call overhead. These include the research & development expenses, the selling, general and administrative (SG&A) expenses, as well as other operating expenses.

Figure 8.1 shows the profit elasticity for the two cost categories for 15 selected US companies from different sectors.[8]

We can interpret these values as follows. If Ford succeeded in cutting its cost of goods sold by 1%, its pre-tax income would rise by 31.3%. At Apple, the corresponding profit increase would be 2.5%. If Ford reduced its overhead costs by 1%, profit would rise by 4.8%, while Apple would achieve a gain of only 0.5%.

It is readily apparent that the profit elasticities show extreme differences. The profits levels are one reason. Cost savings have a disproportionately

---

[5]To be precise, the elasticity is −6, because cost changes and profit changes have different signs. In this case we are looking at the absolute value of the profit elasticity.

[6]Cost increases result in the same percentage changes, but with the opposite sign.

[8]https://www.macrotrends.net/stocks/charts, called up February 6, 2020. Latest available data, most are for the business year 2019, some for 2018.

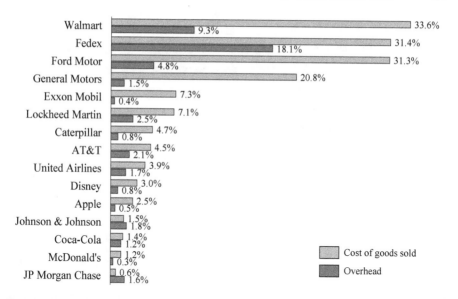

Fig. 8.1 Profit change for selected US companies assuming a 1% change in costs of goods sold or in overhead costs[7]

---

[7]The calculation is as follows: Profit Elasticity in % = cost of goods sold × 0.01/pre-tax income × 100, with an analogous equation for overhead cost. For Lockheed Martin: For cost of goods sold, profit elasticity in % = $51.4 billion × 0.01/$7.2 billion = 7.1%; for overhead, profit elasticity in % = $178 million × 0.01/$7.2 billion = 2.5%.

higher impact on the profits of low-margin companies than they do on the profits of higher-margin companies. Profit appears in the denominator of the elasticity, so a low profit level drives the elasticity higher.

The large differences exist not only across sectors, but also within them. That can be explained by differences in supplier structures and value chains. Using the US data, however, it is not possible to determine separate profit elasticities for material costs and labor costs, because both costs are subsumed into cost of goods sold. But it is clear that material costs account for the bulk of the profit elasticities in Fig. 8.1 for companies such as Walmart, Ford Motor, or General Motors, who all have a significant supplier share in their costs.

German companies generally break out their material and labor costs in their reporting. That allows us to determine the profit elasticities for those two cost categories, as shown in Fig. 8.2 for a selection of German compa-

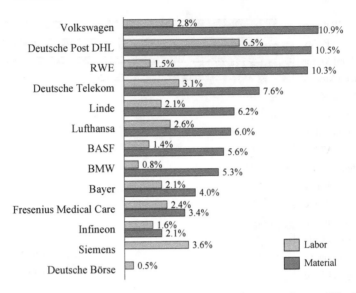

Fig. 8.2 Profit change for selected German companies assuming a 1% change in labor costs or material costs

nies.[9] Please note that the numbers in Figs. 8.1 and 8.2 measure different aspects.

Let's look at BMW in detail. If material costs decline by 1%, the pre-tax income rises by 5.3%. If labor costs fall by 1%, the corresponding profit increase is 0.8%. Increases in the respective costs would lead to the same profit changes in absolute terms, but with the opposite signs.

Similar to the US examples, Fig. 8.2 shows substantial differences across industry sectors. The profit elasticity for material costs for industrial companies is generally higher than the profit elasticity for labor costs. Car manufacturers in particular have a high profit elasticity for material costs. This relationship explains why such companies fight much harder on the procurement side than they do on the labor side to reduce costs. The payback is simply higher. It is also less unpleasant for the companies to risk a strained relationship with suppliers than with their employees. Figure 8.2 shows how important it is for a company to know these elasticities, so that it can focus on using its greatest cost leverage.

If we compare these values with the profit elasticities for price (see Fig. 6.4), it shows that the latter tend to be higher. The explanation is simple: when

---

[9]The numbers are drawn from either the 2018 or the 2017 business year. The calculations are analogous to Fig. 8.1.

profit is positive, the sum of material and labor costs is less than revenue. And this translates to the unit level.

Fixed versus Variable Costs

The way costs are divided into fixed and variable components plays a critical role in how cost changes affect profits. One often neglects, though, that the fixed-variable allocation must be defined for a specific time period. Over the long term—except for situations in which a company has indefinite obligations[10]—all costs are variable. In the short term, however, a very high share of costs can be fixed. These include labor costs within contractual terms such as notice periods. For this reason, the use of costs to make decisions regarding strategy, volume, and price requires the definition of the relevant time period. That could be a season, a business year, or the entire life cycle of a product. Why is the distinction between fixed and variable costs so important for the topic of this chapter, the profit effect of costs? There are several reasons.

Costs and Price Floors

Costs define a lower bound or floor for prices. This corresponds to the lowest price at which a company will offer a product or accept an order. The setting of a price floor depends on the distinction between short- and long-term considerations. Over the longer term, a company should only sell a product when its price will cover both the variable and the fixed costs. The long-term lower bound or floor price is therefore determined by the total unit costs or full costs.

The answer for the short-term situation is different, because fixed costs by definition cannot be reduced and should be covered or "over-covered" to the greatest extent possible. The company earns a contribution to cover its block of fixed costs whenever the selling price is greater than the marginal cost. If the cost function is linear—a condition we will apply here for simplicity's sake—then the marginal cost and the variable unit cost are identical and define the short-term price floor. The difference between price and variable unit cost is called the unit contribution. One could also say that in the short term, it's worthwhile to sell a product whenever it yields a positive unit contribution.

---

[10]An example for obligations in perpetuity could be the requirement to maintain a shuttered mine for an indefinite period.

If differentiated pricing is possible for individual product units—such as the case with custom manufacturing—then the respective marginal costs form the price floor, not the variable unit costs. If a multi-product company accepts an incremental order that can be fulfilled only by not producing a unit of a different product, then it needs to take into account those foregone profits from the second product, the so-called opportunity costs. In such cases, the price floor is equal to the sum of the marginal cost and the opportunity cost.

More broadly speaking, a company can incur opportunity costs as a result of a range of dynamic interrelationships that go beyond the product itself. These costs can arise on the production and on the sales side. In such cases, the price floor has a complex structure and cannot be defined or expressed in a general way.

The most important insights into price floors or lower bounds are:

- Long-term price floor: total unit cost (full cost)
- Short-term price floor:

   1. For uniform prices: variable unit cost
   2. For differentiated prices: marginal cost
   3. For capacity bottlenecks: marginal cost plus opportunity cost

Costs and the Break-Even-Point

The first step in a break-even analysis is to calculate the unit contribution by subtracting the variable unit cost k from the price p. This assumes a linear cost function, i.e. the variable unit cost and the marginal cost are both constant and identical. Alternatively, for a non-linear cost function, one could use the average variable unit costs for a certain volume interval.

The unit contribution d is defined as:

$$d = p - k. \qquad (8.1)$$

The break-even point BEP is determined by dividing the fixed costs C_{fix} by the unit contribution d

$$BEP = C_{fix}/d = C_{fix}/(p - k). \qquad (8.2)$$

This volume level covers the fixed costs exactly, which means the profit is zero. The break-even point is therefore often referred to as the profit threshold. Sales volume above the BEP results in a profit, while the company incurs a loss as long as sales volumes remain below the BEP.

One sees in Eq. (8.2) and in Fig. 8.3 that the relationship between fixed costs and break-even volume is linear. The effects on the break-even volume due to changes in the variable unit costs, however, are non-linear. The data in Fig. 8.3 come from our now-familiar working example with fixed costs of $30 million and a constant price of $100.

At a price of $100, the break-even volume is 750,000 units. The break-even point will rise over-proportionally as variable unit costs increase, and will decline under-proportionally as variable unit costs go down. If we assume a starting value of $60 for variable unit costs, the same percentage change in those costs will drive a more rapid increase in the BEP than the identical percentage increase in fixed costs. But below a BEP of 500,000 units, a decrease in fixed costs has a greater proportional impact on the BEP than a decrease in variable unit costs. The decision on whether investments and

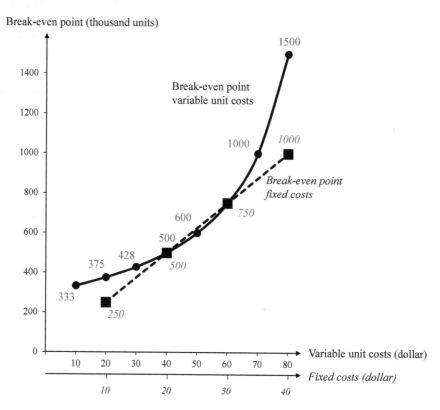

Fig. 8.3 How the break-even point depends on variable unit costs and fixed costs

measures on fixed costs or variable unit costs have greater effects on the BEP will therefore always depend on the prevailing situation.

The BEP is a critical metric for start-ups and for new products. As long as volumes remain below the BEP, cash flow will remain negative and the company will need to seek capital from external sources. For a given price, lower break-even points are easier to reach. The odds improve that the company crosses the profit threshold and doesn't need an injection of capital. In other words, lower variable unit costs or lower fixed costs reduce the risk that the new business or product fails.

The break-even analysis is a practical but imperfect instrument for "yes-no" decisions on start-ups, the launch of an innovation, or the elimination of a product. The imperfection lies in the fact that the analysis does not take into account what happens "beyond" the break-even point.

Another important consequence of the allocation of fixed and variable costs comes from the fact that only marginal cost affects the profit-maximizing price (see Eq. (6.1)). In line with the general principle that decision-making should only consider those variables on which the decision depends, we can say that fixed costs are extraneous because they depend neither on price nor on sales volume. The relevant determinants of the profit-maximizing price are the marginal cost (equal to the variable unit cost, if the cost function is linear) and the price elasticity. That means that if the company cannot determine its marginal cost with sufficient clarity, it cannot determine an optimal price.

Cost Structure

Fixed costs and variable costs are normally positive, although the relationship between the two cost categories can be very different. In extreme cases, one of the two might be negligible or zero. Figure 8.4 shows three very different configurations of fixed and variable costs as well as examples of the types of services for which the respective structures are common.

In each of these cases, the price is constant at $2. In the example of a capital-intensive service, the fixed costs are $200, while the variable unit costs are essentially zero. That puts the break-even point at 100. The profit rises sharply to the right of that volume, as the cost curve remains at a constant level. For the technology-intensive service shown in the middle of Fig. 8.4, we set the fixed costs at $100 and the variable unit costs at $1. The break-even point in this scenario is also 100 units. But an increase in volume beyond the BEP leads to a smaller increase in profit than in the capital-intensive case. In

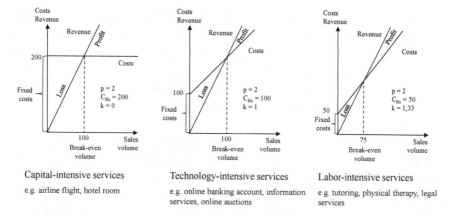

Fig. 8.4 Different structures of fixed and variable costs, with examples from selected industries

the labor-intensive example, the fixed costs are $50 and the variable unit cost is $1.33. At an unchanged price of $2, the break-even point is achieved with just 75 units. But the profit increase to the right of the BEP is much smaller. Each incremental unit sold in the capital-intensive case yields an additional profit of $2, versus $1 in the technology-intensive case and only 67 cents in the labor-intensive case.

The lower the variable unit cost (and generally speaking, marginal cost), the more profitable sales growth becomes. Low variable costs normally come in combination with high fixed costs, a constellation that results in strong pressure to grow by boosting sales volume. In capital-intensive service industries, high capacity utilization is the best route to sustained profitability.

The structure of the two types of costs (fixed and variable) opens up interesting strategic options. In order to reduce variable costs, one must normally accept higher fixed costs. Automation is a good example of that, because it offsets lower variable costs (less labor) with investments in machines, resulting in higher fixed costs. Another good example is the switch from selling via retailers to selling via one's own stores, as many luxury goods and fashion companies have done. This move shifts the cost structure toward higher fixed costs.

But such changes in cost structures also change the company's risk profile and mean that in a time of crisis, a company is left sitting on high fixed costs. In 2009, at the height of the Great Recession, I walked through the mall at the Raffles Hotel in Singapore. All renowned luxury brands were present there with their own stores, whose rents result in high fixed costs. What I did not see, however, were customers. Even in more recent times, many fashion firms have had existential crises and some have not survived. These include

Gerry Weber, Esprit, Charles Vögele, and Miller & Monroe. One important cause for this distress is the enormous rise in fixed costs due to the expansion into company-run stores. Interesting in this context is the finding that cost management is most commonly associated with cost cutting. But often overlooked are the ways that these cost cutting measures alter a company's cost structure. When fixed costs rise as a result, it can restrict a company's room for maneuver if a crisis hits.[11]

In times of continuous growth, companies are always looking for ways to shift their sharply rising variable costs away from independent sales agents, wholesalers, retailers, and logistics to their own capacities. This strategy is advantageous, despite the increase in fixed costs, as long as the growth continues to generate high sales volumes and high revenue. But if sales and revenue growth plateau or decline, the firm is left sitting on the high fixed costs and risks ending up in the red. Reducing the fixed costs is difficult under those circumstances because many of them are tied to longer-term commitments.

Economies of Scale and the Experience Curve

Continuous productivity improvements that lead to cost reductions are an indispensable prerequisite for profit improvement and thus for the survival of a company. Two important determinants of cost reductions are economies of scale and learning effects. Economies of scale mean that unit costs decline with higher production and sales volumes. The more a company produces, the lower its production costs are per unit. This is a static concept. In contrast, learning effects are a dynamic process operationalized in the form of the experience curve. This concept means that the inflation-adjusted unit costs fall by a certain percentage with every doubling of cumulative production. A company needs time to achieve experience-curve effects. In order to achieve economies of scale, sheer size is enough.

Pursuit of economies of scale and experience curve effects have the same consequence, namely, that they put pressure on companies to sell more units. The ensuing lower costs enable companies to cut prices actively, in order to drive even greater unit sales, or to cut prices reactively if competitors attack. In the ideal case, costs decline faster than prices, and the combination of higher contribution margins and higher sales volumes leads to enormous profits. But this strategy does not always succeed. It is not uncommon for

---

[11]Alexander Himme, "Kostenmanagement: Bestandsaufnahme und kritische Beurteilung der empirischen Forschung," *Zeitschrift für Betriebswirtschaft*, September 2009, p. 1075.

prices to fall faster than unit costs, which shrinks contribution margins and can lead to lower profits despite higher sales. Recent research has shown that companies tend to overestimate the cost effects from economies of scale and the experience curve. One should be skeptical of naïve faith in these effects and the sales volume maximization associated with them.

Zero Marginal Costs

As we know from Eq. (6.1), marginal cost is one of the determinants of the optimal price. The profit-maximizing price results from applying a price-elasticity-based markup to marginal cost. One of the special characteristics of the internet is that marginal costs are approaching zero in many cases. The phenomenon of marginal costs at or near zero is nothing new though. Relative to development costs, marginal costs for software and in some cases pharmaceuticals and electronics have often been very low. The same applies for the use of an airline seat or a hotel room that would have otherwise been unoccupied. An additional passenger or guest results in only minimal additional cost.

But online, the phenomenon of "zero marginal costs" has taken on a much greater dimension. Jeremy Rifkin considers the idea to be so revolutionary that it could diminish or even lead to the downfall of capitalism.[12] In his book *The Zero Marginal Cost Society*, he supports this claim with the assertion that prices will eventually approach the level of marginal costs. Thus, if marginal costs are tending toward zero, then prices should as well. No capitalistic entrepreneur will be willing to produce goods and services at those prices. Public or non-profit organizations will need to assume that role, and that would represent the end of capitalism.

Rifkin expands his zero-marginal-cost paradigm to many sectors of the economy. These include energy (solar, wind), the sharing economy, and education through so-called Massive Open Online Courses (MOOCs). In the sharing economy, resources such as available living space or vehicles are shared among users rather than remaining unoccupied or idle. There is no doubt that these phenomena—which are not entirely new but are spreading like wildfire thanks to the internet—are having considerable effects on marginal costs, and thus on businesses and their price models.

It is rare, however, that marginal costs are actually zero. In spite of the title, Rifkin refers in the book to "near-zero marginal costs." If marginal

---

[12]See Rifkin [2].

costs are zero, it does not mean that the profit-maximizing price is also zero. In that case, it is identical to the revenue-maximizing price. At maximum revenue, the price elasticity is -1. The price-elasticity-based markup retains its validity as marginal costs approach zero and the price approaches its revenue-maximizing level.[13] But at very low marginal cost, the markup factor is very high.

An important aspect of zero marginal cost is that, *ceteris paribus*, price and volume increases will have the same positive effect on profit. That results because higher sales volumes do not lead to higher cost. But it is likely that price competition will intensify under those circumstances. The reason is that the short-term lower bound for prices is at the level of marginal cost, i.e. at or close to zero. That is why digital products often have extremely low prices or even have a price of zero.

When marginal cost is zero, a seller who urgently needs liquidity can set its prices slightly above zero and still earn a contribution and generate cash flow. But a firm cannot survive indefinitely with that philosophy. Losses are inevitable if the contributions are not also sufficient to cover fixed cost.

The pressure on sales volumes is enormous when marginal cost is zero. That is especially true when the fixed costs for development and operation of the respective system are high. The supplier is essentially forced to aim for the maximum number of users. The probability is high that monopolies will arise when fixed costs are spread among the highest possible number of users. It is no coincidence that digital companies with low marginal costs earn very high net returns on sales. Alibaba achieves an unbelievable net return of 29.32%, while Facebook's is 26.15% and Alphabet (Google) earns 21.22%.[14] And remember, these return-on-sales figures are *after* taxes!

Zero marginal costs also have massive effects on competition. Over time, traditional suppliers—the ones who sell physical products or provide personal services with higher marginal costs—stand no chance against the digital "zero marginal costs" competitors. YouTube, Netflix, Spotify, Booking.com and similar services have marginalized video stores, movie theaters, traditional radio and television, and travel agents, and in some cases have rendered them obsolete. The situation is different for companies or sectors where systems marginal costs are definitely not at or near zero. Systems marginal costs in this context refer to all of the costs for the provision of the service, and not merely those incurred to operate the digital platform. Such companies include Uber, Flixbus, WeWork, delivery firms, bike and scooter rental companies, and similar offerings. They incur variable costs for drivers, vehicles, repairs and

---

[13]For a detail analysis of this phenomenon, see Simon and Fassnacht [3].
[14]*Fortune*, August 10, 2020.

maintenance, depreciation, etc. It remains to be seen whether these companies earn a sustainable profit and cover their cost of capital. The fundamental difference in comparing and evaluating internet companies is whether their marginal costs are negligible (at or near zero) or significantly different from zero.

To end this section, the zero-marginal-cost condition only applies for a limited interval, even for purely digital services. If a company acquires one, ten, or a hundred new customers, the costs rise negligibly, if at all, and the marginal costs remain essentially at zero. But if the company gains 100,000 or 1 million new customers, it will need to expand its IT capacity and data network. In other words, there is a step change in fixed costs when the number of customers increases sharply. The investments increase the block of fixed costs, and the marginal costs will remain at zero again until the next step change.

Cost Management

Cost management focuses on the composition of costs, and generally implies efforts to reduce costs. Cost accounting, in contrast, provides information on costs. Both categories can be considered sub-areas of controlling. To estimate cost reduction potential, companies employ a number of methods such as benchmarking, target costing, activity-based costing, overhead value analysis, product life cycle costing, design thinking, business process reengineering, or cross-company analyses. Benchmarking and target costing are the most frequently used methods.[15] The applications vary significantly from industry to industry. Cross-company analyses, which include suppliers, are mostly employed by manufacturing industries such as automotive and electronics. In the 1990's, the much-discussed concept of business process reengineering rarely led to the "radical cures" that Hammer and Champy envisioned. Instead the concept's impact was usually limited to process refinements.[16] Digitalization, sometimes called "Industry 4.0", resulted in more radical process innovation.

It is disappointing that academics have not yet produced any convincing and representative proof of a link between cost management and profitability. One often hears about impressive successes from individual projects, but there are no representative studies. One survey of 131 accounting leaders collected

---

[15]See Kajüter [4].
[16]Hammer and Champy [5].

data on the successes of cost-reduction programs. Using that data, one can estimate the following cost reductions:[17]

- Product costs: 5.4%
- Process costs: 7.7%
- After-sales: 2.4%
- Administrative costs: 9.0%.

It is not surprising that the largest cost savings came in administration, but processes also apparently offer considerable rationalization potential. Even when these cost reductions do not seem dramatic, they can have significant impacts when one considers the low returns that we highlighted in previous chapters, with average after-tax return on sales for the Fortune Global 500 in the range of 5 to 6%.

The evidence that cost management affects shareholder value is even thinner. The announcement of cost cutting programs, and job cuts in particular, tends to have a positive resonance on capital markets. But it is not possible to generalize whether the announcements eventually lead to sustained higher shareholder value. That depends most likely on the success of the implementation over the longer term.

Cost Culture

The success of cost management by no means depends solely on organizational measures; employee attitudes and behavior play a decisive role. Amazingly, little is known about these soft factors. One author of a study said: "To the best of my knowledge this is the first study which empirically investigates behavioral factors in the special context of cost reductions."[18] This study confirmed that cost culture, top-management commitment, and employee participation have a significant influence on the success of cost-cutting measures. These findings are highly plausible and not surprising.

A "cost culture" is certainly helpful to meet these challenges. The central element of such a culture is that each leader and each employee shares responsibility for the costs. Robin Cooper describes this culture as follows: "Cost management, like quality, has to become a discipline by virtually every person

---

[17]Himme [6]. The percentage cost reductions were calculated by me based on the ranges provided; they are therefore approximations.
[18]Ibid., p. 204.

in the firm. Systems that create intense downward pressure on all elements of costs are required."[19]

Employee Involvement

Cost-cutting programs regularly face resistance from employees. This is especially true when the cost-cutting measures put jobs at risk. A company can lessen this resistance by informing the employees in a timely manner and integrating them in the process. But employees can also play a more active role in cost management. To this day, the old-fashioned "suggestion box" remains a very important source of ideas for cost-cutting from operations. These suggestions affect product quality, working conditions, processes, and costs. The knowledge of the workers who perform the respective activities can be a very rich source of savings. The suggestions to improve product quality can indirectly lead to lower costs, because they reduce scrappage.

Management Commitment

It is evident that the commitment and the clout of management determine the success of cost-cutting measures. First, the company will overcome resistance only if senior leadership is decisive and adamant. Second, the measures will take time to have an impact, which means management needs staying power. The example that management sets—especially the CEO—plays a central role in the company's cost culture and in the way that employees will react.

If senior leaders spend extravagantly, employees might not understand why they need to cut corners. The CEO is ultimately responsible for avoiding waste. According to an old saying, the boss needs to act when the water faucet in the factory is dripping. Such interventions may only have symbolic character, but the point is that the firm, exemplified by the CEO, avoids waste even on a small scale. Many small savings can add up to a considerable amount.

In my experience, companies differ greatly with respect to these soft factors. I am convinced that cost culture, employee participation, and management commitment have very strong effects on costs in general, as well as on the success of cost-cutting programs. In this regard, they strongly

---

[19]Cooper [7].

		Value			
		Value parameter 1	Value parameter 2	Value parameter 3	Value parameter 4
Cost	Cost parameter 1				
	Cost parameter 2				
	Cost parameter 3				
	Cost parameter 4				

Fig. 8.5 Cost-value-matrix

affect the company's profitability and thus its chances of survival. But I am not claiming that no firm has ever been destroyed by cost-saving efforts. It is possible for a company to "save itself to death" when, for example, the cost-cutting erodes quality. On the other hand, many companies have gone under because they lacked sufficient cost consciousness and did not manage costs effectively.

Effectiveness: Cost-Value Analysis

Effectiveness means doing the right things, while efficiency answers the question of how well things get done. One could say that the value of an activity is the most important aspect of effectiveness, while productivity and costs are the important factors behind efficiency. A useful instrument for improving effectiveness is the cost-value-matrix, which we show in general form in Fig. 8.5.

There are numerous variants of this matrix and the methods behind it: Input-Output-Matrix, Quality Function Deployment, Value Engineering, and Activity Value Analysis.[20] The fundamental steps are similar in all of them. The input factors can include costs, time, employees, or investment budgets. The data and information come from finance or accounting. The value (output) parameters comprise the effects that the customer perceives, such as quality, efficiency, speed, economic viability/feasibility, and similar attributes. "Customers" in this context could be internal or external. Ultimately it is the customers who decide how much value they receive. With respect to profit maximization, one can start from either aspect (cost or value). When costs are the starting point, one should try to maximize the

---

[20] See Chalkiadikis [8].

resulting value. When value is the starting point, then the goal is to minimize costs.

The coefficients in the matrix cells play a central role in the analysis. They capture how an input or cost factor translates into customer value. These coefficients can be determined through technical analyses (i.e., to what extent does a more expensive material prolong product life), expert estimates, or even customer surveys. This matrix, even when it is not filled out completely, yields valuable insights into cost-savings potential. Those input or cost parameters that make only slight contributions to customer value are the first candidates for reduction or elimination. On the flip side, input parameters that show high effectiveness with respect to value-to-customer should be strengthened.

Eradicate Ineffectiveness

As mentioned above, effectiveness is about doing the right things. "Right things" are activities that provide value to the recipient or beneficiary. An activity is ineffective when the coefficients in the cost-value matrix are at or near zero. Ineffectiveness is widespread, as the following examples show.

In a large energy company, we examined how certain internal services were used and what value the intended "customers" derived from them. In question were information, analyses, and other services that a department provided to other internal departments. It turned out that customers rarely if ever made use of a large portion of these services, because they often perceived minimal value. Many of these ineffective offerings could be reduced or even eliminated. Modern information technologies allow a company to determine the actual value and usage of internal services with little effort and rather high precision.

One possible solution for such internal cases is a "pull system," similar to the Japanese Kanban method. The goal is to control the value added at each manufacturing stage of a multi-stage integration chain in a cost-optimized manner. Products or services are not "pushed" to internal customers, but rather "pulled" by them when and only when they need them. It is even better to assign an internal transfer price to the service. This shows whether it is really valued by potential customers.

Ineffectiveness also occurs in relationships with external customers. A paint manufacturer offered its B2B customers 42 different services. Customers highly valued the product-related services and used them extensively. But the opposite was true for general services such as help with legal, tax, or succession issues. For such issues, the customers usually turned to their own tax advisers, lawyers, or other experts. Offering the services generated considerable costs, but minimal revenue. In our project we recommended that the manufacturer eliminate half of the service portfolio, saving significant money without diminishing value-to-customer.

I personally witness a lot of ineffectiveness. Think of all those customer magazines that companies send out. Most of the ones I receive end up directly in the trash or recycling bins. They bring me no value at all, just frustration about the waste. The same applies to reports from banks and investment advisors. The simplest solution would be to replace this "push" system with a "pull" one: offer full paperless service and send printed material only upon request. Large banks would save millions with that simple trick.

Phrases that describe products with ineffective attributes include overengineered, all-in-one, and feature shock.[21] These problems require attention at the earliest phases of concept development. Methods such as Quality Function Deployment and Value Engineering help to avoid product-related ineffectiveness. But sometimes the use of differentiated offers and prices can transform ineffective performance into effective and paid performance. One example is the television function in the BMW 7 series. This function was offered free of charge as part of the first-generation navigation system. Many drivers were unaware the function even existed, and few used it or saw any value in it. Only very specific target groups—such as customers with personal drivers who need to wait in the cars for long periods—derived high value from the television capability. It made sense, then, to offer it separately and charge for it. Starting with the sixth generation of the navigation system, the price for the TV function was set at €1,300. This tactic was not about cost savings but rather about making ineffective performance effective.

Ineffective performance is often hard to identify. That is particularly true for general services and overhead functions, less so for services closely tied to products or customers. But ineffectiveness is by no means synonymous with failure. It is especially difficult to recognize in research and development. Let's look at the example of a researcher in the pharmaceutical industry. If this researcher investigates 99 substances and finds no measurable effects, this is not ineffectiveness, but rather a necessary step that may lead to success with the 100th substance. The failure of a new product introduction doesn't generally get categorized as ineffectiveness, because in many cases, only an actual product launch can uncover what path will lead to success or failure.

---

[21] See Ramanujam and Tacke [9].

Having said that, I suspect that ineffectiveness is a frequent occurrence in R&D, especially in large companies. One indicator of that is the differences in cost per patent. Hidden Champions need an average R&D budget of €529,000 per patent, while large companies require €2.7 million per patent. One explanation for this difference is that projects at large companies tend to be more comprehensive. But there are also fundamental differences in the innovation processes. In blunt terms, one could describe the differences this way: large companies throw big R&D budgets at projects, while Hidden Champions deploy dedicated teams in order to avoid ineffectiveness and develop products with lower costs. There are two positive side effects to the Hidden Champions' approach, namely, faster development times and a significantly higher level of patent use of 80 versus only 20% for large companies.

Efficiency and Productivity

Efficiency means that a particular result is achieved with the least effort and fewest resources possible. That is essentially what profit maximization amounts to. Companies should avoid any waste of resources, labor, and intellectual competencies.

Those are general statements that every responsible business leader will accept and internalize. The list of starting points for improvements is endless. Product and process innovation are the most important ones. Technical progress comes about when the same level of performance is achieved with less use of materials. A transatlantic cable used to require 120,000 tonnes of copper. Today we only need 800 kg of that expensive material to provide even greater transmission capacity.

Good companies know and feel the compulsion to continually increase efficiency and productivity. Some time ago, 13 professors from the Harvard Business School visited Hidden Champions as well as several large companies such as Siemens, Airbus, and BMW in Germany. Shortly afterwards, I asked several of the participants about their impressions of the visit. I received two consistent answers:

- All of the companies strived for continuous improvement, year after year
- The Germans are obsessed with productivity.

The first statement fits to the motto "forever better" that Miele has lived up to for over 120 years. It encompasses everything that Miele does. Behind that motto is the same philosophy as the Japanese Kaizen method, which aims for continual improvement. This applies not only to quality or timeliness, but also to costs.

The second observation recalls a statement made by the head of sales at BMW: "If we increase our productivity by 5% per year, it means that at constant capacity, I need to sell 5% more cars every year." This statement accurately captures the relationship between productivity and growth. Higher productivity, and thus lower costs, allows higher production volumes without the need for additional capacity. They give a firm the option of lowering prices or earning higher margins at constant prices. No company can afford to rest on its achievements in efficiency or productivity. The competition never sleeps, and every pause in the continuous improvement process puts the survival of the company at risk.

Suppliers

Suppliers are often the most important source of cost cuts. This is especially true when a company's own added value is slight. The pressure on suppliers therefore rises with every new cost-cutting initiative. Long-term contracts regularly include objectives for cost cuts, with the benefits passed on to the buyer. Herbert Diess, later CEO of Volkswagen, was extraordinarily effective in this regard in his former role as head of procurement at BMW. One comment noted: "Since he assumed his role four and a half years ago, BMW procurement head Herbert Diess has reduced material costs by a total of €4 billion. He achieved savings targets a year earlier than planned and became a star internally."[22]

Admittedly, though, there are cases in which the extreme pressure on suppliers leads to disadvantages in the medium and long term. It can lead to lower quality, force suppliers from the market, or prompt suppliers to decline business. One manager said on this last point: "I no longer ship to our largest customer. They forced prices down to the absolute minimum, and at the same time they are demanding a bigger range of services from us. I can now reallocate the freed-up capacity more profitably to other customers." The following comment of a service provider echoes that remark: "A large automotive company asks us year after year to bid on work. But because they only outsource work at low prices, we never submit an offer. If we submitted a bid

---

[22] *Handelsblatt*, August 15, 2011.

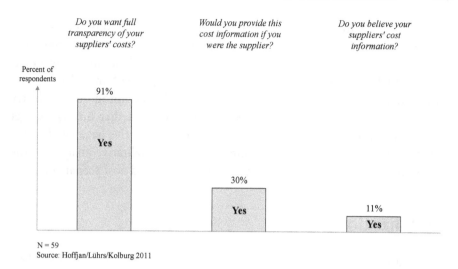

Fig. 8.6 Opinion of buyers regarding open-book pricing (OBP)

and actually won, we already know that we would need to cross-subsidize that work with funds from our core business. We cannot justify that."

The service provider then called out the longer-term effects of accepting such a contract: "Another reason we can't justify it is that once you enter the 'low price' segment, you hardly have any basis anymore to raise your prices. A high-end service provider such as our firm can only sell its time once. We considered hiring less expensive staff to provide 'low-end services,' but we figured out that the move would cause more problems than it would solve. Sometimes the best business is the deal you don't take."

Another leader touched on some additional aspects: "When buyers exert too much pressure on prices, I refer them to our competitors. I lose revenue, but the low prices will weaken the competitors who replace me as a supplier. That is clearly in my interest." But a supplier can afford such measures only when it has a position of power. These measures can backfire over the long term.

One popular tactic among buyers is to demand that the suppliers reveal their costs. This is referred to as open-book pricing (OBP) or open-book accounting. Sometimes buyers will offer to support suppliers in efforts to cut costs further. OBP is controversial. A survey of 59 buyers in the logistics sector yielded the results shown in Fig. 8.6.[23]

The contradictions in the results are fascinating. While 91% of buyers would want their suppliers to reveal their costs, only 30% would be willing

---

[23]Hoffjan et al. [10].

to comply with the demand if they were suppliers. And only one of nine respondents said he or she believes the suppliers' cost information anyway.

A supplier has a strong motivation, of course, to load up its products with the highest possible costs. In projects conducted by Simon-Kucher, we learned that a considerable number of suppliers in the automotive industry have refused to allow customers to see their costs. Whether buyers can get suppliers to cut their costs and prices depends on the relative balance of power in the market. For the reason, we often perform a qualitative analysis of the balance of power in order to estimate realistic price and cost scenarios.

Digitalization

Digitalization plays a vital role in cost management. Measures based on digitalization include cost reductions (e.g. better coordination of production systems, labor cost savings, stock reductions, more efficient administration), and value-to-customer (e.g. faster delivery, stronger personalization, more convenience). Both effects are often achieved simultaneously.

In most cases these measures require a complete reorganization of value-creation processes, in order to exploit the achievable cost reductions and deliver greater value-to-customer. Digitalization and artificial intelligence open up totally new opportunities, but these developments will necessarily lead to some job losses.

Several examples show the huge improvement potential that digital processes can bring. The Finnish Hidden Champion Fastems delivers "manufacturing management systems" which companies uses to integrate individual machines into a production workflow. Prior to integration, these machines have utilization rates in many cases as low as 25 to 30%. After integration, they often reach 50 to 60%. In other words, a factory can achieve the same performance with half the machine park, or can double its production with the existing park.

Trumpf, one of the world's leading companies for machine tools, laser technology, and electronics for industrial applications, can deliver customer-specific tools in four hours thanks to a fully digitalized process. This accelerated timeline saves costs and offers higher value-to-customer. MK Technologies builds installations that manufacture extremely complex forms using investment casting, an alternative technology to 3D printing. These forms used to take a week to manufacture, but MK's installations produce them in four hours. SpaceX, the rocket firm of Elon Musk, uses these MK machines. We also witness similar improvements to complex services. Control

Expert processes car damage claims digitally in a matter of hours and handles more than nine million cases per year. These processes used to take several weeks.

Digitalization is often primarily or exclusively cost-driven. But that view is too narrow. Digitalization offers vast potential for marketing as well. A critical but often neglected aspect is its effects on value-to-customer. The examples above go hand-in-hand with improvements in value-to-customer. But it is not true that digitalization automatically enhances customer value. Around 99% of all consumer apps fail because customers view them as useless. Companies often pay too little attention to how digital innovations affect value-to-customer and loyalty.

Avoiding Arrogance

Ongoing success is the enemy of change and makes cost management difficult, especially with respect to employee acceptance. Employees wonder why they should rationalize and cut costs when everything is going so well. The former CEO of Ciba-Geigy, Heiner Lippuner, expressed the resulting challenge this way: "The wise do things voluntarily in good times that the unwise must do involuntarily in bad times."[24] Actually, a good financial situation should make it easier to implement cost cutting measures, because there are abundant resources for investments, severance, and other expenses.

Success is the mother of arrogance. One should not underestimate the power of this unpleasant phenomenon. I recall a visit to the headquarters of Nokia near Helsinki in 2004. At that time, Nokia had a global share of over 40% in the mobile phone market. Rarely have I encountered more arrogance with respect to invincibility and competitive superiority than during that visit. One comment was: "with 19,000 employees in research and development, we are unbeatable." When such sentiments seep into the thinking of top management, one can hardly expect employees to show any modesty or cost consciousness. Another example is Kodak, which was generating record profits until a few years before its demise as a market-leading firm. A comfortable profit situation is unlikely to motivate management to pursue change.

At General Electric Aircraft Engines, the world market leader for jet engines, I experienced the exact opposite of such exaggerated self-confidence. The CEO at the time, Gerhard Neumann, always had a sign behind his

---

[24]Ciba-Geigy is one of the predecessor firms of Novartis.

desk that read "Feel Insecure."[25] When I visited him, he always stressed the importance of feeling constant insecurity. He said it preserves a willingness to change and keeps both management and employees alert and cost conscious. Noam Chomsky, professor emeritus at MIT, said that a classic strategy of cost cutting and control is the insecurity of employees.[26] He cited a speech by Alan Greenspan before the US Congress in which the former Federal Reserve chairman referred to employee insecurity as a factor behind increased productivity. I doubt, however, that that is the right strategy. Ongoing uncertainty can devolve into cynicism. But an appropriate level of perceived insecurity is definitely preferable to pronounced arrogance.

Costs and Crises

Cost cuts are obviously easier to implement during a crisis. If a firm needs to keep its head above water, there is no alternative to cost cutting. But everyone who has a stake in the company's survival should be onboard.[27] The Great Recession after 2008 offers numerous cases. Trumpf was hit especially hard. Revenue dropped by 23% in the 2008–09 business year, and sank a further 19% in the following year. But Trumpf managed this potentially mortal threat to the firm in exemplary fashion. It pulled every lever it could, from reduced hours to paid leave to the elimination of overtime. At some points, the actual working time was reduced to zero, and the employees instead devoted their time to training and additional qualifications. Trumpf even offered to train the employees of its customers. These measures allowed the firm to retain its qualified employees and accelerate the recovery process once the crisis subsided.

There are three lessons for future crises. First, it is very helpful to have a constructive, cooperative relationship between labor and management. Second, the role of government in terms of financial support cannot be underestimated. Finally, even in times of crisis, the focus should not lie exclusively on cost cutting, but rather on the long-term consequences.

---

[25] See Neumann [11].
[26] "Wir flexibilisieren uns zu Tode," *Frankfurter Allgemeine Zeitung*, January 7, 2015, p. N4.
[27] Simon [12].

Summary

Costs are an enormously important driver of profit, competitiveness, and the ability of a company to survive. In the context of profit, the main focus is cost cutting. One of its special features—compared to the other two profit drivers (price and sales volume)—is that cost-cutting measures primarily affect employees and suppliers. The relative power of the company and of the other affected parties plays a decisive role in the ability to implement cost cutting measures.

The profit elasticity of total costs is roughly on par with that of price. How much fixed and variable costs contribute depends on their relative weightings. Determining which costs are fixed and which are variable always requires the definition of a time period. In the short term, most costs are fixed, but over the long term, nearly all costs are variable.

Break-even analysis is a practical tool for making yes-no decisions on product introductions, investments, or the elimination of products from the portfolio. Changes in variable costs have a non-linear influence on the break-even point, while changes in fixed costs have a linear effect.

Costs are also the basis for lower bounds or floors on prices. When the cost function is linear, the short-term price floor is based on variable unit cost. When the cost function is non-linear, the basis for the floor is marginal cost. Over the long term, the full costs determine the price floor. The full costs are the variable costs and fixed costs spread across the volume.

Marginal costs are one of the two determinants of the profit-maximizing price, which results from a price-elasticity-based markup on marginal cost. The fixed cost has no influence on the profit-maximizing price.

The fixed-variable cost structure has significant effects on profit and volume management. High fixed costs combined with low variable costs heighten the pressure to boost volume. Increasing volume then has a massive impact on profit, because of the high positive unit contribution. This effect is particularly pronounced when marginal costs are at or near zero, a phenomenon that applies to many digital products and services. As a result, the short-term price floor is near zero. Economies of scale and the experience curve work similarly, in that sales volume growth has a very strong effect on profit.

Establishing the form of the cost structure is a strategic challenge. The options can range between two extremes, in which one of the costs (either fixed or variable) is essentially zero and the other comprises 100% of the costs. The chosen structure has an impact on how profit is affected by volume changes and also results in different risk profiles.

Cost accounting generates information on costs and their structure. Cost management, in contrast, involves the active efforts to reduce the costs for a specific activity or level of performance. Too little is known about the long-term successes of cost management. One reason is that companies are reluctant to make cost information available for academic study. Cost cutting programs can generate savings of as much as 10%. That does not appear to be revolutionary, but when compared to the low return on sales that many firms have, improvements of that magnitude have a major impact on profit.

In addition to organizational and methodological measures, a number of soft factors—cost culture, management commitment, and employee participation—play a vital role in the success of cost management programs. Cost cutting efforts should focus on efficiency (we do a thing right, i.e. in a cost-minimal way) as well as on effectiveness (we do the right thing). It is important for the company to avoid wheel-spinning on inefficient or ineffective activities. The ability to successfully implement cost cutting measures on suppliers depends on the relative balance of power between the parties.

Digitalization leads to expectations of enormous cost savings. But digital processes also often lead to higher value-to-customer. The opposite can be the case, however, if digitalization means that customers no longer have personal contact. That is why the digitalization of processes should not only consider pure cost aspects, but also the impact the changes will have on value-to-customer.

In times of crisis, it is easier to implement cost cuts. But this requires good cooperation between labor and management. Even in crisis situations, the objective cannot be solely to cut costs. The company must also take the long-term demand effects of these changes into account.

Arrogance, which is often a byproduct of success, can jeopardize cost consciousness and reduce the willingness to make cost cuts. Without pushing too far, a company should foster some level of insecurity or uncertainty among employees. In the end, only the permanent and relentless effort to maintain a competitive cost level will improve profitability and the company's chances of survival.

References

1. Himme, A. (2009) Kostenmanagement: Bestandsaufnahme und kritische Beurteilung der empirischen Forschung, *Zeitschrift für Betriebswirtschaft*, September, pp. 1051–1098.
2. Rifkin, J. (2015). *The Zero Marginal Cost Society*, New York: Griffin.

3. Simon, H., & Fassnacht, M. (2019). *Price Management: Strategy, Analysis, Decision, Implementation*, New York: Springer Nature, p. 544.

4. Kajüter, P. (2005). Kostenmanagement in der deutschen Unternehmenspraxis– Empirische Befunde einer branchenübergreifenden Feldstudie, *Zeitschrift für betriebswirtschaftliche Forschung*, January, pp. 79–100.

5. Hammer, M., & Champy, J. (1993) *Reengineering the Corporation: A Manifesto for Business Revolution*, New York: Harper Business.

6. Himme, A. (2012). Critical Success Factors of Strategic Cost Reduction, *Journal of Management Control*, p. 200.

7. Cooper, R. (1995). *When Lean Enterprises Collide: Competing through Confrontation*, Boston: Harvard Business School Press, p. 7.

8. Chalkiadikis, L. (2019). *New Product Development with the Use of Quality Function Deployment*, Beau Bassin: Lambert Academic Publishing.

9. Ramanujam, M., & Tacke, G. (2016). *Monetizing Innovation: How Smart Companies Design the Product around the Price*, Hoboken: Wiley.

10. Hoffjan, A., Lührs, S., & Kolburg, A. (2011) Cost Transparency in Supply Chains: Demystification of the Cooperation Tenet, Schmalenbach Business Review, July 15/63, pp. 230–251.

11. Neumann, G. (1984). *Herman the German*, New York: William Morrow.

12. Simon, H. (2010). *Beat the Crisis—33 Quick Solutions for Your Company*, New York: Springer.

Epilogue

In this book I make an impassioned case for profit orientation as a corporate goal and as a mantra for business leaders. I'm deeply convinced that the profit orientation is more effective than any other goal to ensure the survival of a company and serve the welfare not only of the shareholders, but also the stakeholders. When a company turns a profit, it usually benefits the employees, the company's partners along the value chain, banks, the government, and society at large.

In terms of profit performance, many companies are weak and do not earn their cost of capital. Other companies earn fantastic profits and, as a result, achieve correspondingly high market capitalizations. Firms with weak profits face significant risks with respect to their ability to invest and innovate. They become takeover candidates. If the profit weakness persists, it puts their survival in doubt. I consider a strict profit orientation to be indispensable for such firms.

I do not deny that profit orientation is not without its share of problems. These include the conflict between short- and long-term views, which can be difficult to reconcile. Of course I do not advocate that firms extract the most they can from employees, suppliers, and customers in the short term. Some companies do pursue that objective, but one can only go to the well so often. Profit orientation should always be long-term and thus in harmony with the concept of shareholder value. But one must show some modesty in this regard, because what "long term" means is often anything but clear. The future will always be uncertain.

Ethics are and remain the cornerstone of long-term leadership. The words of the second dean of the Harvard Business School—that one should earn "a decent profit decently"—captures that idea in an exemplary way. But there are also gray areas. What is decent and what isn't? Should the price of a drug like Luxturna, which cures a rare eye disease, be $850,000?[1]

Does digitalization make the primacy of profit orientation obsolete? That belief took hold once already, during the New Economy boom around the year 2000. I can recall discussions, even with economists, in which some people claimed that the laws of the "Old Economy" were no longer valid. Click rates, users, or capital burn rates emerged as the new success indicators and displaced profit.

The burst of the New Economy bubble was a tough lesson for these experts, but the effects were apparently only temporary. Around two decades later, we are living through a new era of euphoria in which 84‰ of companies that go public earn no profit, yet in some cases enjoy ridiculously high market valuations. Maybe this time the return to earth (and thus to reality) happens faster, as the developments at WeWork seem to indicate. As for Uber, I'm not going to venture a prognosis. By early 2021, Tesla's market capitalization surpassed that of the rest of the auto industry. Is that justified and will it last? I don't know the answer.

The question remains, though: how can companies be successful even though they make no money for years? Amazon and Salesforce.com are the new archetype in this regard. For me, the question has an easy answer: because investors trust that one day these companies will be very profitable, and therefore they continue to make capital available. Is this smart? We won't know until years from now whether those companies will indeed turn hope and trust into real profits. In these cases, short-term speculation on stock price increases can also play a role. The driving force is the investors' profit motive, which loses none of its relevance. The laws of the old Economy apply in the modern Economy, while new phenomena such as "zero marginal costs" must be taken into account.

Every business leader or entrepreneur must decide what success means for herself or himself. I do not claim any definitional authority in this regard. But I would venture a final hypothesis: If a company does not make any profits in the long term and ultimately perishes as a result, one can hardly describe this enterprise as a success. I have witnessed far too often how low profits or losses demotivated, frustrated, disappointed, and de-energized executives, managers, and employees. And conversely, I have experienced that sustained

---

[1] US price for treatment of both eyes. Prices in Germany and in the UK are €590,000 and £610,000 respectively.

profitability motivated, emboldened, and energized everyone in the company, so that all found fulfillment in their work. My conclusion is therefore that there is no alternative to profit orientation for private companies. After all, no company ever went broke from turning a profit.

CPSIA information can be obtained
at www.ICGtesting.com
Printed in the USA
BVHW012155291021
620345BV00015B/116

9 783030 767013